Lancelot of the Laik

and

Sir Tristrem

Middle English Texts

General Editor

Russell A. Peck
University of Rochester

The Middle English Texts Series is designed for classroom use. Its goal is to make available to teachers and students texts which occupy an important place in the literary and cultural canon but which have not been readily available in student editions. The series does not include those authors such as Chaucer, Gower, Langland, the Pearl-poet, or Malory, whose English works are normally in print in good student editions. The focus is, instead, upon Middle English literature adjacent to those authors that teachers need in compiling the syllabuses they wish to teach. The editions maintain the linguistic integrity of the original work but within the parameters of modern reading conventions. The texts are printed in the modern alphabet and follow the practices of modern capitalization and punctuation. Manuscript abbreviations are expanded, and u/v and j/i spellings are regularized according to modern orthography. Hard words, difficult phrases, and unusual idioms are glossed on the page, either in the right margin or at the foot of the page. Textual notes appear at the end of the text, along with a glossary. The editions include short introductions on the history of the work, its merits and points of topical interest, and also include briefly annotated bibliographies.

Lancelot of the Laik

and

Sir Tristrem

Edited by
Alan Lupack

Published for TEAMS
(The Consortium for the Teaching of the Middle Ages)
in Association with the University of Rochester

by

Medieval Institute Publications
WESTERN MICHIGAN UNIVERSITY

Kalamazoo, Michigan — 1994

Library of Congress Cataloging-in-Publication Data

[Lancelot of the laik]
Lancelot of the laik ; and, Sir Tristrem / edited by Alan Lupack.
p.   cm. -- (Middle English texts)
In Scots.
Lancelot of the laik prepared from the Cambridge University ms.
Kk.1.5.vii, folios 1r-42v and Sir Tristrem from the Auchinleck MS
(Advocates 19.2.1), fols. 281a-299b, in the National Library of
Scotland.
Includes bibliographical references (p.)
ISBN 1-879288-50-8
1. Lancelot (Legendary character)--Romances. 2. Tristan
(Legendary character)--Romances. 3. Arthurian romances.
4. Romances, Scottish. I. Lupack, Alan. II. Sir Tristrem.
III. Series: Middle English texts (Kalamazoo, Mich.)
PR2065.L19 1994
821'.208--dc20   94-27291
                                                              CIP

ISBN 1-879288-50-8

Printed in the United States of America

Cover design by Elizabeth King

Acknowledgments

I have used MS Kk.1.5.vii in the preparation of the edition of *Lancelot of the Laik* by permission of the Syndics of Cambridge University Library.

I have used the Auchinleck MS in the preparation of the edition of *Sir Tristrem* by permission of the Trustees of the National Library of Scotland.

I am grateful to Cambridge University Library and to the National Library of Scotland for allowing me to use these manuscripts.

I am particularly indebted to Russell Peck for his assistance, encouragement, and advice in preparing this edition. His wide-ranging knowledge of medieval literature is impressive. Even more impressive, though, is the generosity and enthusiasm with which he shares that knowledge.

This volume is dedicated
to the memory of
William and Edna Lupack

Contents

Lancelot of the Laik

Introduction

The romance known as *Lancelot of the Laik* survives in only one manuscript, Cambridge University Kk.1.5, and even there it is incomplete, ending abruptly in the middle of the 3487th line. As R. J. Lyall suggests (in "The Lost Literature of Medieval Scotland" in *Bryght Lanternis: Essays on the Language and Literature of Medieval and Renaissance Scotland*, ed. J. Derrick McClure and Michael R. G. Spiller [Aberdeen: Aberdeen University Press, 1989], p. 50), this poem may be the *"Lancelot du Lac* referred to in the *Complaynt of Scotland."* The manuscript dates from very late in the fifteenth century. The writing of the poem has generally been placed not much earlier. Vogel dates it "not earlier than the latter part of 1482" (p. 10). However, this specific date is based on the opinion that the poem's political advice to King Arthur is a response to the problems of the reign of James III of Scotland, advice which R. J. Lyall has demonstrated to be "almost entirely conventional" (p. 25). Nevertheless a part of the poem seems to belong to "a tradition of political advice which enjoyed continuous currency in Scotland between about 1450 and about 1580" (Lyall p. 25), and so was most likely composed not long before the writing of the surviving manuscript.

The poem was written in a Scottish dialect, as is evidenced by a number of terms typical of that dialect and by numerous forms common to Scottish and northern dialects. Among the words indicative of the Scottish are, for example, *anerding* (meaning *adhering*, in line 345), *deden* (Sc. form of *deign*, in line 949), *uall* (meaning *wave*, in line 1317), *feill* (meaning *knowledge*, in line 2854), *radour* (meaning *fear*, in line 3465), as well as the more common words such as *sic* (meaning *such*, as in line 560 and 2115, where the form is *sice*), *the ilk* (=*thilk*, meaning *that*, in line 629), forms in *quh* instead of *wh* (e.g., *quhen*, line 335; *quhar*, line 640; *quhich*, line 1053; *sumquhat*, line 1059; *quhill*, line 1229; *quhat*, line 1253; etc.).

Among the forms found both in Scottish and northern dialects are the third person singular and plural of the present tense in *-s* or *-is* (e.g., *afferis*, in line 1690; *redis*, in line 204; *thei has*, in lines 495–96); the present participle in *-and* (e.g., *thinkand*, line 2173; *prekand*, line 3089; *fechtand*, line 3127); and the third person plural pronoun in *th-* (e.g., *thaim*, line 144, *thei*, line 382). Words typical of northern England and Scotland include *sal* (line 110), with *s* instead of *sh*; *mekil* (line 857);

1

and those retaining the long *a*, where other dialects have shifted to *o* (e.g., *fra*, line 218; *ham*, line 1139; and *hamlynes*, line 2448).

But the dialect that appears in the Cambridge manuscript is far from uniform. Beside *ham* and *hamlynes*, one could cite *homme* (line 897) and *homely* (line 2463). In addition to *fra*, *sal*, and *sic*, one finds *frome* (line 6), *shall* (line 454), and *such* (line 388). The form *thinking* (line 1230) appears as well as *thenkand*.

The mixture of dialectical forms is the result of several factors. There is, of course, the possibility that some of the non-northern forms have been introduced by the scribe. However, other factors are certain to have contributed. By the late fifteenth century, the process of standardization of the written language was well under way. In addition, just as the style and ideas of the author of *Lancelot of the Laik* were influenced by poets like Chaucer and Gower, surely his language must have been as well. It should be noted, however, that Gregory Kratzmann — in *Anglo-Scottish Literary Relations 1430–1550* (Cambridge: Cambridge University Press, 1980), p. 231 — believes that "the fact that *Lancelot* is written in a heavily anglicised form of Scots . . . may well denote an attempt to imitate the language of the [*Kingis*] *Quair* rather than that of Chaucer's poetry." (The *Kingis Quair* was allegedly written by the Scottish King James I while a prisoner in England.)

In accordance with the practice of the Middle English Texts Series, I have expanded abbreviations in the manuscript and have regularized u/v and j/i spellings according to modern orthography. As an extension of this principle I have also regularized the orthography when a *w* in the text would be a *v* in modern orthography and vice versa. Another point of orthography needs mention. The scribe makes use of a *y*-shaped thorn, not an uncommon practice in fifteenth-century texts. Earlier editors have transcribed this as *y* in most instances. Thus Skeat, for example reads "yat" (line 82) where what is clearly intended is "that" and "yi" (line 145) where "thi" is intended. Only in a couple of places in his notes does Skeat indicate that the *y*-shaped letter stands for *th*: his note to line 160 reads, "*yis*, this"; to line 1044: "*oyer*. So in MS.; the *y* representing the old *th*; to line 1187: "*qwheyar*, whether; and to line 1240 "*yarof*, thereof." But generally the letter is merely transcribed as *y* and presented without comment. I have treated this letter according to METS guidelines and transcribed it as *th*.

One other idiosyncracy of the manuscript is worthy of note. The scribe frequently writes *-ing* where one would normally find the ending *-en* (as in an infinitive or a plural form of a verb, or a past participle), e.g., "Fore to avysing" (line 424); "thei waryng into were" (line 443); and "The day is cumyng" (i.e., has come, line 447). Alternatively he often uses *-ine* or *-yne* where one would expect *-ing*, e.g., "bookis longyne to ther artis" (line 433). The inversion of the usual spelling is clear in line

448: "Besichyne them to shewyng ther entent." This feature seems to be scribal rather than dialectal, but I have retained it in my transcription.

Criticism of *Lancelot of the Laik* has generally promoted two opinions about the poem. The former is stated bluntly by Helaine Newstead in her account of the poem in the *Manual of Writings in Middle English*: "The poem has slight claim to literary merit or originality. It is a paraphrase of the first part of the Vulgate *Lancelot* . . . marked by the incompetence that the poet freely admits" (pp. 50–51). This opinion is shared by Robert Ackerman, in his essay on "English Rimed and Prose Romances" in Roger Sherman Loomis's *Arthurian Literature in the Middle Ages*, who calls the poem "a badly conceived rehandling of the first portion of the French Prose *Lancelot*" (p. 491). These two authoritative works merely affirmed what some earlier critics had said. Vogel, for example, said that "in the remarkable history of Arthurian literature," *Lancelot of the Laik* is "perhaps even insignificant" (p. 1).

The second opinion about the poem was first expressed by Vogel. He asserts that the "extremely lengthy 'digression' on the natures and duties of the king . . . is of considerable interest" (p. 1). The interest for Vogel lies in his belief that this amplification of the remarks on kingship in the French source was inspired by "the degraded state of government in Scotland under James III" (p. 5). Ackerman accepts this judgment and says of these references "to the contemporaneous political scene" that "only in this respect is the romance of much interest" (p. 491).

In fact, the passage containing the presumed topical allusions dominate the small body of critical studies of *Lancelot of the Laik*. Every article to deal with the poem since Vogel's 1943 study has focused on this section of the poem. Flora Alexander examines the poem along with other Scottish treatments of Arthur and concludes that the criticism of his reign is not related to fears of English aggression but rather to the inadequacies of James III as a king. Wurtel sees much of the advice as traditional and therefore considers *Lancelot of the Laik* a precursor of the type of courtesy book offering advice to a prince popular in the Renaissance. And R. J. Lyall argues that since the advice to Arthur is almost entirely conventional, this section is not reliable evidence for dating the poem.

The reason the passage of advice to the king receives such attention is that it is the longest expansion of the French source in the surviving text. The Amytans section, which begins with the wise man's appearance in lines 1294 and following and runs to the king's taking of his leave from Amytans in lines 2145–46, dominates the second book of the poem and resonates in the incomplete third book. But to say that it is important is different from considering it the *raison d'etre* of the poem.

Perhaps the reason for the emphasis on this passage as well as for the disparaging comments on the poem as a whole is that *Lancelot of the Laik* is incomplete. As a result, this passage occupies a large percentage of the surviving lines — even though it would not loom so large if the poem were completed as projected. The incompleteness of the poem has presented a problem to critics of medieval literature, many of whom were trained in New Critical reading, which prizes form and structure of complete works. It is no accident that for many years critical discussion of medieval literature focused much of its praise and blame on the structure of the works under consideration. The parallel structure of *Sir Gawain and the Green Knight*, the debate over whether Malory's *Morte d'Arthur* is one book or eight, the relationship of the *Visio* and the *Vita* in *Piers Plowman*, the ordering of Chaucer's tales and the thematic grouping of them, the apparent weakness of the link between the parts of poems like the *Awntyrs of Arthure*, and other such questions have filled many a page in scholarly journals and monographs. These are all important issues, and they have led to important insights. However, the inclination to focus on such issues can easily lead to the slighting of works that have much to offer, especially if those works are structurally incomplete. The *Canterbury Tales* have received so much comment in spite of its incompleteness because parts of the larger work — the individual tales — often have a brilliant completeness of their own, because there are enough of them to let a reader see some of the ways in which they are interconnected, and because the plan for the whole is reasonably clear.

To appreciate an incomplete work like *Lancelot of the Laik*, or any other fragmentary work, one must apply an aesthetics of incompleteness similar to that used in discussion of the *Canterbury Tales* in order to assess it properly. Even the consideration of the significance of Amytans' advice can not be understood without imagining it as part of a larger whole and without considering its relationship to that larger whole. No doubt scholars have been drawn to this passage because it is complete and the full content of Amytans' speech can be analyzed. But to see it in isolation distorts both the poem in which it appears and the passage itself.

Projecting the completed work makes it clear that *Lancelot of the Laik* is not a courtesy book but a romance in which the advice plays an important but subsidiary role. Such projection requires a reader to consider the poet's own statement about the contents and the changes made by him in adapting the French romance. Such an examination provides a basis for challenging the assumptions that *Lancelot of the Laik* lacks originality and literary merit and that it is only of interest because of the passage of political advice given to Arthur.

Lancelot of the Laik has its source in the French Vulgate *Lancelot*. It would, however, be a mistake to call it a translation of the French romance or even "a paraphrase of the first part of the Vulgate *Lancelot*," as the *Manual of Writings in Middle English* calls it (I, p. 51). In the process of creating a verse romance from the prose of the French, the Scottish poet has translated some passages fairly closely, changed details in others, sometimes expanded on the text, sometimes abbreviated it. But the most obvious change he makes is to select a portion of the much longer source and focus on that. It is clear that the poet knew the longer romance, that he is not working from an incomplete manuscript because he recounts in his prologue many of the events that he will not treat. His sense of various parts of the French romance as stories in themselves is made obvious when he says that one of the many incidents he has recounted in his *occupatio* would provide material for a "gret [i.e., long] story" (line 296). In fact, the author of *Lancelot of the Laik* adapts his source in a manner that has been described by Larry Benson (in *Malory's Morte Darthur* [Cambridge: Harvard University Press, 1976], p. 43) as typical of Middle English romancers' "concentration on action, as contrasted to the courtly psychological subtleties of Chrétien de Troyes, their relative lack of interest in mysticism and symbolism of the sort we find in the French Grail romances, and their preference for simple, brief, relatively straightforward narrative lines in contrast to the structural complexities of French works."

Having selected the section of the French romance that he wishes to treat, the author of the English poem does more than paraphrase it. It is generally accepted that he has added significantly to Amytans' advice, but the significance of some of the other differences from the source has not been noted. And even the role of the Amytans section has not been clearly defined in relation to the work as a whole.

Perhaps the strongest indication that *Lancelot of the Laik* must be read as a romance and not as a poem of political advice is found in the Prologue. This section, which has no parallel in the French source, contains the poet's love complaint and a dream vision in which a messenger from the god of Love instructs him either to tell his lady of his love for her or to write a "trety" (narrative) of love or arms — but something joyful and not sorrowful — which will let his lady know that he is in her service. After a disclaimer about his lack of literary talent, which critics have taken too literally, he decides to write for his beloved the story of Lancelot.

However conventional such an opening might be, it clearly puts the following poem in a particular context. The tale of Lancelot is selected because it is the story of a great lover. The implied simile is that the poet's love for the woman for whom the poem is written is like Lancelot's love for Guinevere. Given this context, it would be totally inappropriate for the author to write a courtesy book or to have political advice as his primary emphasis. In fact, the poet explains in the Prologue that Arthur's war with Galiot is important because Lancelot was the reason for Arthur's victory and won the most honor in those wars. And the love of Guinevere was his reward for these achievements (see lines 304–13). Thus Arthur's travails are important primarily to provide a showcase for Lancelot's valor.

The first book supports this contention, for while much of it is devoted to the deeds of Gawain, it is Lancelot who prevents Arthur's forces from being defeated. He proves himself in battle — and he also sees and falls in love with Guinevere. It is for her that he performs the wondrous acts of valor that save the day. He tells himself that he should either deserve her love through his deeds or he should die like a knight. The emphasis is kept on the romance rather than the political element in this book by having the Lady of Melyholt, Lancelot's captor, fall in love with him because of his martial achievements. It is indicative of the method, and perhaps of the theme, employed by the English poet that, as Göller noted (p. 138), he moves the visit of the Lady of Melyholt and her cousin to a point in the narrative immediately following Lancelot's exploits. In the French, this scene occurs after Amytans' advice. The advice and the exploits of Lancelot are interlaced. By placing the visit immediately after the battle, the English author has emphasized that it is knightly conduct that has made Lancelot worthy of the love of a noble lady.

This arrangement of the narrative, without the interlacing of the French source, is one of the elements that contributes to the impression that Book II, the section devoted to Amytans' advice, is central to the story. After all, a major portion of the narrative is devoted to it. It is structured so as to form a separate unit, uninterrupted by the account of Lancelot's exploits. But the focus on Arthur's character does in a general and a specific sense relate to Lancelot. Amytans informs Arthur that victory in battle and the very reign of a king depend on God's will. If Arthur changes his ways and perseveres in virtue, his reign will prosper — and, though Amytans does not say this specifically, the narrative makes it clear that Lancelot is the instrument by which Arthur's power will be maintained.

Even more to the point is the scene in which Amytans advises Arthur to confess all his failings. Arthur returns and claims to have fulfilled the injunction. Amytans says, in effect, didn't you forget to confess how you treated King Ban and his wife; and he adds, "Bot of ther sone . . . / Ne spek Y not" (lines 1450–51). Their son is, of course, Lancelot. The sin to which Amytans refers is his failure to come to the aid of Ban, Arthur's vassal, even though Ban had faithfully rendered service to Arthur when called upon to do so (see the note to line 1448 for a full account of this incident).

Amytans ends his sermon to Arthur by telling the king that it is now up to him to lose or retain his honor and his reign. In response, Arthur says that he has only one concern — whether the knight who defended Arthur's realm (that is, Lancelot) shall be persuaded to enter Galiot's service, as Galiot himself had boasted he would. Arthur asks: "If that shall fall Y pray yhow tellith me, / And quhat he hecht [promised] and of quhat lond is hee" (lines 2139–40). His main concern is that Lancelot, whose name Arthur does not yet learn, should remain in his service and not

6

enter that of his enemy. Obviously Arthur believes that his honor and his reign depend on the knight who fought so valiantly.

The importance of Lancelot to Arthur is emphasized by an interesting verbal echo. In explaining his melancholy humor to Gawain, the king says that it was once assumed that he had in his household "the flour of knichthed and of chevalry" but now he sees that the contrary is true since "the flour of knychthed is away" (lines 2183–85). To speak of the epitome as "the flower" is fairly common in Middle English; in fact the term is used in this sense elsewhere in this poem. However, in this context, in the same book in which the Blessed Virgin is referred to symbolically as a flower — the last such reference being only sixty lines earlier — it is difficult not to associate the two. Just as on a moral and spiritual level, Mary is the "flour that al our gladness sterith" (line 2104) and the "flour of our salvatioune" who shall be Arthur's "succour" and who shall "thi ned redress" (lines 2110–14), so on a worldly level Lancelot is Arthur's succor and salvation.

That the echo is not accidental or coincidental is supported by two facts. First, the reference to Mary as the "flour" is made repeatedly. In lines 2088–2104, ten of the seventeen lines begin with the phrase "this is the flour," as does line 2108; and the word "flour" appears two more times, in lines 2109 and 2123. Secondly, when the term "flour of knychthed" appears in lines 2183 and 2185, it is not translating the French "flors," as the references to Mary as the flower are. Rather the first use of the phrase "flour of Knychthed" translates "toute la proeche terriene," all earthly prowess, (Sommer III, p. 226, lines 28–29) and the second "li mieudres cheualiers del monde," the best knight of the world (line 30). The implied comparison between Lancelot on a worldly level and Mary on a spiritual level is one more way that the poet links the advice of Amytans to his central purpose of emphasizing Lancelot's superiority as knight and lover.

Other changes that the English author made in his source indicate that he has adopted a strategy similar to that used by Malory. He has made changes which are designed to enhance the position and reputation of Lancelot. Of course in the French source Lancelot has a central position; nevertheless, Lancelot's love and valor are even more prominent in the English. For example, the passage in which Lancelot, "byrnyng in loves fyre," battles through the field "lyk to o lyone" and in which Gawain praises him as a knight who does more deeds of valor in a shorter space than he has ever seen (lines 1091–1128) is the English author's addition. So too is Lancelot's complaint, written in five-line stanzas (in lines 699–718), and his lament in lines 1011–28. Likewise, Lancelot's reminder to himself to fight well in the sight of his lady (lines 3270–88) is not found in the French.

Other examples might be added, including places where Lancelot's speeches are expanded from the French source, as is the case with his tribute to Gawain when he thinks Gawain might have died (lines 2749–72) and his exhortation to Arthur's troops (lines 3445–72). The cumulative effect of these changes to the source is to alter the focus from that of the French text, so that the English poem becomes a romance of love and valor, of which virtues Lancelot is the exemplar, rather than a history of the rise and moral fall of Lancelot.

Thus, placing the passage of advice to Arthur in its proper context and observing the changes the author made to his source leads to the conclusion that Amytans' advice is far from the most important or most interesting element of *Lancelot of the Laik*. In fact, one must conclude, focusing on that passage distorts the understanding of the poem.

While the fragmentary nature of the only extant manuscript of the poem makes it impossible to be certain where the emphasis on Lancelot is leading, the poet's method in the surviving portion and his statement in the Prologue about his intent and subject matter allow for some conjecture. In lines 299–313, the author summarizes his "mater." He will tell of the wars between Arthur and Galiot, of how Lancelot "berith the renownn" in these wars — this is the subject of the surviving books and would have continued at least to the end of book three. Then in a bridging section he will tell how Lancelot brings about peace between the two rulers. Finally he will tell — probably in a section at least comparable in length to the first three books — how Venus rewards Lancelot for bringing about "concorde" by allowing him to have his lady's (i.e., Guinevere's) favor. Though not referred to specifically by the poet, a concluding epilogue in which the poet offers his work to his lady and compares his love to that of Lancelot for Guinevere might have ended the work.

Had such a completed romance survived, it is likely that *Lancelot of the Laik* would have had a much higher reputation and would probably have been looked upon as an interesting example of late medieval romance. At the least, critics would have been forced to place Amytans' advice in a proper context and to focus on other aspects of the poem, such as its detailed and sometimes lively battle scenes and the poet's interesting use of direct speech. The poem's novel use of the dream vision is also worthy of attention since the vision provides not a means of understanding for the narrator but rather instruction to make a poem. This advice that a poem might substitute for a direct expression of love seems to suggest a deliberate, conscious artifice as a means of expressing emotion; and this seems to indicate a Renaissance sensibility as much as a medieval one.

A final interesting and original element of the poem is worth noting. Because of the author's purpose to create a poem to express his love, which therefore must be one which "soundith not oneto no hevyness / Bot oneto gladness and to lusteness" (lines 149–50), the love of Lancelot and Guinevere is not linked to the ultimate tragedy of Arthur. It is the only medieval English romance in which such a connection is not made. Malory, of course, makes Lancelot central to his *Morte d'Arthur* but, as the conventional title suggests, his love brings about the downfall of Arthur and his realm. The same is true in the stanzaic *Morte Arthur*, the only other romance in which Lancelot is the central character. There is no other medieval English treatment of Lancelot besides the relatively short ballad "Sir Lancelot du Lake," which recounts Lancelot's battle with Sir Tarquin and does not concern itself with matters of love.

Even in later literature, the story of Lancelot and Guinevere is rarely told without coupling it with the death of Arthur. Tennyson does this in the *Idylls of the King* — though the completed portion of his early Arthurian effort, "Sir Launcelot and Queen Guinevere: A Fragment," focuses on the queen's beauty and only alludes to the tragedy by saying that a man would give "all other bliss / And all his worldly worth" to be able to "waste his whole heart in one kiss / Upon her perfect lips." William Morris, of course, links the tragedy to the love in "King Arthur's Tomb" and "The Defence of Guinevere," as do other poets as diverse as Edwin Arlington Robinson (in his *Lancelot*), Sara Teasdale (in "Guenevere") and John Ciardi (in "Launcelot in Hell"). Playwrights, novelists, and filmmakers follow in this tradition. J. Comyns Carr's *King Arthur*, T. H. White's *The Once and Future King*, and John Boorman's *Excalibur* all link the love of Lancelot and Guinevere to the downfall of Camelot. Thus, though it is based largely on its French source, the poem is quite original in the context of English literature.

The conclusion that one reaches after considering *Lancelot of the Laik* in the context of medieval and other English treatments of Lancelot is the same as that reached when considering the poem in relation to its source and as an example of medieval romance: that it is a far more interesting poem than it has been thought to be and one which deserves wider reading and further study.

Selected Bibliography

Manuscript

Cambridge University Manuscript Kk.1.5.vii, folios 1r–42v.

Previous Editions

The Scottish Metrical Romance of Lancelot du Lak: Now First Printed from a Manuscript of the Fifteenth Century, Belonging to the University of Cambridge. With Miscella-

neous Poems from the Same Volume. Edinburgh: The Maitland Club, 1839. (This edition was reprinted in 1971 by AMS Press.)

Lancelot of the Laik: A Scottish Metrical Romance (About 1490–1500 A.D.). Re-Edited from a Manuscript in the Cambridge University Library, with an Introduction, Notes, and Glossarial Index. Ed. W. W. Skeat. EETS o.s. 6. 1865, 2nd ed. 1870; rpt. London: Oxford University Press for The Early English Text Society, 1965.

Lancelot of the Laik: From Cambridge University Library MS. Ed. Margaret Muriel Gray. STS n.s. 2. Edinburgh: William Blackwood and Sons for the Scottish Text Society, 1912.

Criticism

Ackerman, Robert W. "English Rimed and Prose Romances." In *Arthurian Literature in the Middle Ages: A Collaborative History.* Ed. Roger Sherman Loomis. Oxford: Clarendon Press, 1959. Pp. 480–519 (pp. 491–493 are devoted to *Lancelot of the Laik*). Ackerman considers the poem "a badly conceived rehandling of the first portion of the French Prose *Lancelot*" (p. 491).

Alexander, Flora. "Late Medieval Scottish Attitudes to the Figure of King Arthur: A Reassessment." *Anglia* 93 (1975), 17–34. Alexander examines a number of Scottish works which comment on King Arthur. She concludes about *Lancelot of the Laik* that its criticism of Arthur "is not connected with the national fear of English aggression" (p. 19) and that "the poet's interest is not in national independence, but in the pressing internal problem of the reign of James III" (p. 34).

Göller, Karl Heinz. *König Arthur in der Englischen Literatur des späten Mittelalters.* Gottingen: Vandenhoeck and Ruprecht, 1963. Göller sees *Lancelot of the Laik* as a treatise on statecraft (*"Fürstenspiegel"*) and considers the figure of Arthur as he appears in the poem an *"exemplum malum"* (p. 176).

Lyall, R. J. "Politics and Poetry in Fifteenth and Sixteenth Century Scotland." *Scottish Literary Journal* 3.2 (December 1976), 5–29. Lyall concludes that the discussion of kingship in *Lancelot of the Laik* and a number of other Scottish poems of the fifteenth century is "almost entirely conventional" and warns that "a mere interest in the nature of good government does not provide a basis for dating a poem" (p. 25).

Introduction

Lyall, Roderick J. "Two of Dunbar's Makars: James Affleck and Sir John the Ross." *The Innes Review* 27 (1976), 99–109. Lyall offers "a suggestion . . . rather than proof" (p. 99) of the identities of two poets named in Dunbar's *Lament for the Makaris*, James Affleck and John the Ross. Affleck, a variant of Auchinleck, has been considered to be the author of the *Quair of Jelousy*, and Skeat has suggested that the same author wrote *Lancelot of the Laik*. Lyall does not believe that "common authorship of these works can be assumed" but suggests that "James Auchinleck the son of Sir John of that Ilk can be considered a likely candidate as Dunbar's James Affleck" (pp. 108–09)

Skeat, Walter W. "The Author of 'Lancelot of the Laik.'" *The Scottish Historical Review* 8 (1911), 1–4. Skeat argues, on the basis of similarities in "style, prosody, vocabulary, grammar, and phonology," (p. 1) that the author of the *Quair of Jelousy*, identified by D. Laing as James Auchinleck (Dunbar's James Affleck) is also the author of *Lancelot of the Laik*.

Vogel, Bertram. "Secular Politics and the Date of *Lancelot of the Laik*." *Studies in Philology* 40.1 (Jan. 1943), 1–13. Vogel contends that Amytans' speech on kingship may be "the most important element of the Scots poem"(p. 13). He believes that it was probably "the degraded state of government in Scotland under James III which immediately impelled the poet not only to select this particular romance . . . but more, to translate this particular portion of the story selected, and to amplify the political comments contained in the original" (p. 5). The historical background that he sees in the poem leads him to date it "not earlier than the latter part of 1482" (p. 10).

Wurtele, Douglas. "A Reappraisal of the Scottish *Lancelot of the Laik*." *Revue de l'Université d'Ottowa* 46 (1976), 68–82. Wurtele argues that *Lancelot of the Laik* is more than a topical poem responding to "the political climate generated by the long minorities of James II and James III" (p. 69). He notes parallels to the *Secreta Secretorum* and the *Confessio Amantis* and concludes that "Amytans' sermon, far from constituting a blemish on the poem, puts the work in the ranks of these and other seriously meant books of instruction" (p. 80) and marks the poem as "an early attempt, through use of the Arthurian romance tradition, at the kind of superior 'courtesy book' to be produced in the next century by Castiglione, Ascham, Elyot, and, supremely, Spenser" (p. 74).

The Romans of Lancelot of the Laik

	The soft morow ande the lustee Aperill,	*morning; pleasant*
	The wynter set, the stormys in exill,	*past*
	Quhen that the brycht and fresch illumynare[1]	
	Uprisith arly in his fyré chare	*chariot*
5	His hot courss into the orient,	
	And frome his spere his goldine stremis sent	*sphere*
	Wpone the grond, in maner off mesag	*Upon the earth*
	One every thing, to ualkyne thar curage,	*On; awaken their spirit*
	That natur haith set wnder hire mycht,	*power*
10	Boith gyrss and flour and every lusty uicht,	*grass; vigorous person*
	And namly thame that felith the assay	*especially; attack*
	Of lufe, to schew the kalendis of May,	*love; reveal; (see note)*
	Throw birdis songe with opine vox one hy	*open voice (i.e., aloud)*
	That sessit not one lufaris for to cry,	*ceases; lovers*
15	Lest thai forghet, throw slewth of ignorans,	*through sloth*
	The old wsage of Lovis observans.	*custom; rite*
	And fromme I can the bricht face asspy,	*from the time that; bright*
	It deuit me no langare fore to ly,	*helps*
	Nore that love schuld sleuth into me finde,	*sloth in me*
20	Bot walkine furth, bewalinge in my mynde	*walk forth*
	The dredful lyve endurit al to longe,	*life*
	Sufferans in love of sorouful harmys stronge,	*Suffering; grievous*
	The scharpe dais and the hevy yerys	*trying days; distressing years*
	Quhill Phebus thris haith passith al his speris,[2]	
25	Uithoutine hope ore traistinge of comfort.	*Without; reliance on*
	So be such meine fatit was my sort.[3]	
	Thus in my saull rolinge al my wo,	*soul; meditating on*
	My carful hart carving cann in two	*(see note)*

---

[1] *When the bright and new[ly returned] source of light*

[2] *While Phoebus [the sun] has thrice gone through his circuit*

[3] *So, in such a way, fated was my lot*

	The derdful suerd of lovis hot dissire;	*sword*
30	So be the morow set I was afyre	*by morning*
	In felinge of the access hot and colde,	*ague fit*
	That haith my hart in sich a fevir holde;	*such*
	Only to me thare was nonne uthir ess	*other pleasure*
	Bot thinkine qhow I schulde my lady pless.	*Except thinking how*
35	The scharp assay and ek the inwart peine	*assault; also*
	Of dowblit wo me neulyngis cann constrein	*doubled; afresh*
	Quhen that I have remembrit one my thocht	*When*
	How sche, quhois bewté al my harmm haith wrocht,	*whose*
	Ne knouith not how I ame wo-begonne,	
40	Nor how that I ame of hire servandis onne.	*one of her servants*
	And in myself I cann nocht fynde the meyne	*way*
	Into quhat wyss I sal my wo compleine.	*In what manner; shall; lament*
	Thus in the feild I walkith to and froo,	
	As thochtful wicht that felt of nocht bot woo,	*person*
45	Syne to o gardinge, that wess weil besenn [1]	
	Of quiche the feild was al depaynt with grenn.	*which; colored*
	The tendyre and the lusty flouris new	
	Up throue the grenn upone thar stalkis grew	
	Aghane the sone, and thare levis spred,	*In the sunlight*
50	Quharwith that al the gardinge was iclede.	*Wherewith; adorned*
	That Pryapus, into his tyme before,	*in*
	In o lustear walkith nevir more.	*In a more fertile [one]*
	And al about enveronyt and iclosit	*surrounded and enclosed*
	One sich o wyss, that none within supposit	*In such a way*
55	Fore to be senn with ony uicht thareowt.	*by any person outside*
	So dide the levis clos it all about.	
	Thar was the flour, thar was the Quenn Alphest,	*(see note)*
	Rycht wering being of the nychtis rest,	*weary*
	Wnclosing ganne the crownel for the day;	*Unclosed the diadem*
60	The brycht sone illumynit haith the spray,	*slender twigs*
	The nychtis sobir ande the most schowris,	*gentle; moist showers*
	As cristoll terys withhong upone the flouris	*tears hung*
	Haith upwarpith in the lusty aire,	*drawn up; pleasant*
	The morow makith soft, ameyne, and faire.	*morning; pleasant*

---

[1] *Then [I walked] to a garden, which was beautiful*

65	And the byrdis thar mychty voce out-throng	*cast forth*
	Quhill al the wood resonite of thar songe	*Until; resounded with*
	That gret confort till ony uicht it wer	*to any person*
	That plessith thame of lustenes to here.	*joy[ful sound] to hear*
	Bot gladness til the thochtful, ever mo	*to the melancholy*
70	The more he seith, the more he haith of wo.	
	Thar was the garding with the flouris ovrfret,[1]	
	Quich is in posy fore my lady set,[2]	
	That hire represent to me oft befor	*symbolized her*
	And thane also; thus al day gan, be sor	*(see note); by sorrow*
75	Of thocht, my gost with torment occupy,	*spirit*
	That I becamme into one exasy,	*trance*
	Ore slep, or how I wot; bot so befell	*before I knew how*
	My wo haith done my livis gost expell,	*spirit*
	And in sich wiss weil long I can endwr;[3]	
80	So me betid o wondir aventur.	*befell a wondrous adventure*
	As I thus lay, rycht to my spreit uas senn	*spirit was seen*
	A birde, that was as ony lawrare grenn,	*laurel*
	Alicht and sayth into hir birdis chere,	*Alighted; bird's way*
	"O woful wrech that levis into were!	*who lives in doubt*
85	To schew the thus the god of Love me sent	
	That of thi service no thing is content,	*Who with; is not at all*
	For in his court yhoue levith in disspar	*you live in despair*
	And uilfully sustenis al thi care	
	And schapith no thinge of thine awn remede[4]	
90	Bot clepith ay and cryith apone dede.	*call constantly; death*
	Yhow callith the birdis be morow fro thar bouris;	*in the morning; bowers*
	Yhoue devith boith the erbis and the flouris	*You deafen*
	And clepit hyme unfaithful King of Love.	*call*
	Yow devith hyme into his rigne abufe;	*deafen; in his kingdom above*
95	Yhow tempith hyme, yhoue doith thiself no gud;	*tempt*
	Yhoue are o monn of wit al destitude.	*a man*

[1] *There was the garden profusely adorned with flowers*

[2] *Which is in poetry (i.e., figuratively) presented for my lady*

[3] *And in such a state I endured very long*

[4] *And do nothing to bring about your own cure*

Wot yhoue nocht that al livis creatwre [1]

Haith of thi wo into his hand the cwre? *cure*

And set yhoue clep one erbis and one treis, *although you call on*

100 Sche heris not thi wo, nore yhit sche seis; *hears; nor sees it*

For none may know the dirkness of thi thocht *despondency*

Ne blamyth her thi wo sche knowith nocht.

And it is weil accordinge it be so *quite fitting*

He suffir harme, that to redress his wo *[That] he should suffer*

105 Previdith not; for long ore he be sonde, [2]

Holl of his leich, that schewith not his uound. [3]

And of Ovid the autor schall yhow knaw,

Of lufe that seith, for to consel or schow, [4]

The last he clepith althir best of two; *(see note)*

110 And that is suth and sal be ever mo. *the truth*

And Love also haith chargit me to say *commanded*

Set yhoue presume, ore beleif, the assay *(see note)*

Of his service, as it wil ryne ore go, *run or*

Preswme it not, fore it wil not be so;

115 Al magré thine a servand schal yow bee. *(see note)*

And as tueching thine adversytee, *concerning*

Complen and sek of the ramed, the cwre; *Lament; moan; remedy; cure*

Ore, gif yhow likith, furth thi wo endure." *longer*

And, as me thocht, I ansuerde againne *it seemed to me I replied*

120 Thus to the byrde, in wordis schort and plane:

"It ganyth not, as I have harde recorde, *It avails; heard said*

The servand for to disput with the lord;

Bot well he knowith of al my uo the quhy *woe the reason*

And in quhat wyss he hath me set, quhar I *in what manner; where*

125 Nore may I not, nore can I not attane, [5]

Nore to hir hienes dare I not complane." *her majesty; lament*

"Ful," quod the bird, "lat be thi nyss dispare, *Fool; foolish*

For in this erith no lady is so fare, *earth; fair*

---

[1] *Do you not know that the creator of all life*

[2] *Makes no provision; for [it is] a long time before he will be healthy*

[3] *Sound of body, who does not reveal his wound*

[4] *Who speaks of love, between keeping it secret or revealing it*

[5] *Neither am able nor know how to attain*

	So hie estat, nore of so gret empriss	*Of such high degree; renown*
130	That in hireself haith uisdome ore gentrice,	*nobility*
	Yf that o wicht, that worthy is to be	*a person*
	Of Lovis court schew til hir that he	*show to her*
	Servith hire in lovis hartly wyss	*heartfelt*
	That schall tharfor hyme hating or dispiss.	*hate or despise*
135	The god of Love thus chargit the, at schort,	*in short*
	That to thi lady yhoue thi wo report.	
	Yf yhoue may not, thi plant schall yhou urit.	*complaint; write*
	Se, as yhoue cane, be maner oft endit	*Say; in the manner; written*
	In metir, quhich that no man haith susspek,	*holds suspect*
140	Set ofttyme thai contenyng gret effecc;[1]	
	Thus one sume wyss yhow schal thi wo dwclar.	*in some way*
	And for thir sedulis and thir billis are[2]	
	So generall and ek so schort at lyte	*also; (see note)*
	And swme of thaim is lost the appetit,	*passion*
145	Sum trety schall yhoue for thi lady sak,	*narrative; lady's sake*
	That wnkouth is, als tak one hand and mak[3]	
	Of love ore armys or of sum othir thing	
	That may hir oneto thi remembryng brynge,	
	Qwich soundith not oneto no hevyness[4]	
150	Bot oneto gladness and to lusteness	*pleasure*
	That yhoue belevis may thi lady pless,	*you believe; please*
	To have hir thonk and be oneto hir ess	*thanks; pleasure*
	That sche may wit in service yhow art one.	*know*
	Faire weil," quod sche, "thus schal yhow the dispone	*conduct yourself*
155	And mak thiself als mery as yhoue may;	
	It helpith not thus fore to wex alway."	*to be so [sad] always*
	With that the bird sche haith hir leif tak,	*her leave taken*
	For fere of quich I can onone to wak.	*I woke up at once*
	Sche was ago, and to myself thocht I	*gone*
160	Quhat may this meyne? Quhat may this signify?	
	Is it of troucht or of illusioune?	*truth*

---

[1] *Although often they contain much significance*

[2] *And since letters and petitions such as these are*

[3] *That [previously] unknown is, so as to undertake and write*

[4] *Which does not cause any sorrow*

Bot finaly, as in conclusioune,
Be as be may, I schal me not discharge [1]

Sen it apperith be of Lovis charg — *Since it appears to be Love's mandate*
165 And ek myne hart nonne othir bissynes — *concern*
Haith bot my ladice service, as I gess. — *lady's; suppose*
Among al utheris I schal one honde tak — *undertake*
This litil occupatioune for hire sak.
Bot hyme I pray, the mychty gode of Love,
170 That sitith hie into his spir abuf — *high in his sphere above*
(At command of o wyss quhois visioune — *(see note)*
My gost haith takin this opunioune)
That my lawboure may to my lady pless — *effort; be pleasing*
And do wnto hir ladeschip sum ess — *her ladyship; pleasure*
175 So that my travell be nocht tynt, and I — *work; wasted*
Quhat utheris say setith nothing by. — *What; care nothing for*
For wel I know that be this worldis famme — *by*
It schal not be bot hurting to my namme
Quhen that thai here my febil negligens — *When; hear*
180 That empit is and bare of eloquens, — *empty*
Of discressioune, and ek of retoryk, — *discrimination*
The metire and the cuning both elyk — *skill at versification; craft; alike*
So fere discording frome perfeccioune, — *far differing*
Quhilk I submyt to the correccioune — *Which*
185 Of thaim the quhich that is discret and wyss — *those who are; wise*
And enterit is of Love in the service, — *[who] have entered*
Quhich knouyth that no lovare dare withstonde: — *Who know; oppose*
Quhat Love hyme chargit he mot tak one honde, — *he must undertake*
Deith or defamm or ony maner wo. — *[Whether it be] death or disgrace*
190 And at this tyme with me it stant rycht so — *just so*
As I that dar makine no demande — *to make; countermand*
To quhat I wot it lykith Love commande. [2]
Tueching his chargis, as with-al destitut, [3]
Within my mynd schortly I conclud
195 For to fulfyll, for ned I mot do so. — *necessarily I must*

---

[1] *However it might be, I shall not free myself from my responsibility*

[2] *To what I know it pleases Love to command*

[3] *Concerning his commands, as [one who is] entirely destitute*

     Thane in my thocht rolling to and fro

     Quhare that I myhct sum wnkouth mater fynde — *original subject*

     Quhill at the last it fell into my mynd — *Until finally*

     Of o story, that I befor had sene,

200 That boith of love and armys can contenn, — *consisted*

     Was of o knycht clepit Lancelot of the Laik, — *called; Lake*

     The sone of Bane was, King of Albanak,

     Of quhois fame and worschipful dedis — *whose; renowned*

     Clerkis into diverss bukis redis, — *in various books read*

205 Of quhome I thynk her sumthing for to writ — *whom [= Lancelot]*

     At Lovis charge, and as I cane endit, — *as I am able to compose*

     Set men tharin sal by experiens — *Since*

     Know my consait and al my negligens. — *frame of mind*

     Bot for that story is so pasing larg, — *exceedingly long*

210 Oneto my wit it war so gret o charg — *a demand*

     For to translait the romans of that knycht.

     It passith fare my cunyng and my mycht;

     Myne ignorans may it not comprehende.

     Quharfor thareone I wil me not depend — *(see note)*

215 How he was borne, nore how his fader deid

     And ek his moder, nore how he was denyed

     Efter thare deth, presumyng he was ded,

     Of al the lond, nore how he fra that stede — *from; place*

     In sacret wyss wnwyst away was tak — *without its being known; taken*

220 And nwrist with the Lady of the Lak. — *raised by*

     Nor, in his youth, think I not to tell

     The aventouris, quhich to hyme befell,

     Nor how the Lady of the Laik hyme had

     Oneto the court, quhare that he knycht was mad. — *where; made*

225 None wist his nome nore how that he was tak — *name; taken*

     By love and was iwondit to the stak — *(see note)*

     And throuch and throuch persit to the hart — *pierced*

     That al his tyme he couth it not astart; — *could; escape*

     For thare of Love he enterit in service

230 Of Wanore throuch the beuté and franchis, — *Guinevere; nobility*

     Throuch quhois service in armys he has urocht — *wrought*

     Mony wonderis, and perellis he has socht. — *sought out*

     Nor how he thor, into his young curage — *there; in; heart*

     Hath maid avoue and into lovis rage — *sworn an oath; frenzy*

18

235	In the revenging of o wondit knycht	
	That cumyne was into the court that nycht.	
	Into his hed a brokin suerd had he	*In*
	And in his body also mycht men see	
	The tronsione of o brokine sper that was,	*truncheon; broken*
240	Quhich no man out dedenyt to aras;	*deigned to pull out*
	Nor how he haith the wapnis out tak	
	And his avow apone this wis can mak,	*in this manner made*
	That he schuld hyme reveng at his poware	*to the best of his ability*
	One every knycht that lovith the hurtare	*the one who did the harm*
245	Better thane hyme, the quhich that uas iwond.	*was wounded*
	Throw quich avoue in armys hath ben founde	
	The deth of mony wereoure ful wicht;	*warrior very valiant*
	For, fro tho vow was knowing of the knycht,	*since the; known*
	Thare was ful mony o pasage in the londe	*many a combat*
250	By men of armys kepit to withstond	*retained*
	This knycht, of quhome thai ben al set afyre	*by whom*
	Thaim to reveng in armys of desir.	*(see note)*
	Nor how that thane incontynent was send	*immediately*
	He and Sir Kay togidder to defend	
255	The Lady of Nohalt, nore how that hee	
	Governit hyme thare, nore in quhat degré.	*Conducted himself*
	Nor how the gret pasing vassolag	*surpassing valor*
	He eschevit throue the outragouss curag,	*achieved; extravagant*
	In conquiryng of the sorowful castell.	
260	Nor how he passith doune in the cavis fell	*dreadful*
	And furth the keys of inchantment brocht,	*brought*
	That al distroyt quhich that thare uas urocht.	*was wrought*
	Nore howe that he reskewit Sir Gawane,	
	With his nine falouss into presone tane.	*companions; taken*
265	Nore mony uthere diverss adventure,	*various*
	Quhich to report I tak not in my cwre.	*as my responsibility*
	Nore mony assemblay that Gawane gart be maid [1]	
	To wit his name; nor how that he hyme hade	*know; kept himself*
	Wnwist and hath the worschip and empriss;	*Unknown; renown*
270	Nor of the knychtis into mony diverss wyss	*various ways*

---

[1] *Nor many an encounter that Gawain caused to be made*

Throuch his avoue that hath thare dethis found.   *vow*
Nor of the sufferans that by Lovis wounde   *suffering*
He in his travel sufferith avermore.   *travail*
Nor in the Quenis presens how tharfor
275   By Camelot, into that gret revare,   *river*
He was ner dround. I wil it not declare   *drowned*
How that he was in lovis hevy thocht   *sad*
By Dagenet into the court ibrocht;
Nor how the knycht that tyme he cane persew,   *pursued*
280   Nor of the gyantis by Camelot he slew;
Nor wil I not her tell the maner how
He slew o knycht, by natur of his vow,
Off Melyholt; nore how into that toune
Thar came one hyme o gret confusione   *mixture*
285   Of pupil and knychtis al enarmyt;   *people; armed*
Nor how he thar haith kepit hyme wnharmyt;
Nor of his worschip, nor of his gret prowes,   *valor*
Nor his defens of armys in the pres;   *press of battle*
Nor how the Lady of Melyhalt that sche
290   Came to the feild and prayth hyme that he
As to o lady to hir his suerd hath yold,   *yielded*
Nor how he was into hir keping hold.   *detained*
And mony uthir nobil deid also   *deeds*
I wil report quharfor I lat ovrgo.   *why I disregard them*
295   For quho thaim lykith forto specyfy   *relate fully*
Of one of thaim mycht mak o gret story.   *long*
Nor thing I not of his hye renown   *think*
My febil wit to makin mensioune.
Bot of the weris that was scharp and strong,   *were bitter and fierce*
300   Richt perellouss, and hath enduryt long;
Of Arthur in defending of his lond
Frome Galiot, sone of the fair Gyonde
That brocht of knychtis o pasing confluens   *a great gathering*
And how Lancelot of Arthuris hol defens
305   And of the ueris berith the renownn;   *wars*
And how he be the wais of fortoune   *by*
Tuex the two princis makith the accorde   *Between; agreement*
Of al there mortall weris to concorde;   *end peacefully*
And how that Venus, siting hie abuf,   *high above*

310	Reuardith hyme of travell into love	*for his labors in love*
	And makith hyme his ladice grace to have,	*lady's favor*
	And thankfully his service can resave:	*did accept*
	This is the mater quhich I think to tell.	*which*
	Bot stil he mot rycht with the lady duell	
315	Quhill tyme cum eft that we schal of hym spek.	
	This process mot closine benn and stek, [1]	
	And furth I wil oneto my mater go.	*subject*
	Bot first I pray and I besek also	*beseech*
	Oneto the most conpilour to support,	*greatest author; for support*
320	Flour of poyetis, quhois nome I wil report	*Flower of poets*
	To me nor to nonn uthir it accordit	
	Into our rymyng his namm to be recordit;	*In our rhyming*
	For sum suld deme it of presumpsioune	*judge it presumptuous*
	And ek our rymyng is al bot derysioune	
325	Quhen that remembrit is his excellens	
	So hie abuf that stant in reverans.	*who stands in reverence*
	The fresch enditing of his Laiting toung	*vivid writing; Latin*
	Out throuch this world so wid is yroung	*celebrated*
	Of eloquens and ek of retoryk.	
330	Nor is nor was nore never beith hyme lyk;	*will be [one] like him*
	This world gladith of his suet poetry.	*delightful*
	His saul i blyss conservyt be forthy; [2]	
	And yf that ony lusty terme I wryt	*pleasant phrase*
	He haith the thonk therof and this endit.	*(see note)*

EXPLICIT PROLOGUS, ET INCIPIT PRIMUS LIBER. [3]

BOOK I

335	Quhen Tytan withe his lusty heit	*(see note); pleasant warmth*
	Twenty dais into the Aryeit	
	Haith maid his courss and all with diverss hewis	*various colors*
	Aparalit haith the feldis and the bewis,	*boughs*

---

[1] *This exposition must be closed and concluded*

[2] *May his soul be saved in the joy [of heaven] on account of that*

[3] *The Prologue ends and the first book begins*

	The birdis amyd the erbis and the flouris	*plants; flowers*
340	And one the branchis makyne gone thar bouris,	*made their nests*
	And be the morow singing in ther chere [1]	
	Welcum the lusty sessone of the yere.	*pleasant season*
	Into this tyme the worthi conqueroure	*In*
	Arthure, wich had of al this worlde the floure	
345	Of chevelry anerding to his crown —	*adhering (see note)*
	So pasing war his knychtis in renoune —	*excellent were*
	Was at Carlill; and hapynnit so that hee	*it chanced that*
	Sojornyt well long in that faire cuntree,	*Stayed*
	Into whilk tyme into the court thai heire	*At which; in; hear*
350	None aventure, for wich the knyghtis weire	*were*
	Anoit all at the abiding thare.	*Annoyed*
	Forwhy beholding one the sobir ayre	
	And of the tyme the pasing lustynes [2]	
	Can so thir knyghtly hartis to encress	*intensify*
355	That thei Shir Kay oneto the King haith sende	
	Beseiching hyme he wold vichsaif to wende	*deign to go*
	To Camelot the cetee, whare that thei	
	Ware wont to heryng of armys day be day. [3]	
	The King forsuth, heryng thare entent,	*hearing*
360	To thare desir, be schort avysment,	*after brief consideration*
	Ygrantid haith; and so the king proponit	*asserted*
	And for to pas hyme one the morne disponit.	*depart; intended*
	Bot so befell hyme that nycht to meit	*dream*
	An aperans, the wich oneto his spreit	*apparition; mind*
365	It semyth that of al his hed the hore	*from; head; hair*
	Of fallith and maid desolat; wharfore	*bald*
	The King therof was pensyve in his mynd	*troubled*
	That al the day he couth no resting fynde	*was able*
	Wich makith hyme his jorneye to delaye.	
370	And so befell apone the thrid day,	
	The bricht sone pasing in the west	
	Hath maid his courss and al thing goith to rest.	

---

[1] *And in the morning singing as is their manner*

[2] *Because observing the pleasant air / And the surpassing joy of the season*

[3] *Were accustomed to hear of arms day by day (i.e., every day)*

The Kinge, so as the story can devyss,   *did relate*
He thoght ageine apone the samyne wyss: *same manner (see note)*
375   His uombe out fallith uith his hoil syde   *stomach; whole*
Apone the ground and liging hyme besid,   *(see note)*
Throw wich anon out of his slep he stert,   *Because of; sprang up*
Abasit and adred into his hart.   *Startled and terrified*
The wich be morow oneto the Qwen he told,   *in the morning*
380   And she ageine to hyme haith ansuer yolde.   *given*
"To dremys, sir, shuld no man have respek,   *give heed*
For thei ben thingis veyn, of non affek."   *worthless; efficacy*
"Well," quod the King, "God grant it so befall."
Arly he ross and gert oneto hyme call   *Early; had summoned to him*
385   O clerk, to whome that al his hevynes   *worry*
Tweching his drem shewith he express,   *Concerning; clearly*
Wich ansuer yaf and seith oneto the Kinge: *Who; gave*
"Shir, no record lyith to such thing;   *Sir; authority*
Wharfor now, shir, I praye yow tak no kep   *heed*
390   Nore traist into the vanyteis of slep.   *worthless things*
For thei are thingis that askith no credens   *call for no credence*
But causith of sum maner influens,   *[are] caused by*
Empriss of thoght, ore superfleuytee,   *Pre-occupation; (see note)*
Or than sum othir casualytee."   *Rather than some other cause*
395   "Yit," quod the King, "I sal nocht leif it so."   *believe*
And furth he chargit mesingeris to go   *commanded*
Throgh al his realm, withouten more demande,   *delay*
And bad them stratly at thei shulde comande   *urgently that*
All the bishopes and makyng no delay
400   The shuld appere be the tuenty day   *They; by; twentieth*
At Camelot with al thar hol clergy   *(see note)*
That most expert war for to certefye   *explain*
A mater tueching to his gost be nyght.   *concerning his spirit*
The mesag goith furth with the lettres right.

405   The King eftsone, within a litill space,   *soon; time*
His jornay makith haith frome place to place,
Whill that he cam to Camelot. And there   *Until*
The clerkis all, as that the chargit were,   *they were commanded*
Assemblit war and cam to his presens,
410   Of his desir to uiting the sentens.   *to know the gist*

	To them that war to hyme most speciall	
	Furth his entent shauyth he al hall;	*he reveals completely*
	By whois conseil of the worthiest	
	He chesith ten, yclepit for the best,	*chooses; named as*
415	And most expert and wisest was supposit,	*were considered*
	To qwhome his drem all hail he haith disclossit —	*wholly*
	The houre, the nyght, and al the cercumstans —	*details*
	Besichyne them that the signifycans	*Beseeching*
	Thei wald hyme shaw, that he mycht resting fynde	*show; respite*
420	Of it, the wich that occupeid his mynde.	*From*
	And one of them with al ther holl assent [1]	
	Saith, "Shire, fore to declare our entent	*Sir*
	Upone this matere, ye wil ws delay	
	Fore to avysing oneto the ninth day."	*deliberate*
425	The King therto grantith haith, bot hee	
	Into o place that strong was and hye,	
	He closith them whare thei may nowhare get	
	Unto the day, the wich he to them set.	*Until*
	Than goith the clerkis sadly to avyss	*diligently to deliberate*
430	Of this mater, to seing in what wyss	*see; manner*
	The Kingis drem thei shal best specefy.	*explain*
	And than the maistris of astronomy	
	The bookis longyne to ther artis set.	*pertaining; (see note)*
	Not was the bukis of Arachell forget,	
435	Of Nembrot, of Danghelome, thei two,	
	Of Moyses, and of Herynes allsoo.	
	And seking be ther calcolacioune	*calculation*
	To fynd the planetis disposicioune,	*(see note)*
	The wich thei fond ware wonder evill yset	*were very ill-situated*
440	The samyne nyght the King his sweven met.	*dreamed his dream*
	So ner the point socht thei have the thing, [2]	
	Thei fond it wonder hevy to the King,	*very troublesome*
	Of wich thing thei waryng into were	*were in doubt*
	To shew the King for dreid of his danger.	*fear of his power*
445	Of ane accorde thei planly have proponit	*one; proposed*

---

[1] *And one of them, with their unanimous agreement*

[2] *In such detail have they analyzed the thing (i.e., the dream)*

24

	No worde to show, and so thei them disponit.	*say; they intended*
	The day is cumyng and he haith fore them sent,	*has come*
	Besichyne them to shewing ther entent.	*declare their understanding*
	Than spak thei all and that of an accorde:	*unanimously*
450	"Shir, of this thing we can no thing recorde,	*report*
	For we can noght fynd intil our sciens	*in our learning*
	Tweching this mater ony evydens."	*Concerning; any clue*
	"Now," quod the King, "and be the glorius Lorde,	*by*
	Or we depart ye shall sumthing recorde;	*Before; report*
455	So pas yhe not, nor so it sall not bee."	*leave you; shall*
	"Than," quod the clerkis, "grant ws dais three."	*days*
	The wich he grantid them, and but delay	*without delay*
	The term passith; nothing wold the say,	*they*
	Wharof the King stondith hevy cherith;	*heavy-hearted*
460	And to the clerkis his visag so apperith	*countenance*
	That all thei dred them of the Kingis myght.	
	Than saith o clerk, "Sir, as the thrid nyght	*third*
	Ye dremyt, so giffis ws delay	*give*
	The thrid tyme and to the thrid day."	
465	By whilk tyme thei fundyng haith the ende	*have found*
	Of this mater, als far as shal depend	*be the concern*
	To ther sciens; yit can thei not avyss	*Of; devise [something]*
	To schewing to the King be ony wyss.	*reveal; in any way*
	The day is cum; the King haith them besocht;	*summoned*
470	Bot one no wyss thei wald declar ther thoght.	
	Than was he wroth into hisself and noyt	*annoyed*
	And maid his vow that thei shal ben distroyt.	
	His baronis he commandit to gar tak	*to have taken*
	Fyve of them oneto the fir stak	*fire-stake*
475	And uther fyve be to the gibbot tone;	*gallows; taken*
	And the furth with the Kingis charg ar gone.	*they*
	He bad them into secret wyss that thei	
	Shud do no harm but only them assey.	*put them to the test*
	The clarkis, dredful of the Kingis ire	*fearful*
480	And saw the perell of deth and of the fyre,	
	Fyve, as thei can, has grantit to record,	*agreed to report*

25

That uther herde and ben of ther accorde. [1]
And al thei ben yled oneto the King
And shew hyme thus as tueching of this thing.   *reveal to him; concerning*
485 "Shir, sen that we constrenyt ar by myght   *since*
And to shaw wich that we knaw nothing aricht,
For thing to cum preservith it allan [2]
To Hyme the wich is every thing certann   *Him to whom*
Excep the thing that til our knawleg Hee   *to*
490 Hath ordynat of certan for to bee.   *surely*
Therfor, shir King, we your magnificens
Beseich it turne till ws to non offens
Nor hald ws nocht as learis, thoght it fall   *charlatans though*
Not in this mater, as that we telen shall."
495 And that the King haith grantit them, and thei
Has chargit one, that one this wiss sall seye. [3]
"Presumyth, shir, that we have fundyne so: *ascertained*
All erdly honore ye nedist most forgo   *earthly; necessarily*
And them the wich ye most affy intyll   *put faith in*
500 Shal failye yow, magré of ther will;   *in spite of their*
And thus we have into this matere founde."   *in*
The King, qwhois hart was al wyth dred ybownd,   *whose; fettered*
And askit at the clerkis if thei fynde   *asked of*
By there clergy that stant in ony kynde   *their study*
505 Of possibilitee fore to reforme   *change*
His desteny, that stud in such a forme,   *was shaped in such a way*
If in the hevyne is preordynat
On such o wiss his honor to translat.   *remove*
The clerkis saith, "Forsuth, and we have sene   *In truth*
510 O thing wharof, if we the trouth shal menn,   *tell*
Is so obscure and dyrk til our clergye   *dark to our learning*
That we wat not what it shal signefye   *know*
Wich causith ws we can it not furth say."
"Yis," quod the King, "as lykith yow ye may,   *if you wish*
515 For wers than this can nat be said for me."   *worse*

---

[1] *The other [five] heard and are in agreement with them*
[2] *For [knowledge of] things to come is reserved solely*
[3] *Have designated one who will speak in this manner*

26

Thane saith o maistir, "Than suthly thus finde we: *truly*
Thar is nothing sal sucour nor reskew;
Your worldly honore nedis most adew,   *necessarily must depart*
But throuch the watrye lyone, and ek fyne,   *Except through the watery lion; end*
520 On throuch the liche and ek the wattir syne,   *physician; then*
And throuch the conseill of the flour; God wot   *flower; knows*
What this shude menn, for mor ther-of we not."   *mean; know not*
No word the King ansuerid ayane,   *in response*
For al this resone thinkith bot in veyne.   *seems to be to no effect*
525 He shawith outwart his contenans
As he therof takith no grevans;   *offense*
But al the nyght it passid nat his thoght. [1]
The dais courss with ful desir he socht, [2]
And furth he goith to bring his mynd in rest
530 With mony o knyght unto the gret forest.
The rachis gon wncopelit for the deire [3]
That in the wodis makith nois and cheir;   *bark and sport*
The knychtis with the grewhundis in aweit   *greyhounds*
Secith boith the planis and the streit.   *clearings; narrow paths*
535 Doune goith the hart, doune goith the hynd also.
. . . .
The swift grewhund, hardy of assay;   *proven hardy*
Befor ther hedis nothing goith away.   *heads; escapes*
The King of hunting takith haith his sport
540 And to his palace home he can resort   *he returned*
Ayan the noon. And as that he was set   *At noon*
Uith all his noble knyghtis at the met,   *meal*
So cam therin an agit knyght; and hee   *aged*
Of gret esstat semyt for to bee,   *rank*
545 Anarmyt all, as tho it was the gyss,   *Armed; then; custom*
And thus the King he salust one this wiss.   *greeted*

"Shir King, oneto yow am Y sende
Frome the worthiest that in world is kend   *known*

---

[1] *But all night it was not out of his thoughts*

[2] *The coming of day he eagerly longed for*

[3] *The hunting dogs were unleashed upon the wild animals*

27

	That levyth now of his tyme and age,	*Who lives*
550	Of manhed, wisdome, and of hie curag,	
	Galiot, sone of the fare Gyande.	
	And thus, at short, he bidis yow your londe	*in short*
	Ye yald hyme ovr, without impedyment	*hand over to him; delay*
	Or of hyme holde, and if tribut and rent.	*(see note); give tribute*
555	This is my charge at short, whilk if youe lest	*it pleases you*
	For to fulfill, of al he haith conquest	
	He sais that he most tendir shal youe hald."	*dear*
	By short avys the King his ansuer yald:[1]	
	"Schir knycht, your lorde wondir hie pretendis	*aspires*
560	When he to me sic salutatioune sendis;	*such greeting*
	For I as yit, in tymys that ar gone,	
	Held never lond excep of God alone	
	Nore never thinkith til erthly lord to yef	*give*
	Trybut nor rent, als long as I may lef."	*live*
565	"Well," quod the knycht, "ful sor repentith me;	*it grieves me*
	Non may recist the thing the wich mone bee.	*resist; which must be*
	To yow, sir King, than frome my lord am I	
	With diffyans sent, and be this resone why:	*a declaration of war*
	His purpos is, or this day moneth day,	*before a month from today*
570	With all his ost, planly to assay	*host; attack*
	Your lond with mony manly man of were	*war*
	And helmyt knychtis, boith with sheld and spere	*helmed*
	And never thinkith to retwrn home whill	*until*
	That he this lond haith conquest at his will	*conquered*
575	And ek Uanour the Quen, of whome that hee	*Guinevere*
	Herith report of al this world that shee	
	In fairhed and in vertew doith excede,	*beauty*
	He bad me say he thinkis to possede."	*possess*
	"Schir," quod the King, "your mesag me behufis	*it behooves me*
580	Of resone and of curtasy excuss;	
	But tueching to your lord and to his ost,	*concerning*
	His powar, his mesag and his bost,	*army; boast*
	That pretendith my lond for to distroy,	*aspires*
	Tharof as yit tak I non anoye;	

---

[1] *After considering only a short time, the King gave his answer*

28

585	And say your lord one my behalf, when hee
	Haith tone my lond, that al the world shal see
	That it shal be magré myne entent."
	With that the knycht, withouten leif, is went,
	And richt as he was pasing to the dure
590	He saith, "A Gode! What wykyt adventure
	Apperith!" With that his hors he nome —
	Two knichtis kepit, waiting his outcome.
	The knicht is gon; the King he gan inquere
	At Gawan and at other knychtis sere
595	If that thei knew or ever hard recorde
	Of Galiot, and wharof he wes lorde.
	And ther was non among his knychtis all
	Which ansuerd o word into the hall.
	Than Galygantynis of Walys rase,
600	That travelit in diverss londis has,
	In mony knychtly aventur haith ben.
	And to the King he saith, "Sir, I have sen
	Galiot, which is the farest knycht
	And hiest be half a fut one hycht
605	That ever I saw, and ek his men accordith;
	Hym lakid nocht that to a lord recordith.
	For uisare of his ag is non than hee
	And ful of larges and humylytee.
	An hart he haith of pasing hie curag
610	And is not twenty-four yer of age.
	And of his tyme mekil haith conquerit:
	Ten kingis at his command ar sterit.
	He uith his men so lovit is, Y gess,
	That hyme to pless is al ther besynes. [1]
615	Not say I this, sir, into the entent
	That he, nor none wnder the firmament,
	Shal pouere have ayane your majestee;
	And or thei shuld, this Y sey for mee —
	Rather I shall knychtly into feild
620	Resave my deith anarmyt wnder sheld.

Glosses (right margin):

- 586 taken
- 587 in spite of my intention
- 588 leave, has gone
- 589 door
- 591 took
- 592 guarded [it]; departure
- 594 Of; of various other knights
- 595 heard an account
- 599 rose
- 604 tallest by; in height
- 605 are similar
- 606 pertains
- 607 wiser
- 608 generosity
- 611 in his time much
- 612 ruled
- 613 with (i.e., by)
- 616 under heaven
- 617 Shall avail against
- 618 before
- 620 Receive; armed

---

[1] *That to please him is all they are concerned about*

29

	This spek Y lest." The King, ayan the morn,	*(see note)*
	Haith uarnit huntaris baith with hund and horne	*notified*
	And arly gan oneto the forest ryd	*early; ride*
	With mony manly knyghtis by his sid	
625	Hyme for to sport and comfort with the dere	*wild animals*
	Set contrare was the sesone of the yere	*Although unfavorable*
	His most huntyng was atte wyld bore.	*of the*
	God wot a lustye cuntree was it thoore	*knows; pleasant; there*
	In the ilk tyme. Weil long this noble King	*In that time*
630	Into this lond haith maid his sujornyng.	*sojourn*
	Frome the Lady was send o mesinger	*sent*
	Of Melyhalt, wich saith one this maner,	
	As that the story shewith by recorde:	
	"To yow, sir King, as to hir soveran lorde,	
635	My lady hath me chargit for to say	*commanded*
	How that your lond stondith in affray	*is under attack*
	For Galiot, sone of the fare Gyande,	*son*
	Enterit is by armys in your land;	*by force of arms into*
	And so the lond and cuntré he anoyth	*vexes*
640	That quhar he goith planly he distroyth	
	And makith al obeisand to his honde	*obedient to him*
	That nocht is left wnconquest in that lond,	*unconquered*
	Excep two castellis longing to hir cwre,	*under her dominion*
	Wich to defend she may nocht long endure.	
645	Wharfor, sir, in wordis plan and short,	*plain*
	Ye mon dispone your folk for to support."	*must use*
	"Wel," quod the King, "oneto thi lady say	
	The neid is myne; I sall it not delay.	
	But what folk ar thei nemmyt for to bee	*said to be*
650	That in my lond is cumyne in sich degree?"	*in such a way*
	"An hundreth thousand boith uith sheld and spere	
	On hors ar armyt, al redy for the were."	*war*
	"Wel," quod the King, "and but delay this nycht,	*without delay*
	Or than tomorn as that the day is lycht	*Before the morning when*
655	I shal remuf; ther shal nothing me mak	*depart*
	Impedyment my jorney for to tak."	
	Than seith his knychtis al with one assent,	
	"Shir, that is al contrare our entent;	*in opposition to*

30

	For to your folk this mater is wnwist	*unknown*
660	And ye ar here ovr few for to recist	*too few to resist*
	Yone power and youre cuntré to defende.	
	Tharfor abid and for your folk ye send,	*wait*
	That lyk a king and lyk a weriour	
	Ye may susten in armys your honoure."	
665	"Now," quod the King, "no langer that I yeme	*care for*
	My crowne, my septure, nor my dyademe	*scepter*
	Frome that I here ore frome I wnderstand	*From [the time] that*
	That ther by fors be entrit in my land	
	Men of armys, by strenth of vyolens,	
670	If that I mak abid or resydens	*If I hesitate or delay*
	Into o place langar than o nycht	*In*
	For to defend my cuntré and my rycht."	
	The King that day his mesage haith furth sent	
	Throuch al his realme and syne to rest is went.	*Through; then*
675	Up goith the morow; wp goith the brycht day;	
	Wp goith the sone into his fresh aray.	*in his new adornment*
	Richt as he spred his bemys frome northest,	
	The King wprass withouten more arest	*arose; delay*
	And by his awn conseil and entent	
680	His jornaye tuk at short avysment.	*undertook quickly*
	And but dulay he goith frome place to place	*without delay*
	Whill that he cam nere whare the lady was	*Until*
	And in one plane apone o rever syde	*river*
	He lichtit doune, and ther he can abide.	*dismounted; stayed*
685	And yit with hyme to batell fore to go	
	Seven thousand fechteris war thei and no mo.	*soldiers; more*
	This was the lady, of qwhome befor I tolde	*whom*
	That Lancilot haith into hir kepinge holde,	
	But for to tell his pasing hevynesse,	*great grief*
690	His peyne, his sorow, and his gret distresse	
	Of presone and of loves gret suppris,	*prison; oppression*
	It war to long to me for to devys.	*recount*
	When he remembrith one his hevy charge	
	Of love, wharof he can hyme not discharge,	*free himself*
695	He wepith and he sorowith in his chere;	*was sorrowful of demeanor*

31

	And every nyght semyth hyme o yere.	*a year*
	Gret peité was the sorow that he maad,	*pity*
	And to hymeself apone this wiss he saade:	*said*

"Qwhat have Y gilt, allace, or qwhat deservit [1]
700 That thus myne hart shal uondit ben and carvit   *wounded; slashed*
   One by the suord of double peine and wo?
   My comfort and my plesans is ago;   *gone*
To me is nat that shuld me glaid reservit. [2]

"I curss the tyme of myne nativitee,   *birth*
705 Whar in the heven it ordinyd was for me   *ordained*
   In all my lyve never til have eess   *to have ease*
   But for to be example of disess;   *distress*
And that apperith that every uicht may see.   *so that every person*

"Sen thelke tyme that I had sufficians   *Since that; sufficiency*
710 Of age and chargit thoghtis sufferans,   *heeded; affliction*
   Nor never I continewite haith o day   *had the space of one day*
   Without the payne of thoghtis hard assay;   *assault*
Thus goith my youth in tempest and penans.   *penance*

"And now my body is in presone broght,   *prison*
715 But of my wo, that in regard is noght, [3]
   The wich myne hart felith evermore.
   O deth, allace! Whi hath yow me forbore   *alas; overlooked*
That of remed haith the so long besoght?" [4]

Thus nevermore he sesith to compleine,   *ceases*
720 This woful knyght that felith not bot peine   *nothing but pain*
   So prekith hyme the smert of loves sore   *afflicts; pain; sorrow*
   And every day encressith more and more.
And with this lady takine is also   *by*

---

[1] *What have I done wrong or what [have I done] to deserve*

[2] *Nothing that should give me joy remains to me*

[3] *But that [being in prison] is nothing in comparison with my woe*

[4] *Who have so long pleaded to you for a remedy*

	And kepit whar he may nowhare go	
725	To haunt knychthed, the wich he most desirit.	*engage in knightly deeds*
	And thus, his hart with dowbil wo yfirite,	*burned*
	We lat hyme duel here with the lady still	*remain*
	Whar he haith laisere for to compleine his fyll.	*leisure*
	And Galiot in this meynetyme he laie	*meantime*
730	By strong myght o castell to assay	*besiege*
	With many engyne and diverss wais sere	*various*
	For of fute folk he had a gret powere	*foot soldiers; army*
	That bowis bur and uther instrumentis,	*carried; other weapons*
	And with them lede ther palyonis and ther tentis,	*pavilions*
735	With mony o strong chariot and cher	*cart*
	With yrne qwhelis and barris long and sqwar,	*iron wheels; square*
	Well stuffit with al maner apparell	*stocked; equipment*
	That longith to o sege or to batell,	*pertains*
	Wharwith his ost was closit al about	
740	That of no strenth nedith hyme to dout.	*fear*
	And when he hard the cumyne of the King	*coming*
	And of his ost and of his gaderyng,	*host; mustering*
	The wich he reput but of febil myght	*considered*
	Ayanis hyme for to susten the ficht,	*Against*
745	His consell holl assemblit he, but were,	*whole; without a doubt*
	Ten kingis with other lordis sere,	*various*
	And told theme of the cuming of the King	
	And askit them there consell of that thing.	
	Hyme thoght that it his worschip wold degrade	*It seemed to him*
750	If he hymeself in propir persone raide	*in [his own] person rode*
	Enarmyt ayane so few menyé	*a host so small in number*
	As it was told Arthur fore to bee.	*As it was said Arthur's was*
	And thane the Kyng An Hundereth Knychtis cold	*called*
	(And so he hot, for nevermore he wolde	*was named*
755	Ryd of his lond but in his cumpany	*without [having]*
	O hundyre knyghtis ful of chivellry),	*hundred*
	He saith, "Shir, ande I one hond tak,	*if I undertake*
	If it you pless, this jorney shal I mak."	
	Quod Galiot, "I grant it yow, but ye	
760	Shal first go ryd, yone knychtis ost and see."	
	Withouten more he ridith ovr the plan	*more [ado]; field*

And saw the ost and is returnyd ayann   *again*
And callit them mo than he hade sen, forwhy   *because*
He dred the reprefe of his cumpany.   *reproof*
765 And to his lord apone this wys saith hee:
"Shir, ten thousand Y ges them for to bee."
And Galiot haith chargit hyme to tak
Als fell folk and for the feld hyme mak.   *many*
And so he doith and haith them wel arayt;   *marshalled*
770 Apone the morne his banaris war displayt.   *banners*

Up goth the trumpetis with the clariouns;   *(see note)*
Ayaine the feld blawen furth ther sownis,   *Across; sounds*
Furth goth this king with al his ost anon.
Be this the word wes to King Arthur gone,   *By [means of]*
775 That knew nothing, nor wist of ther entent;   *understood*
But sone his folk ar oneto armys went.
But Arthur by report hard saye   *by rumor heard it said*
How Galiot non armys bur that day;   *carried*
Wharfor he thoght of armys nor of sheld
780 None wald he tak, nor mak hyme for the feld.   *head for the field*
But Gawane haith he clepit, was hyme by,   *called*
In qwhome rignith the flour of chevelry,   *whom is found the flower*
And told one what maner and one what wyss
He shuld his batelles ordand and devys,   *arrange and array his troops*
785 Beseching hyme wisly to forsee   *prepare*
Againe thei folk, wich was far mo than hee.   *For that army; more*
He knew the charg and passith one his way
Furth to his horss and makith no dulay.   *delay*
The clariounis blew and furth goth al ononn   *at once*
790 And ovr the watter and the furd ar gonne.   *ford*
Within o playne upone that other syd,
Ther Gawan gon his batellis to devide,   *forces*
As he wel couth, and set them in aray,   *knew how*
Syne with o manly contynans can say,   *Then; countenance*
795 "Ye falowis wich of the Round Table benn,   *companions*
Through al this erth whois fam is hard and sen,   *fame; heard; seen*
Remembrith now it stondith one the poynt,   *on the brink*
Forwhy it lyith one your speris poynt,   *Wherefore*
The wellfare of the King and of our londe;

800	And sen the sucour lyith in your honde	*since*
	And hardement is thing shall most availl	*courage; help [to keep]*
	Frome deth ther men of armys in bataill,	*these*
	Lat now your manhed and your hie curage	
	The pryd of al thir multitude assuage;	*lessen*
805	Deth or defence, non other thing we wot."	*know*
	This fresch king, that Maleginis was hot,	*bold; called*
	With al his ost he cummyne ovr the plann;	
	And Gawan send o batell hyme agann	*a battalion*
	In myde the berde, and festinit in the stell	*(see note)*
810	The sperithis poynt, that bitith scharp and well;	*spear's*
	Bot al to few thei war and mycht nocht lest	*hold out against*
	This gret rout that cummyth one so fast.	*army*
	Than haith Sir Gawan send, them to support,	
	One othir batell with one knychtly sorte,	*battalion; knightly band*
815	And syne the thrid, and syne the ferde also;	*then; third; fourth*
	And syne hymeself oneto the feld can go	*to the field went*
	When that he sauch thar latter batell steir,	*(see note)*
	And the ten thousand cummyne, al thei ueir.	*were*
	Qwhar that of armes previt he so well,	*he proved himself*
820	His ennemys gane his mortall strokis fell.	*(see note)*
	He goith ymong them in his hie curage	
	As he that had of knyghthed the wsage	*who had practised knighthood*
	And couth hyme weill conten into o shour;	*(see note)*
	Againe his strok resistit non armour.	
825	And mony knycht that worth ware and bolde	*worthy*
	War thore with hyme of Arthuris houshold	*there*
	And knyghtly gan oneto the feld them bere,	*conduct themselves*
	And mekil wroght of armys into were.	*greatly; in war*
	Sir Gawan than upone such wyss hyme bure,	*conducted himself*
830	This othere goith al to discumfitoure.	*defeat*
	Sevyne thousand fled and of the feld thei go,	*from the battlefield*
	Wharof this king into his hart was wo,	*in; sorrowful*
	For of hymeself he was of hie curage.	
	To Galiot than send he in mesag	
835	That he shuld help his folk for to defende	
	And he to hyme hath thirté thousand sende,	
	Wharof this king gladith in his hart	*rejoiced*
	And thinkith to reveng all the smart	*suffering*

	That he tofor haith suffirit and the payne.	
840	And al his folk returnyt is ayayne	*again*
	Atour the feld and cummyne thilk as haill.	*Over; thick*
	The swyft horss goith first to the assall.	*attack*
	This noble knyght that seith the grete forss	*who sees*
	Of armyt men that cummyne upone horss	
845	Togiddir semblit al his falowschip	*assembled*
	And thoght them at the sharp poynt to kep [1]	
	So that thar harmm shal be ful deir yboght.	*loss; dearly paid for*
	This uthere folk with straucht courss hath socht	*direct charge; gone*
	Out of aray atour the larg felld.	*In a disorderly manner throughout*
850	Thar was the strokis festnit in the shelde;	*delivered*
	Thei war resavit at the speris end.	*greeted*
	So Arthuris folk can manfully defend;	
	The formest can thar lyves end conclude.	*first*
	Whar sone assemblit al the multitude,	
855	Thar was defens, ther was gret assaill;	*assault*
	Richt wonderfull and strong was the bataill	*difficult*
	Whar Arthuris folk sustenit mekil payn	*much*
	And knychtly them defendit haith againe.	*defended themselves in return*
	Bot endur thei mycht apone no wyss	*in no way*
860	The multitude and ek the gret suppriss.	*also; injury*
	But Gawan, wich that setith al his payn	*who devoted all his efforts*
	Upone knyghthed, defendid so againe	*To*
	That only in the manhede of this knyght	*courage*
	His folk rejosit them of his gret myght,	*army rejoiced in*
865	And ek abasit hath his ennemys;	*also humbled*
	For throw the feld he goith in such wyss	*through*
	And in the press so manfully them servith	*in the thick of battle*
	His suerd atwo the helmys al tokervith,	*cuts up*
	The hedis of he be the shouderis smat; [2]	
870	The horss goith, of the maister desolat.	*deprived*
	But what avaleth al his besynes,	*exertion*
	So strong and so insufferable uas the press?	*battle*
	His folk are passit atour the furdis ilkon,	*across the fords*

---

[1] *And intended to keep them in the perilous vanguard*

[2] *The heads he smote off at the shoulders*

	Towart thar bretis and to ther luges gon,	*parapet; tents*
875	Whar he and many worthy knyght also	
	Of Arthuris houss endurit mekill wo	*much sorrow*
	That never men mar into armys uroght	*did greater deeds in arms*
	Of manhed; yit was it al for noght.	*courage*
	Thar was the strenth, ther was the pasing myght	*surpassing*
880	Of Gawan, wich that whill the dirk nyght	*until the dark*
	Befor the luges faucht al hyme alonn,	*tents; fought all by himself*
	When that his falowis entrit ware ilkonn,	*each one*
	On Arthuris half war mony tan and slan.	*Arthur's side; taken; slain*
	And Galotis folk is hame returnyd againe,	
885	For it was lait. Away the ostis ridith,	*late*
	And Gawan yit apone his horss abidith	*remains*
	With suerd in hond when thei away uar gon;	*were gone*
	And so forwrocht hys lymmys uer ilkon	*exhausted with toil; limbs*
	And wondit ek his body up and doune,	
890	Upone his horss right thore he fel in swoune.	*there; a swoon*
	And thei hyme tuk and to his lugyne bare.	*lodging*
	Boith King and Qwen of hyme uare in dispare;	
	For thei supposit, throw marvellis that he uroght,	*wrought*
	He had hymeself to his confusione broght.	*death*
895	This was nereby of Melyhalt, the hyll	
	Whar Lanscelot yit was with the lady still.	
	The knychtis of the court pasing homme;	*go home*
	This ladiis knychtis to hir palice com	*lady's*
	And told to hir how that the feld was uent	*had gone*
900	And of Gawan and of his hardyment	*valor*
	That mervell was his manhed to behold.	*courage*
	And sone thir tithingis to the knycht uas told	*tidings*
	That was with wo and hevyness opprest,	*sorrow and sadness*
	So noyith hyme his sujorne and his rest.	*troubles*
905	And but dulay one for o knycht he send	*without delay*
	That was most speciall with the lady kend.	*favorably by; known*
	He comyne and the knycht unto hyme said,	
	"Displess you not, sir, be yhe not ill paid,	*you; ill-pleased*
	So homly thus I yow exort to go	*directly*
910	To gare my lady spek o word or two	*cause my lady to speak*
	With me that am a carful presonere."	*wretched prisoner*

	"Sir, your commande Y shall, withouten were,	*without a doubt*
	Fulfill." And to his lady passit hee,	*went*
	In lawly wyss besiching hir that she	*gracious manner*
915	Wald grant hyme to pas at his request	*go*
	Unto hir knycht stood wnder hir arest.	*[who] was in her custody*
	And she, that knew al gentilless aright,	
	Furth to his chamber passit wight the licht.	*with the light; (see note)*

	And he aross and salust curtasly	*greeted*
920	The lady and said, "Madem, her I,	
	Your presoner, besekith yow that yhe	*beseech*
	Wold mersy and compassione have of me	
	And mak the ransone wich that I may yeif.	*(see note); give*
	I waist my tyme in presone thus to leife	*live*
925	Forwhy I her on be report be-told	*(see note)*
	That Arthur, with the flour of his housholde,	*best*
	Is cummyne here and in this cuntré lyis	
	And stant in danger of his ennemyis	*from*
	And haith assemblit; and eft this shalt bee	*engaged in combat*
930	Within short tyme one new assemblee.	*battle*
	Tharfor, my lady, Y youe grace besech	
	That I mycht pas, my ranson for to fech,	*go; get*
	Fore I presume thar longith to that sort [1]	
	That lovid me and shal my nede support."	*Who*

935	"Shire knycht, it stant nocht in sich dugree; [2]	
	It is no ransone wich that causith me	
	To holden yow or don yow sich offens.	
	It is your gilt, it is your violens	
	Wharof that I desir nothing but law,	
940	Without report, your awnn trespas to knaw."	*rumor*
	"Madem, your plesance may ye wel fulfill	*desire; satisfy*
	Of me that am in presone at your will.	
	Bot of that gilt I was for til excuss	*I was blameless*

---

[1] *For I presume there exist people of such a type*

[2] *Sir knight, that's not the way things stand*

For that I did of verrey nede behwss —[1]

945 It tuechit to my honore and my fame;   *concerned*

I mycht nocht lefe it but hurting of my nam,[2]

And ek the knycht was mor to blam than I.

But ye, my lady, of your curtessy,

Wold ye deden my ransone to resave   *deign; receive*

950 Of presone so I my libertee myght have,

Y ware yolde evermore your knyght   *I would be dedicated [as]*

Whill that I leif with al my holl myght.   *As long as I live*

And if so be ye lykith not to ma   *make*

My ransone, if me leif to ga   *give me leave to go*

955 To the assemblé, wich sal be of new;   *shall; shortly*

And, as that I am feithful knycht and trew,

At nycht to yow I enter shall againe —

But if that deth or other lat certann,   *Unless; obstacle*

Throw wich I have such impediment   *Through*

960 That I be hold, magré myne entent."   *in spite of*

"Sir knycht," quod she, "I grant yow leif, withthy   *leave provided that*

Your name to me that ye wil specify."

"Madem, as yit sutly I ne may   *truly*

Duclar my name, one be no maner way;

965 But I promyt, als fast as I have tyme   *promise; as soon*

Convenient or may uithouten cryme,   *wickedness*

I shall." And than the lady saith hyme tyll,

"And I, schir knycht, one this condiscione will

Grant yow leve, so that ye oblist bee   *you are bound*

970 For to return as ye have said to me."

Thus thei accord. The lady goith to rest.   *agree*

The sone discending closit in the uest.   *sets*

The ferd day was devysit for to bee   *fourth*

Betuex the ostis of the assemblee.   *Between the armies; battle*

975 And Galiot richt arly by the day   *quite early in*

Ayane the feld he can his folk aray.[3]

---

[1] *For what I did was necessary because of a true need*

[2] *I could not avoid it without harming my reputation*

[3] *He arranged his forces facing the battlefield*

	And fourty thousand armyt men haith he	
	That war not at the othir assemblé	*encounter*
	Commandit to the batell for to gon.	
980	"And I myself," quod he, "shal me dispone	*plan [to go]*
	Onto the feild againe the thrid day,	
	Wharof this were we shal the end assay."	*war; undertake*

	And Arthuris folk that come one every syd,	
	He for the feld can them for to provide,	
985	Wich ware to few againe the gret affere	*performance*
	Of Galiot yit to susten the were.	
	The knychtis al out of the ceté ross	*emerged from the city*
	Of Melyholt, and to the semblé gois.	*battle*
	And the lady haith, into sacret wyss,	*secret*
990	Gart for hir knycht and presoner dewyss	*Had . . . prepared*
	In red al thing that ganith for the were:	*are useful for war*
	His curseir red, so was boith scheld and spere.	*warhorse*
	And he to qwham the presone hath ben smart	*whom; painful*
	With glaid desir apone his cursour start.	*on his warhorse leapt*
995	Towart the feld anon he gan to ryd	
	And in o plan hovit one rever syde.	*waited; river*
	This knycht, the wich that long haith ben in cag,	*confinement*
	He grew into o fresch and new curage,	
	Seing the morow blythfull and amen,	*morning; delightful; pleasant*
1000	The med, the rever and the uodis gren,	*meadow; woods*
	The knychtis in armys them arayinge,	
	The baneris ayaine the feld displayng.	
	His youth in strenth and in prosperytee	
	And syne of lust the gret adversytee,	*desire*
1005	Thus in his thocht remembryng at the last	
	Efterward one syd he gan his ey to cast	*aside; eye*
	Whar ovr a bertes lying haith he sen	*parapet*
	Out to the feld luking was the Qwen.	
	Sudandly with that his gost astart	*(see note)*
1010	Of love anone haith caucht hyme by the hart.	
	Than saith he, "How long shall it be so,	
	Love, at yow shall wirk me al this wo,	*that*
	Apone this wyss to be infortunat,	
	Hir for to serve the wich thei no thing wate	*who however; knows*

40

1015	What sufferance I in hir wo endure[1]	
	Nor of my wo nor of myne adventure?	*lot*
	And I wnworthy ame for to attane	
	To hir presens nor dare I noght complane.	*lament*
	Bot, hart, sen at yow knawith she is here	*since that*
1020	That of thi lyve and of thi deith is stere,	*Who; life; ruler*
	Now is thi tyme, now help thiself at neid	
	And the devod of every point of dred	*rid yourself*
	That cowardy be none into the senn;	*cowardice; seen in you*
	Fore and yow do, yow knowis thi peyne, I weyn.	*if; I suppose*
1025	Yow art wnable ever to attane	
	To hir mercy or cum be ony mayne.	*(see note)*
	Tharfor Y red hir thonk at yow disserve[2]	
	Or in hir presens lyk o knycht to sterf."	*die*
	With that confusit with an hevy thocht	
1030	Which ner his deith ful oft tyme haith hyme socht,	
	Devoydit was his spritis and his gost,	*Departed; thoughts; soul*
	He wist not of hymeself nor of his ost	*knew*
	Bot one his horss, als still as ony ston.	
	When that the knychtis armyt war ilkon,	
1035	To warnnyng them up goith the bludy sown	*To warn; sound*
	And every knyght upone his horss is bown,	*ready*
	Twenty thousand armyt men of were.	*war*
	The King that day he wold non armys bere;	
	His batellis ware devysit everilkon	*arranged every one*
1040	And them forbad out ovr the furdis to gon.	*over the fords*
	Bot frome that thei ther ennemys haith sen,	*from (the time) that*
	Into such wys thei couth them noght sustenn.	*In this way*
	Bot ovr thei went uithouten more delay	
	And can them one that other sid assay.	*fight*
1045	The Red Knycht still into his hevy thoght	*in*
	Was hufying yit apone the furd and noght	*lingering*
	Wist of himeself; with that a harrold com	*Knew; herald*
	And sone the knycht he be the brydill nom	*took*
	Saying, "Awalk! It is no tyme to slep.	*Awake*

---

[1] *What suffering I, in sorrow because of her, endure*

[2] *Therefore I advise that you earn her thanks*

1050	Your worschip more expedient uare to kep." [1]	
	No word he spak, so prikith hyme the smart	*afflicts; pain*
	Of hevynes that stood unto his hart.	*grief*
	Two screwis cam with that, of quhich onn	*(see note)*
	The knychtis sheld rycht frome his hals haith tonn;	*neck; taken*
1055	That uthir watter takith atte last	*other one water; at the*
	And in the knychtis ventail haith it cast.	*(see note)*
	When that he felt the uatter that uas cold,	*water*
	He wonk and gan about hyme to behold	*blinked*
	And thinkith how he sumquhat haith mysgonn.	*gone astray*
1060	With that his spere into his hand haith ton,	*taken*
	Goith to the feild withouten uordis more.	
	So was he uare whare that there cam before	*aware*
	O manly man he was into al thing	
	And clepit was the Ferst-Conquest King.	*called*
1065	The Red Knycht with spuris smat the sted;	*struck the horse*
	The tother cam that of hyme hath no drede.	*other*
	With ferss curag ben the knychtis met.	*fierce courage*
	The king his spere apone the knycht hath set	
	That al in peciss flaw into the felde.	*flew*
1070	His hawbrek helpit, suppos he had no scheld.	*even though*
	And he the king into the scheld haith ton	*in; taken (i.e., struck)*
	That horss and man boith to the erd ar gon.	*So that; ground*
	Than to the knycht he cummyth, that haith tan	*who had taken*
	His sheld, to hyme deliverith it ayane,	
1075	Besiching hyme that of his ignorance,	*because of*
	That knew hyme nat, as takith no grevance.	*to take no offense*
	The knycht his scheld but mor delay haith tak	*without*
	And let hyme go and nothing to hyme spak.	
	Than thei the wich that so at erth haith sen	*on the ground*
1080	Ther lord, the Ferst-Conquest King, Y menn,	
	In haist thei cam, as that thei uar agrevit;	*distressed*
	And manfully thei haith ther King relevit.	*rescued*
	And Arthuris folk, that lykith not to byde,	*stand around*
	In goith the spuris in the stedis syde.	*steed's*

---

[1] *It would be more expedient to pay heed to your honor*

1085	Togiddir thar assemblit al the ost,	*charged*
	At whois meting many o knycht was lost.	
	The batell was richt crewell to behold,	
	Of knychtis wich that haith there lyvis yolde.	*given up*
	Oneto the hart the spere goith throw the scheld;	*heart*
1090	The knychtis gaping lyith in the feld.	*open-mouthed*
	The Red Knycht, byrnyng in loves fyre,	
	Goith to o knycht als swift as ony vyre,	*(see note)*
	The wich he persit throuch and throuch the hart.	
	The spere is went; with that anon he start [1]	
1095	And out o suerd into his hond he tais.	*sword; takes*
	Lyk to o lyone into the feld he gais,	*lion; goes*
	Into his rag smyting to and fro:	*In; rage*
	Fro sum the arm, fro sum the nek in two;	*From*
	Sum in the feild lying is in swoun,	*swoon*
1100	And sum his suerd goith to the belt al dounne.	
	For qwhen that he beholdith to the Qwen,	*when he looks upon*
	Who had ben thore his manhed to have sen,	*there; courage*
	His doing into armys and his myght,	*deeds of arms*
	Shwld say in world war not such o wight.	*a person*
1105	His falouschip siche comfort of his dede	*companions such; from*
	Haith ton that thei ther ennemys ne dreid	*taken; do not fear*
	But can themself ay manfoly conten [2]	
	Into the stour that hard was to susten.	*In the combat; endure*
	For Galyot was o pasing multitude	*Galiot's; great*
1110	Of previt men in armys that war gude,	*proven*
	The wich can with o fresch curag assaill	*Who did*
	Ther ennemys that day into batell,	*in*
	That ne ware not the uorschip and manhede	*So that were it not for*
	Of the Red Knycht, in perell and in dreid	
1115	Arthuris folk had ben, uithouten uere. [3]	*without a doubt*
	Set thei uar good, thei uar of smal powere.	
	And Gawan, wich gart bryng hymeself befor	*who had himself brought*
	To the bertes, set he was uondit sore,	*parapet; although; wounded*

---

[1] *The spear is destroyed [literally gone]; with that [occurrence], he immediately leapt [to action]*

[2] *But constantly conducted themselves courageously*

[3] *Although they were good [warriors], they were a small force*

Whar the Qwen uas and whar that he mycht see
1120 The manere of the ost and assemblé.   *army; battle*
And when that he the gret manhed haith sen
Of the Red Knycht, he saith oneto the Qwen,
"Madem, yone knycht into the armys rede,   *in the red armor*
Nor never I hard nore saw into no sted   *heard; in any place*
1125 O knycht, the wich that into schortar space   *in a shorter time*
In armys haith mor forton nore mor grace,   *success; prowess*
Nore bettir doith boith with sper and scheild;
He is the hed and comfort of our feild."   *leader*
"Now, sir, I traist that never more uas sen   *trust*
1130 No man in feild more knyghtly hyme conten.   *bear himself*
I pray to Hyme that everything hath cure,
Saif hyme fro deth or wykit adventure."   *Save; accident*
The feild it was rycht perellus and strong   *[fighting on the] field*
On boith the sydis and continewit long,   *lasted*
1135 Ay from the sone the uarldis face gan licht   *Ever since; world's*
Whill he was gone and cumyne uas the nycht.   *Until*
And than o forss thei mycht it not asstart: *then perforce; avoid*
On every syd behovit them depart.   *they had to withdraw*
The feild is don and ham goith every knycht;   *homeward*
1140 And prevaly, unwist of any wicht,   *secretly, unknown by any person*
The way the Red Knycht to the ceté taiis,   *city takes*
As he had hecht, and in his chambre gais.   *promised; goes*
When Arthure hard how the knycht is gon,   *heard*
He blamyt sore his lordis everilkone;   *every one*
1145 And oft he haith remembrit in his thoght
What multitud that Galiot had broght.
Seing his folk that ware so evil arayt,   *harshly treated*
Into his mynd he stondith al affrayt   *disturbed*
And saith, "I traist ful suth it sal be founde,   *completely true*
1150 My drem richt as the clerkis gan expound;   *just as*
Forwhy my men failyeis now at neid   *fail*
Myself, my londe, in perell and in dreide."

And Galiot upone hie worschip set,   *on high honor fixed his mind*
And his consell anon he gart be fet.   *council; he had summoned*
1155 To them he saith, "With Arthur weil ye see   *well*
How that it stant and to qwhat degré,   *what*

44

Aganis ws that he is no poware. *force*
Wharfor, me think, no worschip to ws ware *it seems to me; honor*
In conqueryng of hyme nor of his londe;
1160 He haith no strenth, he may ws not uithstonde.
Wharfor, me think it best is to delay
And resput hyme for a tuelmonneth day[1]
Whill that he may assemble al his myght; *Until*
Than is mor worschip aganis hyme to ficht."
1165 And thus concludit, thoght hyme for the best.[2]
The uery knychtis passing to there rest; *weary; go*
Of Melyholt the Ladeis knychtis ilkone[3]
Went home and to hir presens ar thei gon,
At qwhome ful sone than gan scho to inquere *From whom; she*
1170 And al the maner of the ostis till spere: *to ask about*
How that it went and in what maner wyss,
Who haith most worschip and who is most to pryss. *to be esteemed*
"Madem," quod thei, "o knycht was in the feild —
Of red was al his armour and his sheld —
1175 Whois manhed can al otheris to exced; *Whose courage*
May nan report in armys half his deid; *half of what he did*
Ne wor his worschip, shortly to conclud, *Were it not for*
Our folk of help had ben al destitud. *entirely lacking*
He haith the thonk, the uorschip in hyme lyis *thanks*
1180 That we the feld defendit in sich wyss."
The lady thane oneto hirself haith thocht,
"Whether is yone my presonar ore noght, *that [man]*
The suthfastness that shal Y wit onon." *truth; know soon*
When every wight unto ther rest war gon *had gone*
1185 She clepith one hir cwsynes ful nere,[4]
Wich was to hir most speciall and dere,
And saith to hir, "Qwhethar if yone bee *Whether that man might be*
Our presoner, my consell is we see." *decision*
With that the maden in hir hand hath ton *taken*

---

[1] *And grant a respite to him until a year from today*

[2] *And so he resolved, it seemed to him for the best*

[3] *Each one of the knights of the Lady of Melyhalt*

[4] *She calls one of her very close relatives*

45

1190	O torche and to the stabille ar thei gon	
	And fond his sted lying at the ground,	*on*
	Wich wery was, ywet with mony wounde.	*bloodied*
	The maden saith, "Upone this horss is sen	*On [the evidence of]*
	He in the place quhar strokis was hath benn;	*where sword-strokes*
1195	And yhit the horss, it is nocht wich that hee	*not the one that*
	Furth with hyme hade;" the lady said, "per Dee,	*by God*
	He usyt haith mo horss than one or two.	*has used*
	I red oneto his armys at we go."	*advise; that*
	Tharwith oneto his armys ar thei went.	
1200	Thei fond his helm, thei fond his hawbrek rent;	*coat of mail slashed*
	Thei fond his scheld was fruschit al to nocht.	*smashed*
	At schort, his armour in sich wyss uas urocht	*In short; worked upon*
	In every place that no thing was left haill	*undamaged*
	Nore never eft accordith to bataill.	*after would be of use in battle*
1205	Than saith the lady to hir cusyness,	*female relative*
	"What sal we say, what of this mater gess?"	
	"Madem, I say thei have nocht ben abwsyt;	*misused*
	He that them bur, schortly he has them usyt."	*wore, for a short time*
	"That may ye say, suppos the best that levis	*although; lives*
1210	Or most of worschip intil armys previs	
	Or yhit haith ben in ony tyme befornn,	
	Had them in feld, in his mast curag, bornn."[1]	
	"Now," quod the lady, "will we pass and see	
	The knycht hymeself and ther the suth may we	*truth*
1215	Knaw of this thing." Incontynent them boith	*Immediately*
	Thir ladeis unto his chambre goith.	*Of these ladies*
	The knycht al wery fallyng was on slep;	*had fallen asleep*
	This maden passith in and takith kep.	*goes in and observes*
	Sche sauch his brest with al his schowderis bare	*saw; shoulders*
1220	That bludy war and woundit her and thare.	*here and there*
	His face was al tohurt and al toschent;	*wounded; disfigured*
	His nevis swellyng war and al torent.	*fists were swollen; cut up*
	Sche smylyt a lyt and to hir lady said,	*little*

---

[1] *That may you say, as if the best man that lives / Or the one who proves himself most worthy in arms / Or the one who has been [most worthy in arms] up to now, in any time before / Had worn them on the battlefield, in his greatest valor*

"It semyth weill this knycht hath ben assaid." [1]

1225	The lady sauch and rewit in hir thoght	*saw; pitied*
	The knychtis worschip wich that he haith uroght.	*wrought*
	In hire remembrance Loves fyré dart	
	With hot desyre hir smat oneto the hart.	*struck*
	And than a quhill, withouten wordis mo,	*more*
1230	Into hir mynd thinking to and fro,	
	She studeit so and at the last abraid	*pondered; started*
	Out of hir thocht and sudandly thus said.	
	"Withdraw," quod she, "one syd a lyt the lyght	*aside; a little*
	Or that I pass that I may kyss the knyght."	*Before I go*
1235	"Madem," quod sche, "what is it at ye menn?	*that you say*
	Of hie worschip ovr mekill have ye senn	*too much; seen*
	So sone to be supprisit with o thoght.	*overwhelmed by*
	What is it at yhe think? Preswm ye noght	*that you*
	That if yon knycht wil walkin and persaif	*awaken and perceive*
1240	He shal tharof nothing bot evill consaif,	*infer*
	In his entent ruput yow therby	*opinion regard*
	The ablare to al lychtness and foly?	*more capable of; frivolity*
	And blam the more al utheris in his mynd	*(see note)*
	If your gret wit in sich desire he fynde?"	
1245	"Nay," quod the lady, "nothing may I do,	
	For sich o knycht may be defam me to."	*[a cause of] dishonor*
	"Madem, I wot that for to love yone knycht —	
	Considir his fame, his worschip and his mycht —	
	And to begyne as worschip wil devyss,	*as honor will prescribe*
1250	Syne he ayaine mycht love yow one such wyss	*[And] then he in return*
	And hold yow for his lady and his love,	
	It war to yow no maner of reprwe.	*It would be; disgrace*
	But quhat if he appelit be and thret	*(see note)*
	His hart to love and elliswhar yset?	
1255	And wel Y wot, madem, if it be so,	*know*
	His hart hyme sal not suffir to love two,	
	For noble hart wil have no dowbilness.	*two-timing*
	If it be so, yhe tyne yowr lov, I gess.	*you will lose*
	Than is yourself, than is your love refusit,	

---

[1] *It seems this knight has been well tested*

1260	Your fam is hurt, your gladness is conclusit.	*reputation; ended*
	My consell is therfore yow to absten	*withhold yourself*
	Whill that to yow the verray rycht be senn	*Until; true nature*
	Of his entent, the wich ful son yhe may	
	Have knawlag if yow lykith to assay."	*it pleases you to try*
1265	So mokil to hir lady haith she uroght [1]	
	That at that tyme she haith returnyt hir thocht	*turned away*
	And to hir chambre went, withouten more,	*without more ado*
	Whar love of new assaith hir ful sore.	*anew assails*
	So well long thei speking of the knycht,	*speak*
1270	Hir cusynace hath don al at she mycht	*female relative; that*
	For to expel that thing out of hir thocht.	*eliminate*
	It wil not be. Hir labour is for nocht.	
	Now leif we hir into hir newest pan,	*leave; in; pain*
	And to Arthur we wil retwrn agann.	

EXPLICIT PRIMUS LIBER; INCIPIT SECUNDUS. [2]

BOOK II

1275	The clowdy nyght, wndir whois obscure	*darkness*
	The rest and quiet of every criatur	
	Lyith sauf, quhare the gost with besyness	*safe; spirit diligently*
	Is occupiit with thoghtfull hevynes.	*anxiety*
	And, for that thocht furth schewing uil his mycht,	*will show*
1280	Go farewel rest and quiet of the nycht.	
	Artur, I meyne, to whome that rest is nocht,	
	But al the nycht supprisit is with thocht.	*oppressed*
	Into his bed he turnyth to and fro,	*In*
	Remembryng the apperans of his wo,	*vision*
1285	That is to say, his deith, his confusioune,	*shame*
	And of his realme the opin distruccioune,	
	That in his wit he can nothing provide	*plan*
	Bot tak his forton thar for to abyd.	

---

[1] *So much has she worked upon her lady*

[2] *The first book ends; the second begins*

48

Up goith the son, up goith the hot morow. [1]

1290 The thoghtful King, al the nycht to sorow,   *Who saw; feet; leapt up*
     That sauch the day, upone his feit he start,   *Who saw; feet; leapt up*
     And furth he goith, distrublit in his hart.   *disturbed*
     A quhill he walkith in his pensyf gost,   *pensive spirit*
     So was he ware thar cummyne to the ost   *aware; host*
1295 O clerk, with whome he was aqwynt befor —   *acquainted*
     Into his tyme non better was ybore —   *In; had been born*
     Of qwhois com he gretly uas rejosit,   *whose arrival*
     For into hyme sum comfort he supposit.   *in (i.e., from); expected*
     Betuex them was one hartly affeccioune.   *Between; a heartfelt*
1300 Non orderis had he of relegioune;   *He was not a clergyman*
     Famus he was and of gret excellence
     And rycht expert in al the seven science,   *(see note)*
     Contemplatif and chast in governance,   *in conduct*
     And clepit was the Maister Amytans.   *called*
1305 The King befor his palyoune one the gren,   *pavilion; grassy field*
     That knew hyme well and haith his cummyn senn   *arrival*
     Uelcummyt hyme and maid hyme rycht gud chere.   *greeted him cordially*
     And he agane, agrevit as he were,   *in return, as if he were annoyed*
     Saith, "Nothir of thi salosing nor the   *greeting nor of you*
1310 Ne rak I nocht, ne charg I nocht," quod hee. [2]
     Than quod the King, "Maister, and for what why   *reason*
     Ar ye agrevit or quhat tresspas have I   *annoyed*
     Commytit so that I shal yow disples?"
     Quod he, "Nothing it is ayane myn ess   *contrary to my comfort*
1315 But only contrare of thiself alway,   *against yourself*
     So fare the courss yow passith of the way. [3]
     Thi schip that goth apone the stormy uall,   *wave*
     Ney of thi careldis, in the swelf it fall   *(see note); whirlpool*
     Whar she almost is in the perell drent;   *drowned*
1320 That is to say, yow art so far myswent   *astray*
     Of wykitness upone the urechit dans   *affair*
     That yow art fallyng in the storng vengans   *strong (i.e., fierce)*

---

[1] *The sun rises; the warm morning dawns*

[2] *"I do not heed, nor do I care about," said he*

[3] *So fair is the path you depart from*

	Of Goddis wreth that shal the son devour.	*wrath; you soon*
	For of His strok approchit now the hour	
1325	That boith thi ringe, thi ceptre and thi crounn	*reign; scepter*
	From hie estat He smyting shal adoune.	*shall strike down*
	And that accordith well, for in thi thocht	*is fitting*
	Yow knawith not Hyme, the wich that haith the wrocht	*made you*
	And set the up into this hie estat	
1330	From povert. For, as theselvyne wat,	*as you yourself know*
	It cummyth al bot only of His myght	*all comes only from*
	And not of the nor of thi elderis richt	*from you; ancestors'*
	To the discending as in heritage,	*as an inheritance*
	For yow was not byget onto spousag.	*begotten in wedlock*
1335	Wharfor yow aucht His biding to obserf,	*ought*
	And at thy mycht yow shuld Hyme pless and serf.	*as far as you can*
	That dois yow nat, for yow art so confussit	*befuddled*
	With this fals warld that thow haith Hyme refusit	
	And brokine haith His reul and ordynans,	
1340	The wich to the He gave in governans.	*under your authority*
	He maid the King, He maid the governour,	*made you*
	He maid the so and set in hie honour	
	Of realmys and of peplis sere;	*various*
	Efter His love thow shuld them reul and stere	*rule and govern*
1345	And wnoppressit kep into justice	*restrain under the law*
	The wykit men and pwnyce for ther vice.	*punish [them]*
	Yow dois nothing bot al in the contrare	
	And suffrith al thi puple to forfare.	*allow; be ruined*
	Yow haith non ey but one thyne awn delyt [1]	
1350	Or quhat that plesing shall thyne appetyt.	*please*
	In the defalt of law and of justice,	*In the absence of*
	Wndir thi hond is sufferyt gret suppriss	*oppression*
	Of fadirless and modirless also,	
	And wedwis ek sustenit mekill wo.	*widows also; much*
1355	With gret myschef oppressit ar the pure;	*suffering; poor*
	And thow art causs of al this hol injure,	*entire injustice*
	Wharof that God a raknyng sal craf	*accounting; demand*
	At the, and a sore raknyng sal hafe.	*From you; bitter accounting*

---

[1] *You only look out for your own pleasure*

50

	For thyne estat is gevyne to redress	*remedy*
1360	Thar ned and kep them to rychtwysness.	*Their; in righteousness*
	And thar is non that ther complantis heris;	*hears*
	The mychty folk and ek the flattereris	
	Ar cheif with the and doith this oppressioun.	*most important*
	If thai complen, it is ther confussioune.	*[thai=the poor]; ruin*
1365	And Daniell saith that who doith to the pure	*poor*
	Or faderless or modirless, enjure	*injustice*
	Or to the puple that ilke to God doth hee;	*same [thing]*
	And al this harme sustenit is throw the.	*through you*
	Yow sufferith them, oppressith and anoyith.	*inflict pain on them*
1370	So yow art causs; throw the thei ar distroyth.	
	Than, at thi mycht, God so distroys yow.	*in your grandeur*
	What shal He do agane? Quhat shal yow	
	When he distroys by vengance of his suerd	
	The synaris fra the vysagis of the erde?	*sinners; face of the earth*
1375	Than utraly yow shall distroyt bee;	*utterly*
	And that richt weill apperis now of thee,	
	For yow allon byleft art solitere.	*are left forsaken*
	And the wyss Salamon can duclar,	
	'Wo be to hyme that is byleft alone;	
1380	He haith no help.' So is thi forton gonne.	*fortune*
	For he is callit, with quhom that God is nocht,	
	Allone. And so thi wykitness haith wrocht	
	That God Hymeself, He is bycummyn thi fo.	*has become your enemy*
	Thi pupleis hartis haith thow tynt also.	*have you lost*
1385	Thi wykitness thus haith the maid alon	
	That of this erth thi fortone is ygonn.	
	Yow mone thi lyf, yow mone thi uorschip tyne	*must; honor lose*
	And eft to deth that never shal haf fyne."	*afterwards [go]; end*

	"Maister," quod he, "of yowre benevolens	
1390	Y yow besech that tueching myn offens	*concerning*
	Yhe wald vichsaif your consell to me if	*grant; to give me*
	How I sal mend and ek hereftir leif."	*also; live*
	"Now," quod the Maister, "and I have mervell qwhy	*why*
	Yow askith consail and wil in non affy	*have faith*
1395	Nor wyrk tharby; and yhit yow may in tym,	*act according to it*
	If yow lykith to, amend the cryme."	

51

	"Yhis," saith the King, "and suthfastly I will	*Yes; truly*
	Your ordynans in everything fulfyll."	
	"And if the list at consail to abide, [1]	
1400	The remed of thi harme to provyde,	
	First, the begyning is of sapiens	*wisdom*
	To dreid the Lord and His magnificens.	*fear; grandeur*
	And what thow haith in contrar Hyme ofendit,	
	Whill yow haith mycht, of fre desir amendit.	
1405	Repent thi gilt, repent thi gret trespass;	
	And remembir one Goddis richwysness,	*righteousness*
	How for to Hyme that wykitness anoyt	*vexes*
	And how the way of synaris He distroit.	
	And if ye lyk to ryng wnder his pess	*reign; peace*
1410	The vengans of His mychty hond yow sess,	*cease*
	This schalt yow do, if yow wil be perfit.	*blameless*
	First mone yow be penitent and contrit	*must*
	Of everything that tuechith thi consiens,	*concerns your conscience*
	Done of fre will or yhit of neglygens.	*(see note)*
1415	Thi neid requirith ful contretioune,	*contrition*
	Princepaly, without conclusioune.	*First of all; end*
	With humble hart and gostly bysyness,	*spiritual diligence*
	Syne shalt yow go devotly the confess	*Then; to confess yourself*
	Therof unto sum haly conffessour	*holy*
1420	That the wil consail tueching thin arour,	*advise about your sin*
	And to fulfill his will and ordynans	
	In satisfaccione and doing of pennans,	
	And to amend al wrang and al injure	*injustice*
	By the ydone til every creature,	*Done by you to*
1425	If yow can into thi hart fynde	*in your heart*
	Contretioune, well degest into thi mynd.	*digest [it]*
	Now go thi weie, for if it leful were	*way; lawful*
	Confessioune to me, I shuld it here."	*To confess; hear*
	Than Arthur, richt obedient and mek,	*meek*
1430	Into his wit memoratyve can seik	*Searched his memory*
	Of every gilt wich that he can pens	*think of*

---

[1] *And if it pleases you to abide by [my] advice*

Done frome he passith the yeris of innocens; [1]
And as his Maister hyme commandit hade,
He goith and his confessione haith he maad

1435 Richt devotly with lementable chere.   *sorrowful demeanor*
The maner wich quho lykith for to here   *hear*
He may it fynd into the holl romans.   *in the whole romance*
Off confessione o pasing cercumstans   *a wealth of details*
I can it not; I am no confessour.   *I know it not*

1440 My wyt haith evil consat of that labour,   *poorly conceived of*
Quharof I wot I aucht repent me sore.   *For which I know*
The King wich was confessit, what is more,
Goith and til his Maister tellith hee
How every syne into his awn degree   *sin in its own turn*

1445 He shew that mycht occuryng to his mynde.   *told that might occur*
"Now," quod the Maistere, "left thow aght behynde   *anything out*
Of Albenak the uorschipful King Ban,
The wich that uas into thy service slan,   *slain*
And of his wif disherist eft also?   *deprived of her inheritance*

1450 Bot of ther sone, the wich was them fro,
Ne spek Y not." The King in his entent   *in his heart*
Abasyt was and furthwith is he went   *Embarrassed*
Agane and to his confessour declarith.
Syne to his Maister he ayane reparith,   *Then; returns*

1455 To quhome he saith, "I aftir my cunyng   *according to my skill*
Your ordinans fulfillit in al thing.
And now right hartly Y beseich and prey
Yhe wald vichschaif sumthing to me say   *vouchsafe*
That may me comfort in my gret dreid

1460 And how my men ar falyet in my neid   *failed*
And of my dreme, the wich that is so dirk."   *dream*
This Master saith, "And thow art bound to uirk   *act*

At my consail, and if yow has maad   *According to*
Thi confessione, as yow before hath said,

1465 And in thi conciens thinkith persevere,   *intend to*
As I presume that thow onon shalt here   *soon; hear*

---

[1] *Done from the time when he passed the age of innocence*

That God Hymeself shal so for the provide,

Thow shal remayne and in thi ring abyd.   *reign*

And why thi men ar falyet at this nede,

1470 At short this is the causs, shalt yow nocht dred,   *In short*

Fore yow to Gode was frawart and perwert.   *turned away; perverse*

Thi ryngne and the He thocht for to subvart.   *reign; undermine*

And yow sal knaw na power may recist   *resist*

In contrar quhat God lykith to assist.   *Against*

1475 The vertw nore the strenth of victory,

It cummyth not of man, bot anerly   *only*

Of Hyme, the wich haith every strinth; and than

If that the waiis plessit Hyme of man,   *ways*

He shal have forss againe his ennemys.   *against*

1480 Aryght agan apone the samyne uyss,   *Indeed; in the same way*

If he displess unto the Lord, he shall   *is displeasing*

Be to his fais a subjet or a thrall,   *foes*

As that we may into the Bible red   *in; read*

Tueching the folk He tuk Hymeself to led   *Concerning; lead*

1485 Into the lond, the wich He them byhicht.   *promised*

Ay when thei yhed into His ways richt,   *Always; went in*

Ther fois gon befor there suerd to nocht;

And when that thei ayanis Hyme hath urocht,   *against; worked*

Thei war so full of radur and disspare   *fear*

1490 That of o leif fleing in the air,   *a leaf floating*

The sound of it haith gart o thousand tak   *made*

At onys apone themself the bak   *[take the back upon oneself=flee]*

And al ther manhed uterly foryhet,   *courage; forget*

Sich dreid the Lord apone ther hartis set.

1495 So shalt yow know no powar may withstond

Ther God Hymeself hath ton the causs on hond. [1]

And the quhy stant in thyne awn offens   *reason*

That al thi puple falyhet off defens.   *failed*

And sum are falyeing magré ther entent;   *in spite of*

1500 Thei ar to quhom yow yevyne hath thi rent,   *given; (see note)*

Thi gret reuard, thi richess and thi gold

And cherissith and held in thi houshold.

---

[1] *Where God Himself has taken up the cause*

Bot the most part ar falyheit the at wyll, *failed you deliberately*
To quhome yow haith wnkyndness schawin till, *shown to*
1505 Wrong and injure and ek defalt of law *injustice; lack*
And pwnysing of qwhich that thei stand aw, *punishment; they stand in awe*
And makith service but reward or fee, *without; (see note)*
Syne haith no thonk bot fremmytness of the. *thanks; coldness*
Such folk to the cummyth bot for dred, *only out of fear*
1510 Not of fre hart the for to help at nede.
And what avalith owthir sheld or sper *either*
Or horss or armoure according for the were *suitable for the war*
Uithouten man them for to stere and led? *govern and lead*
And man, yow wot, that uantith hart is ded *you know; lacks courage*
1515 That into armys servith he of noght. *So that in*
A coward oft ful mekil harm haith uroght. *very much*
In multitude nore yhit in confluens *(see note)*
Of sich is nowther manhed nore defens. *courage nor protection*
And so thow hath the rewlyt that almost *governed yourself*
1520 Of al thi puple the hartis ben ylost
And tynt richt throw thyne awn mysgovernans *squandered; misconduct*
Of averice and of thyne errogans. *arrogance*
What is o prince, quhat is o governoure
Withouten fame of worschip and honour? *renown*
1525 What is his mycht, suppos he be a lorde, *although*
If that his folk sal nocht to hyme accorde? *be in sympathy*
May he his rigne, may he his holl empire *reign*
Susten al only of his owne desyre
In servyng of his wrechit appetit
1530 Of averice and of his awn delyt
And hald his men wncherist in thraldome? *unloved in servitude*
Nay! that shal sone his hie estat consome, *waste*
For many o knycht therby is broght ydoune *down*
All uteraly to ther confusioune. *utterly; destruction*
1535 For oft it makith uther kingis by *other; nearby*
To wer on them in trast of victory. *make war; assurance*
And oft als throw his peple is distroyth *also through (i.e., by)*
That fyndith them agrevit or anoyth.
And God also oft with His awn swerd
1540 Punysith ther vysis one this erd. *vices; earth*
Thus falith not: o king but governans, *without control (see note)*

55

Boith realme and he goith oneto myschans."   *go to ruin*

      As thai war thus speking of this thinge,   *were*
      Frome Galiot cam two knychtis to the King.
1545   That one the King of Hundereth Knychtis was;
      That other to nome "The Fyrst-Conquest King" he has   *as a name*
      As first that Galyot conquerit of one.   *(see note)*
      The nerest way oneto the King thei gon,
      And up he ross as he that wel couth do   *knew how to do*
1550   Honor to qwhome that it afferith to.   *is suitable to*
      And yhit he wist not at thei kingis were;   *yet; knew not that*
      So them thei boith and uyth rycht knyghtly cher   *demeanor*
      Reverendly thei salust hyme and thane   *greeted*
      The King of Hunder Knyghtis he began
1555   And said hyme, "Sir, to yow my lord ws sende,
      Galiot, whilk bad ws say he wende   *who bade us; thought*
      That of this world the uorthiest king wor yhe,   *you were*
      Gretest of men and of awtoritee.   *power*
      Wharof he has gret wonder that yhe ar
1560   So feblé cummyne into his contrare   *inadequately; against him*
      For to defend your cuntré and your londe,
      And knowith well yhe may hyme nocht withstonde.
      Wharfor he thinkith no worschip to conquere   *honor in conquering you*
      Nore in the weris more to persyvere.   *wars*
1565   Considdir yowr wakness and yowr indegens, [1]
      Aganis hyme as now to mak defens.
      Wharfore, my lord haith grantit by us here
      Trewis to yhow and resput for o yhere,   *Truce; respite; a year*
      If that yhow lykith by the yheris space   *it pleases you; year's time*
1570   For to retwrn ayane into this place,
      Her to manteine yhour cuntré and withstand   *defend*
      Hyme with the holl power of yhour lond.   *whole*
      And for the tyme the trewis shal endure,   *truce*
      Yhour cuntré and yhour lond he will assurre;   *render safe*
1575   And wit yhe yhit his powar is nocht here.   *know*
      And als he bad ws say yhow by the yhere   *also; within the year*

---

[1] *Consider your weakness and your lack [of sufficient manpower]*

	The gud knycht wich that the red armys bure	*wore*
	And in the feild maid the discumfiture,	*caused the defeat*
	The whilk the flour of knychthed may be cold,	*flower; called*
1580	He thinkith hyme to have of his houshold."	*intends*
	"Well," quod the King, "I have hard quhat yhe say;	*heard what you*
	But if God will and ek if that I may,	*also*
	Into sich wyss I think for to withstond,	*In such a way*
	Yhour lord shall have no powar of my londe."	*control*
1585	Of this mesag the King rejosing hass	*rejoiced*
	And of the trewis wich that grantit was,	*truce*
	Bot anoyt yhit of the knycht was he,	
	Wich thei avant to have in such dogré. [1]	
	Ther leif thei tuk, and when at thei war gon,	*leave*

	This Maister saith, "How lykith God dispone	*it pleases; to arrange*
1590	Now may yhow se and suth is my recorde.	*true; statement*
	For by Hyme now is makith this accorde,	*made; peace*
	And by non uthir worldly providens	
	Sauf only grant of His bynevolans,	*Except; favor; benevolence*
1595	To se if that the lykith to amend	*it pleases you*
	And to provid thi cuntré to defend.	
	Wharfor yow shalt into thi lond home fair	*go home*
	And governe the as that I shall declaire:	
	First, thi God with humble hart yow serfe	*serve*
1600	And His comand at al thi mycht obserf;	*with all your might*
	And syne, lat pass the ilk blessit wonde	*then; very; scepter*
	Of lowe with mercy justly throw thi londe.	*law*
	And Y beseich to qwhome yow sal direke	*give*
	The rewle upone the wrangis to correk	*authority; wrongs*
1605	That yow be nocht in thi electioune blynde;	*choice*
	For writin it is and yow sal trew it fynde	
	That be thei for to thonk or ellis blame	
	And towart God thi part shal be the samm;	*(see note)*
	Of ignorans shalt yow nocht be excusit,	*Ignorance is no defense*
1610	Bot in ther werkis sorly be accusit.	
	For thow shuld ever chess apone sich wyss	*choose*

---

[1] *Whom they boast of as having such power*

The minsteris that rewll haith of justice: *administration*
First, that he be descret til wnderstond
And lowe and ek the mater of the londe, *Both law; also; nature*
1615 And be of mycht and ek autoritee —
For puple ay contempnith low degré — *always*
And that of trouth he folow furth the way; *follows directly the path*
That is als mych as he lovyth trewth alway
And haitith al them the wich sal pas therfro. *stray from it [truth]*
1620 Syne, that he God dreid and love also. *Then (i.e., secondly)*
Of averice bewar with the desyre,
And of hyme full of hastyness and fyre; *rashness; passion*
Bewar tharfor of malice and desire
And hyme also that lovith no medyre. *moderation (see note)*
1625 For al this abhominable was hold *held*
When justice was into the tymis olde. *in*
For qwho that is of an of thir byknow, [1]
The lest of them subvertith all the low *least; law*
And makith it wnjustly to procede.
1630 Eschew tharfor, for this sal be thi meid *Avoid; reward*
Apone the day when al thing goith aright, *are set right*
Whar none excuss hidyng schal the lyght, *hide*
But He the Jug, that no man may susspek, *Judge; have doubts about*
Everything ful justly sal correk. *correct*
1635 Bewar tharwith, as before have I told,
And chess them wysly that thi low shal hold. *law; defend*
And als I will that it well oft be sen, *wish*
Richt to thiself how thei thi low conten, *law conduct*
And how the right and how the dom is went *justice; judgment*
1640 For to inquer that yow be delygent.
And punyss sor, for o thing shal yow know, *punish grievously*
The most trespas is to subvert the low, *greatest fault; law*
So that yow be not in thar gilt accusit
And frome the froit of blissit folk refusit. *reward; excluded*
1645 And pas yow shalt to every chef toune *important town*
Throwout the boundis of thi regioune
Whar yow sall be, that justice be elyk *alike*

---

[1] *For whoever is accustomed to one of these [vices]*

	Without divisione baith to pur and ryk.	*distinction; poor; rich*
	And that thi puple have awdiens	*judicial hearing*
1650	With thar complantis and also thi presens,	
	For qwho his eris frome the puple stekith	*who; shuts*
	And not his hond in ther support furth rekith,	*stretches out*
	His dom sall be ful grevous and ful hard	*judgment*
	When he sal cry and he sal nocht be hard.	*heard*
1655	Wharfor thyne eris ifith to the pwre, [1]	
	Bot in redress of ned and not of injure.	*injustice*
	Thus sall thei don of ressone and knawlag.	*reasonably and knowingly*
	"But kingis when thei ben of tender ag,	*young age*
	Y wil not say I trast thei ben excusit,	*trust*
1660	Bot schortly thei sall be sar accusit	*grievously*
	When so thei cum to yheris of resone	*the age of reason*
	If thei tak not full contrisioune	*contrition*
	And pwnyss them that hath ther low mysgyit.	*misguided*
	That this is trouth it may not be denyit;	
1665	For uther ways thei sal them not discharg	*free from guilt*
	. . . .	
	One estatis of ther realm that shold	
	Within his youth se that his low be hold.	*be kept*
	And thus thow the, with mercy, kep alway	*you yourself*
1670	Of justice furth the ilk blessit way.	*aforementioned blessed*
	"And of thi wordis beis trew and stable,	*trustworthy*
	Spek not to mych, nore be not vareable.	*too much*
	O kingis word shuld be o kingis bonde	
	And said it is, a kingis word shuld stond.	*once it is said*
1675	O kingis word, among our faderis old,	
	Al-out more precious and more sur was hold	*Altogether*
	Than was the oth or seel of any wight.	*oath or seal; person*
	O king of trouth suld be the verray lyght, [2]	
	So treuth and justice to o king accordyth.	*are fitting*
1680	And als, as thir clerkis old recordith,	*also*

---

[1] *Therefore give your ears (i.e., a hearing) to the poor*

[2] *A king should be the very light of truth*

59

	"In tyme is larges and humilitee	*generosity*
	Right well according unto hie dugré	*suitable to high*
	And plessith boith to God and man also.	
	Wharfor I wil incontinent thow go	*want you to go immediately*
1685	And of thi lond in every part abide,	*sojourn*
	Whar yow gar fet and clep one every sid [1]	
	Out of thi cuntreis and ek out of thi tounis,	*(see note)*
	Thi dukis, erlis and thi gret baronis,	
	Thi pur knychtis and thi bachleris,	*poor; (see note)*
1690	And them resauf als hartly as afferis	*receive; as is fitting*
	And be themself yow welcum them ilkon.	*individually; each one*
	Syne, them to glaid and cheris, thee dispone [2]	
	With festing and with humyll contynans.	*feasting; humble behavior*
	Be not pensyve, nore proud in arrogans,	*melancholy*
1695	Bot with them hold in gladnes cumpany.	
	Not with the rich nor myghty anerly,	*only*
	Bot with the pure worthi man also,	*poor honorable*
	With them thow sit, with them yow ryd and go.	*ride and walk*
	I say not to be ovr fameliar,	*overly familiar*
1700	For, as the most philosephur can duclar,	*greatest; declared*
	To mych to oyss familiaritee	*Too; use*
	Contempnyng bryngith oneto hie dugré;	*Contempt*
	Bot cherice them with wordis fair depaynt,	*ornamented*
	So with thi pupelle sal yow the aquaynt.	*acquaint yourself*
1705	Than of ilk cuntré wysly yow enquere	*each; seek out*
	An agit knycht to be thi consulere,	*counselor*
	That haith ben hold in armys richt famus,	*held to be*
	Wyss and discret, and nothing invyus.	*envious*
	For there is non that knowith so wel, iwyss,	*indeed*
1710	O worthy man as he that worthi is.	
	When well long haith yow swjornyt in a place	*sojourned*
	And well acqueynt the uith thi puple has,	
	Than shalt thow ordand and provid the	*prepare; provide yourself*
	Of horss and ek of armour gret plenté,	*With*
1715	Of gold and silver, tressore and cleithing,	*With*

---

[1] *Where you [should] have summoned and called in every region*

[2] *Then, to gladden and cheer them, conduct yourself*

And every riches that longith to o king. — *pertains*
And when the lykith for to tak thi leif, — *it pleases you; leave*
By largess thus yow thi reward geif, — *With generosity; give*
First to the pure worthy honorable — *poor*
1720 That is til armys and til manhed able. [1]
Set he be pur, yhit worschip in hyme bidith. — *Although; poor; resides*
If hyme the horss one wich thiselvyne ridith — *Give*
And bid hyme that he rid hyme for yhour sak; — *ride*
Syne til hyme gold and silver yow betak: — *Then; entrust*
1725 The horss to hyme for worschip and prowes,
The tresor for his fredome and larges. — *liberality; generosity*
If most of riches and of cherising — *Give; affection*
Eftir this gud knycht berith uitnesing. — *(see note)*
Syne to thi tennandis and to thi vavasouris — *(see note)*
1730 If essy haknays, palfrais and cursouris, — *Give gentle; (see note)*
And robis sich as plesand ben and fair. — *such; attractive*
Syne to thi lordis, wich at mychty aire, — *who are powerful*
As dukis, erlis, princis and ek kingis,
Yow if them strang, yow if them uncouth thingis, [2]
1735 As diverss jowellis and ek preciouss stonis, — *Such as unusual gems*
Or halkis, hundis, ordinit for the nonis, [3]
Or wantone horss that can nocht stand in stable. — *unbroken*
Thar giftis mot be fair and delitable. — *must; delightful*
Thus first unto the uorthi pur yow if — *poor; give*
1740 Giftis that may ther poverté releif, — *relieve*
And to the rich iftis of plesans — — *gifts of pleasure*
That thei be fair, set nocht of gret substans. — *although not; amount*
For riches askith nothing bot delyt,
And povert haith ay ane appetyt, — *always one*
1745 For to support ther ned and indigens. — *indigence*
Thus shall yow if and makith thi dispens. — *give; presents*
And ek the Quen, my lady, shalt also
To madenis and to ladeis, quhar yhe go, — *maidens; wherever*
If and cheriss one the samyne wyss; — *Give; show favor in*

---

[1] *Who is capable of deeds of arms and of courage*

[2] *Give them exotic, give them marvelous things*

[3] *Or hawks or hounds provided for the occasion*

1750	For into largess al thi welfar lyis.	*in generosity*
	And if thi giftis with sich continans	*give; such bearing*
	That thei be sen ay gifyne uith plesans.	*always to be given gladly*
	The wyss man sais, and suth it is approvit,	*it is proven true*
	Thar is no thonk, thar is no ift alowit,	*thanks; gift recognized*
1755	Bot it be ifyne into sich manere —	*given in such*
	That is to say, als glaid into his chere —	*as glad in his demeanor*
	As he the wich the ift of hyme resavith;	*gift; receives*
	And do he not, the gifar is dissavith. [1]	
	For who that iffis as he not if wald, [2]	
1760	Mor profit war his ift for to withhald.	*it would be; gift*
	His thonk he tynith and his ift also.	*thanks; loses; gift*
	Bot that thow ifith, if with boith two,	*what you give, give*
	That is to say, uith hart and hand atonis.	*together*
	And so the wys man ay the ift disponis.	*this way; gift grants*
1765	Beith larg and iffis frely of thi thing,	*generous; give liberally*
	For largess is the tresour of o king	*generosity*
	And not this other jowellis nor this gold	
	That is into thi tresory withholde.	*in*
	Who gladly iffith, be vertew of larges,	*gives by*
1770	His tresory encresis of richess	
	And sal aganne the mor al-out resave. [3]	
	For he to quhome he gevith sall have	*whom*
	First his body, syne his hart with two,	*heart also*
	His gudis al for to dispone also	*dispose of*
1775	In his service; and mor atour he shall	*moreover*
	Have o thing, and that is best of all:	
	That is to say, the worschip and the loss	*honor and the fame*
	That upone larges in this world furth goss.	*goes*
	And yow shal knaw the lawbour and the press	*urgency*
1780	Into this erth about the gret richess	*In*
	Is ony bot apone the causs we see	
	Of met, of cloth, and of prosperitee.	*food; clothing*
	All the remanant stant apone the name	

---

[1] *And if he does not do so, the giver is deluded*

[2] *For whoever gives as if he did not want to give*

[3] *And shall in return so much the more altogether receive*

	Of purches, furth apone this worldis fame.	*wealth also*
1785	And well yow wot, in thyne allegians	*know*
	Ful many is, the wich haith sufficians	*who have enough*
	Of everything that longith to ther ned.	*pertains to*
	What haith yow more, qwich them al to-lede,	*(see note)*
	For al thi realmys and thi gret riches	
1790	If that yow lak of worschip the encress?	*profit*
	Well less al-out, for efter thar estate	*altogether*
	Thei have uorschip and kepith it algat;	*all the while*
	And yow degradith al thyne hie dugree	
	That so schuld shyne into nobelitee,	*in*
1795	Throuch vys and throw the wrechitness of hart.	*vice; miserliness*
	And knowis yow not what sall by thi part,	*be*
	Out of this world when yow sal pass the courss?	*make your way*
	Fair well, iwyss; yow never shall recourss	*indeed; return from*
	Whar no prince more shall the subejet have	*vassal*
1800	But be als dep into the erd ygrave,	*as deeply in the earth buried*
	Sauf vertew only and worschip wich abidith	*Except for; lives on*
	With them, the world apone the laif devidith.	*(see note)*
	And if he, wich shal eftir the succed,	*who shall after you*
	By larges spend, of quhich that yhow had dreid,[1]	
1805	He of the world comendit is and prisit,	*praised*
	And yow stant furth of everything dispisit.	*despised*
	"The puple saith and demyth thus of thee:	*judge*
	'Now is he gone, a verray urech was hee,	*true wretch*
	And he the wich that is our king and lord	
1810	Boith vertew haith and larges in accorde.	*generosity together*
	Welcum be he!' And so the puple soundith.	*cry*
	Thus through thi viss his vertew mor aboundith,	*vice; is magnified*
	And his vertew the more thi vice furth schawith.	*reveals*
	Wharfor yhe, wich that princes ben yknawith,	*who; are known to be*
1815	Lat not yhour urechit hart so yhow dant	*daunt*
	That he that cummyth next yhow may avant	*after you may boast*
	To be mor larg, nore more to be commendit;	*generous*
	Best kepit is the riches well dispendit.	*(see note)*

---

[1] *Generously give, which you feared doing*

	O yhe, the wich that kingis ben, fore sham	
1820	Remembrith yhow this world hath bot o naamm	*one name [for you]*
	Of good or evill, efter yhe ar gone.	*after you*
	And wysly tharfor chessith yhow the tonn	*you that one*
	Wich most accordith to nobilitee	*is becoming*
	And knytith larges to yhour hie degré.	*unites generosity*
1825	For qwhar that fredome in o prince ringnis,	*liberality; reigns*
	It bryngith in the victory of kingis	
	And makith realmys and puple boith to dout	*fear*
	And subectis of the cuntré al about.	
	And qwho that thinkith ben o conquerour,	*thinks to be*
1830	Suppos his largess sumqwhat pas mysour,	*Though; surpass moderation*
	Ne rak he nat bot frely iffith ay; [1]	
	And as he wynyth beis uar alway	*prospers is always on guard*
	To mych nor yhit to gredy that he hold,	
	Wich sal the hartis of the puple colde	*make cold*
1835	And lov and radour cummyth boith two	*fear*
	Of larges. Reid and yhe sal fynd it so.	*Read*
	Alexander, this lord the warld that wan,	*who conquered the world*
	First with the suerd of larges he began	
	And as he wynith ifith largely;	*conquers gives generously*
1840	He rakith nothing bot of chevelry	*cares; but for*
	Wharfor of hyme so passith the renown	
	That many o cetee and many o strang townn	*a foreign town*
	Of his worschip that herith the recorde	*which hears the report*
	Dissirith so to haveing sich o lorde	*have such*
1845	And offerith them withouten strok of spere,	*present themselves*
	Suppos that thei war manly men of were,	*Although; were; war*
	But only for his gentilless that thei	*courtliness*
	Have hard. And so he lovit was alway	*heard*
	For his larges, humilitee and manhed	*generosity; courage*
1850	With his awn folk that nevermore, we reid,	*read*
	For al his weris nor his gret travell,	*wars; travail*
	In al his tym that thei hyme onys faill.	*once fail*
	Bot in his worschip al thar besynes	*to his honor all their effort*
	Thei set and levith into no distres.	*devote; desert [him]*

---

[1] *Let him not care, but generously give always*

1855	Wharthrow the suerd of victory he berith.	
	And many prince full oft the palm werith,	*(see note)*
	As has ben hard, by largess of before, [1]	
	In conqueringe of rignis and of glore.	*kingdoms; glory*
	And wrechitnes richt so, in the contrar,	*miserliness; on*
1860	Haith realmys maid ful desolat and barre	
	And kingis broght doun from ful hie estat,	
	And who that red ther old bukis wat. [2]	
	The vicis lef, the vertew have in mynde	*vices abandon*
	And takith larges in his awn kynd,	*practice generosity (see note)*
1865	Amyd standing of the vicis two,	*Standing between*
	Prodegalitee and averice also.	
	Wharfor herof it nedith not to more,	*to [say] more*
	So mych therof haith clerkis urit tofore.	*written formerly*
	Bot who the vertw of larges and the law	
1870	Sal chess mot ned considir well and knaw	*choose must necessarily*
	Into hymeself and thir thre wnderstande:	*these three [things]*
	The substans first, the powar of his land	*amount; wealth*
	Whome to he iffith and the causs wharfore,	*To whom he gives*
	The nedful tyme awatith evermore.	*urgent*
1875	Kepith thir thre; for qwho that sal exced	*Heed these*
	His rent, he fallith sodandly in nede.	*income; suddenly*
	And so the king that onto myster drowis,	*into poverty draws*
	His subjettis and his puple he ovrthrawis	
	And them dispolyeith boith of lond and rent.	*despoils*
1880	So is the king, so is the puple schent.	*ruined*
	Forquhi the voice it scrikth up ful evyne [3]	
	Without abaid and passith to the hevyne	*delay*
	Whar God Hymeself resavith ther the crye	*receives*
	Of the oppresioune and the teranny	
1885	And uith the suerd of vengans doun ysmytith,	
	The wich that carvith al to sor and bitith	*too grievously*
	And hyme distroyth, as has ben hard or this	*heard before*
	Of every king that wirkith sich o mys.	*commits such an offense*

---

[1] *As has been heard, because of generosity in former times*

[2] *And whoever read these old books knows [it is so].*

[3] *Therefore the voice, it shrieks quite directly up*

	For ther is few eschapith them; it sall	*few who escape*
1890	Boith upone hyme and his successione fall.	
	For He, forsuth, haith ifyne hyme the wond [1]	
	To justefy and reull in pece his lond,	*make justice in*
	The puple all submytit to his cure.	*care*
	And he agan oneto no creatur	*in return*
1895	Save only shall unto his Gode obey.	
	And if he passith so far out of the wey,	
	Them to oppress, that he shuld reul and gid	*guide*
	Ther heritag, there gwdis to devide,	*their goods*
	Ye, wnder whome that he most nedis stond,	*(see note)*
1900	At correccioune sal strek his mychty hond,	
	Not every day, bot shal at onys fall	
	On hym, mayhap, and his successione all.	*perhaps*
	In this, allace, the blyndis of the kingis	*blindness (see note)*
	And is the fall of princis and of rygnis.	*downfall; kingdoms*
1905	The most vertew, the gret intellegens,	*greatest virtue*
	The blessit tokyne of wysdom and prudens	*sign*
	Iss, in o king, for to restren his honde	
	Frome his pupleis riches and ther lond.	
	Mot every king have this vice in mynd	*Must; advice*
1910	In tyme and not when that he ned fynde.	*finds need*
	And in thi larges beith war, I pray,	*beware*
	Of nedful tyme, for than is best alway.	*time of need*
	Avyss the ek quhome to that thow salt if,	*Consider; shall give*
	Of there fam and ek how that thei leif;	*their reputation; love*
1915	And of the vertws and vicious folk also,	*virtuous; evil*
	I the beseich devidith well thir two	*distinguish well between these*
	So that thei stond nocht in o degree.	
	Discreccioune sall mak the diversitee	*Discernment; distinction*
	Wich clepith the moder of al vertewis.	*is called; mother*
1920	And beith war, I the beseich of this,	*beware*
	That is to say of flatry, wich that longith	*flattery; is native*
	To court and al the kingis larges fongith.	*generosity seizes*
	The vertuouss man no thing tharof resavith.	*receives*
	The flattereris now so the king dissavith	*deceive*

---

[1] *For he, in truth, has given him the scepter*

1925	And blyndith them that wot nothing, iwyss,	*who know; indeed*
	When thei do well or quhen thei do omyss,	*amiss*
	And latith kingis oft til wnderstonde	*prevent; from understanding*
	Thar vicis and ek the faltis of ther lond.	
	Into the realme about o king is holde	*In; considered*
1930	O flatterere were than is the stormys cold,	*worse*
	Or pestelens, and mor the realme anoyith;	*harms*
	For he the law and puple boith distroyith.	
	And into principall ben ther three thingis	*And mainly are there*
	That caussith flattereris stonding with the kingis:	

1935	"And on, it is the blyndit ignorans	*one (i.e., the first)*
	Of kingis wich that hath no governans	*moral discipline*
	To wnderstond who doith sich o myss;	*commits such an offense*
	But who that farest schewith hym, iwyss,	*indeed*
	Most suffisith and best to his plesans. [1]	
1940	Wo to the realme that havith sich o chans!	*such a fate*

	"And secundly, quhar that o king is	
	Veciuss hymeself, he cherissith, ywys,	*Evil; loves indeed*
	Al them the wich that oneto vicis soundith	*have to do with vices*
	Wharthrow that vicis and flattery ek aboundith.	

1945	"The thrid is the ilk schrewit harrmful vice,	*very accursed*
	Wich makith o king within hymeself so nyce	*foolish*
	That al thar flattry and ther gilt he knowith	
	Into his wit and yhit he hyme withdrowith	*In; refrains*
	Them to repref and of ther vicis he wot; [2]	
1950	And this it is wich that dissemblyng hot	*is called*
	That in no way accordith for o king.	*is appropriate to*
	Is he not set abuf apone his ringne	*throne*
	As soverane his puple for to lede?	*lead*
	Whi schuld he spare or quhom of schuld he dred	
1955	To say the treuth, as he of right is hold?	*obliged*
	And if so ware that al the kingis wold	*it were*

---

[1] *Is most adequate and most pleasing to him [the king]*

[2] *To reprove them even though he knows of their vices*

	When that his legis comytit ony vyce	*vassals*
	As beith not to schamful nore to nyce	*too shameful; foolish*
	That thei presume that he is negligent	
1960	But als far as he thinkith that they mysswent	*erred*
	But dissemblyng reprevith as afferis	*Without; as is appropriate*
	And pwnice them quhar pwnysing requeris,	*punishment is necessary*
	Sauf only mercy in the tyme of ned.	*Except only for [granting]*
	And so o king he schuld his puple led	
1965	That no trespass that cummyth in his way	
	Shuld pass his hond wnepwnist away,	*unpunished*
	Nor no good deid into the samyn degree,	*by the same token*
	Nore no vertew suld wnreuardid bee.	*unrewarded*
	Than flattry shuld, that now is he, be low,	*high*
1970	And vice from the kingis court withdrow.	
	His ministeris that shuld the justice reull	*administer*
	Shuld kep well furth of quiet and reull [1]	
	That now, God wat, as it conservit is,	*knows; maintained*
	The stere is lost and al is gon amys.	*control*
1975	And vertew shuld hame to the court hyme dress	*home; make his way*
	That exillith goith into the wildernes.	*exiled*
	Thus if o king stud lyk his awn degree,	*was as he should be*
	Vertwis and wyss than shuld his puple bee	
	Only set by vertew hyme to pless	*fixed on virtue*
1980	And sore adred his wisdom to displess.	*grievously afraid*
	And if that he towart the vicis draw,	*toward evil*
	His folk sall go on to that ilk law.	
	What shal hyme pless, thai wil nocht ellis fynd	
	Bot therapon setith al ther mynde.	
1985	Thus only in the vertew of o king	
	The reull stant of his puple and his ringne,	*control; reign*
	If he be wyss and, but dissemblyng, schewis,	*without; reveals*
	As I have said, the vicis oneto schrewis. [2]	
	And so thus, sir, it stant apone thi will	*it is dependent on*
1990	For to omend thi puple or to spill,	*improve; ruin*
	Or have thi court of vertewis folk or fullis.	*Either; sinners*

---

[1] *Should well maintain peace and order*

[2] *As I have said, the wicked to be worthless people*

Sen yow art holl maister of the scoullis,   *Since; schools*
Teichith them and thei sal gladly leir —   *learn*
That is to say, that thei may no thing heir   *hear*
1995 Sauf only vertew towart thyn estat.   *Except; about your position*
And cheriss them that vertews ben algait.   *virtuous; at all times*
And thinkith what that vertew is to thee:
It plessith God, uphaldith thi degree."   *rank*

"Maister," quod he, "me think rycht profitable   *it seems to me*
2000 Yowr conseell is and wonder honorable
For me and good. Rycht well I have consavit   *understood*
And in myne hartis inwartness resavit.   *inner recess received*
I shall fulfill and do yowr ordynans   *decree*
Als far of wit as I have suffisans.   *sufficient quantity*
2005 Bot Y beseich yow intil hartly wyss   *in a heartfelt way*
That of my drem yhe so to me devyss,   *interpret*
The wich so long haith occupeid my mynd,
How that I shal no maner sucour fynd
Bot only throw the wattir lyon and syne   *watery lion; then*
2010 The leich that is withouten medysyne;   *physician*
And of the consell of the flour; wich ayre   *flower; are*
Wonderis lyk that no man can duclar."   *declare*

"Now, sir," quod he, "and I of them al thre
What thei betakyne shal I schaw to the.   *signify; reveal to you*
2015 Such as the clerkis at them specefiit,
Thei usit nothing what thei signefiit.[1]
The wattir lyone is the God verray.   *watery lion; true God*
God to the lyone is lyknyt many way;   *comparable in many ways*
But thei have Hyme into the wattir senn;
2020 Confusit were ther wittis al, Y wenn.   *I suppose*
The wattir was ther awn fragelitee   *own moral weakness*
And thar trespas and thar inequitee   *iniquity*
Into this world, the wich thei stond yclosit;[2]
That was the wattir wich thei have supposit   *imagined*

---

[1] *The way the clerks interpreted them, / They said nothing about what they [truly] signified*

[2] *In this world, [in] which they stand (i.e., are) enclosed*

2025	That haith there knowlag maad so inperfyt.	*made; imperfect*
	Thar syne and ek ther worldis gret delyt,[1]	
	As clowdy wattir was evermore betwenn	
	That thei the Lyone perfitly hath nocht senn,	*seen*
	Bot as the wattir wich was ther awn synne	*own sin*
2030	That evermor thei stond confusit in.	
	If thei haith stond into religionn clen,	*in; pure*
	Thei had the Lyone not in watter sen	
	Bot clerly up into the hevyne abuf,	*in; above*
	Eternaly whar He shal not remufe.	*depart*
2035	And evermore in uatter of syne was Hee,	*(see note)*
	Forequhi it is imposseble for to bee.	*(see note)*
	And thus the world, wich that thei ar in	
	Yclosit is in dyrknes of ther syne;	*darkness; sin*
	And ek the thikness of the air betwen	
2040	The Lyone mad in uattir to be sen.	
	For it was nocht bot strenth of ther clergy	*knowledge*
	Wich thei have here (and it is bot erthly)	
	That makith them there resouns devyss	*devise*
	And se the Lyone thus in erthly wyss.	
2045	This is the Lyone, God and Goddis Sone,	
	Jhesu Crist, wich ay in hevyne sal wonne.	*always; dwell*
	For as the lyone of every best is king,	*beast*
	So is He lord and maister of al thing,	
	That of the Blessit Vyrgyne uas ybore.	*born*
2050	Ful many a natur the lyone haith, quharfore	
	That he to God resemblyt is, bot I	
	Lyk not mo at this tyme specify.	
	This is the Lyone — tharof have yow no dred —	
	That shal the help and comfort in thi ned.	
2055	"The sentens here now woll I the defyne	*meaning*
	Of Hyme, the Lech withouten medysyne,	*Physician*
	Wich is the God that everything hath uroght.	*made*
	For yow may know that uther is it noght	
	As surgynis and fesicianis, wich that delith	*physicians; treat*

---

[1] *Their sin and also their great delight in the world (i.e., worldly things)*

2060	With mortell thingis and mortell thingis helyth	*heal*
	And al thar art is into medysyne,	
	As it is ordanit be the mycht devyne,	*by the divine power*
	As plasteris, drinkis, and anounytmentis seir,	*potions; various*
	And of the qualyté watyng of the yher	*(see note); year*
2065	And of the planetis disposicioune	*(see note)*
	And of the naturis of compleccyoune,	
	And in the diverss changing of hwmowris.	
	Thus wnder reull lyith al there cwris.	*(see note); cures*
	And yhit thei far as blynd man in the way,	*yet; fare; on the road*
2070	Oft quhen that deith thar craft list to assay.	*death; chooses to test*
	Bot God, the wich that is the soveran Lech,	*Physician*
	Nedith no maner medysyne to sech;	*to practice*
	For ther is no infyrmyté nore wound	
	Bot as Hyme lykith al is holl and sound.	*healed and cured*
2075	So can He heill infyrmytee of thoght,	*heal*
	Wich that one erdly medesyne can noght.	*an earthly*
	And als the saul that to confusioune goith	*damnation*
	And haith with hyme and uther parteis boith,[1]	
	His dedly wound God helyth frome the ground.	*heals; source*
2080	Onto his cure no medysyne is found.	
	This is His mycht that nevermore shall fyne,	*end*
	This is the Leich withouten medysyne.	
	And if that yhow at confessioune hath ben	*have been*
	And makith the of al thi synnis clen,	*absolved*
2085	Yow art than holl and this ilk samyn is He	*then healed; very same*
	Schall be thi leich in al necessitee.	*[Who] shall*
	"Now of the flour Y woll to the discernn.	*flower; to you explain*
	This is the flour that haith the froyt eternn;	*fruit*
	This is the flour, this fadith for no schour;	*fades; shower*
2090	This is the flour of every flouris floure;	
	This is the flour of quhom the Froyt uas bornn;	*Fruit*
	This ws redemyt efter that we war lornn;	*were lost*
	This is the flour that ever spryngith new;	*grows*
	This is the flour that changith never hew;	*color*

---

[1] *And has with him also other companions as well*

2095	This is the Vyrgyne; this is the blessit flour	
	That Jhesu bur that is our Salveour,	*gave birth to; Savior*
	This flour wnwemmyt of hir virginitee;	*spotless*
	This is the flour of our felicitee;	
	This is the flour to quhom ue shuld exort;	*appeal*
2100	This is the flour not sessith to support	
	In prayere, consell, and in byssynes	*diligence*
	Us catifis ay into our wrechitnes	*wretches always in*
	Onto hir Sone, the quich hir consell herith;	*hears*
	This is the flour that al our gladness sterith,	*controls*
2105	Throuch whois prayer mony one is savit,	*many a one*
	That to the deth eternaly war resavit	*would be consigned*
	Ne war hir hartly suplicatioune;	*Were it not for her heartfelt*
	This is the flour of our salvatioune,	
	Next hir Sone, the froyt of every flour;	*After her Son*
2110	This is the sam that shal be thi succour	
	If that the lykith hartly reverans	*it pleases you heartily*
	And service yeld oneto hir excellens,	
	Syne worschip hir with al thi byssyness.	*Then; diligence*
	Sche sal thi harm, sche sall thi ned redress.	*your need redress*
2115	Sche sal sice consell if oneto the two,	*such advice give*
	The Lyone and the soverane Lech also,	
	Yow sall not ned thi dremm for to dispar	*despair about*
	Nor yhit no thing that is in thi contrare.	*to your misfortune*
	Now," quod the Maister, "yow may well wnderstand	
2120	Tueching thi drem as I have born on hande	*as I have asserted*
	And planly haith the mater al declarith	*meaning*
	That yhow may know of wich yow was disparith.	*were in despair*
	The Lech, the Lyone, and the flour also,	
	Yow worschip them, yow serve them evermo	
2125	And ples the world as I have said before.	
	In governans thus stondith al thi glore.	*moral control; glory*
	Do as yow list, for al is in thi honde	*it pleases you*
	To tyne thiself, thi honore and thi londe	*lose*
	Or lyk o prince, o conquerour or king	
2130	In honore and in worschip for to ringe."	*reign*
	"Now," quod the King, "I fell that the support	*feel*
	Of yhour consell haith don me sich comfort,	

	Of every raddour my hart is into ess;	*fear*
	To yhour command, God will, Y sal obess.	*obey*
2135	Bot o thing is yneuch wnto me:	*enough for*
	How Galiot makith his avant that he	*boast*
	Shall have the knycht that only by his honde	
	And manhed was defendour of my londe,	
	If that shall fall Y pray yhow tellith me,	*shall come about*
2140	And quhat he hecht and of quhat lond is hee.”	*is called*

	“What that he hecht, yow shall no forther know;	*is called*
	His dedis sall herefterwart hyme schaw.	*reveal*
	Bot contrar the he shall be found no way.	*opposed to you*
	No more tharof as now Y will the say.”	*for now*
2145	With that the King haith at his Maistir tone	*from; taken*
	His leve, oneto his cuntré for to gonne.	*leave*
	And al the ost makith none abyde	*delay*
	To passing home anone thei can provid. [1]	
	And to Sir Gawane thei haith o lytter maad,	*for; litter made*
2150	Ful sore ywound, and hyme on with them haade. [2]	

	The King, as that the story can declar,	
	Passith to o ceté that was right fair	*Goes*
	And clepit Cardole, into Walis was,	*called; in*
	For that tyme than it was the nerest place	*then*
2155	And thar he sojornyt twenty-four days	*remained*
	In ryall festing, as the auttore says.	*royal feasting; author*
	So discretly his puple he haith cherit	*gladdened*
	That he thar hartis holy haith conquerit.	*entirely*
	And Sir Gawan, helyt holl and sound	*healed healthy and well*
2160	Be fiftene dais he was of every wounde.	*In*
	Right blyth therof into the court war thei	*happy; in*
	And so befell the twenty-fourth day	
	The King to fall into o hevynes	*dejection*
	Right ate his table siting at the mess.	*meal*
2165	And Sir Gawan cummyth hyme before	

---

[1] *To go home as soon as they can make provision*

[2] *Very seriously wounded, and on [the litter] had (i.e., took) him with them*

73

And saide hyme, "Sir, yhour thoght is al to sore,

Considering the diverss knychtis sere   *various*

Ar of wncouth and strang landis here."   *unknown and foreign*

The King ansuert, as into matalent,   *as if in anger*

2170   "Sir, of my thocht or yhit of myne entent

Yhe have the wrang me to repref; forquhy   *reprove because*

Thar levith none that shuld me blam, for I   *lives*

Was thinkand one the worthiest that levyt   *thinking; who lives*

That al the worschip into armys prevyt,   *displayed*

2175   And how the thonk of my defens he had   *thanks for*

And of the vow that Galiot haith mad.

But I have sen, when that of my houshold   *seen*

Thar was, and of my falowschip, that wold

If that thei wist, quhat thing shuld me pless,   *knew*

2180   Thei wald nocht leif for travell nor for ess.   *leave; (see note)*

And sumtyme it preswmyt was and said

That in my houshold of al this world I had

The flour of knychthed and of chevalry.   *flower*

Bot now tharof Y se the contrarye,

2185   Sen that the flour of knychthed is away."

"Schir," quod he, "of resone suth yhe say;   *reasonably the truth*

And if God will, in al this warld so round

He sal be soght, if that he may be found."

Than Gawan goith with o knychtly chere;   *demeanor*

2190   At the hal dure he saith in this maner: *door*

"In this pasag who lykith for to wend?   *expedition; go*

It is o jorné most for to comend   *journey most commendable*

That in my tyme into the court fallith,   *in; befalls*

To knyghtis wich that chevellry lovith

2195   Or travell into armys for to hant.   *travail in arms to practice*

And lat no knycht fra thynefurth hyme avant[1]

That it denyith." With that onon thei ross,   *refuses; immediately; arose*

Al the knychtis, and frome the burdis goss.   *tables go*

The King that sauch, into his hart was wo   *saw in; sad*

2200   And said, "Sair Gawan, nece, why dois yow so?   *nephew*

Knowis yow nocht I myne houshold suld encress

---

[1]*And let no knight from this time forth boast about himself*

74

Lancelot of the Laik

	In knychthed and in honore and largess?	
	And now yow thinkith mak me dissolat	*intend to make me deprived*
	Of knychtis and my houss transulat	*remove*
2205	To sek o knycht and it was never more	*seek*
	Hard sich o semblé makith o before." [1]	
	"Sir, quod he, "als few as may yhow pless,	
	For what I said was nothing for myne ess,	*not for my comfort*
	Nor for desir of falouschip, forwhy	*because*
2210	To pass alone, but cumpany, think I,	*go; without*
	And ilk knycht to pass o sundry way.	*each; go; different*
	The mo thei pass the fewar eschef thay,	*(see note)*
	Bot thus shal pas no mo bot as yhow lest."	*go no more than you like*
	"Takith," quod he, "of quhom yhe lykith best,	
2215	Fourty in this pasag for to go."	*on this expedition*
	At this command and Gawan chesit so	*then Gawain chose*
	Fourty, quhich that he lovit and that was	
	Richt glaid into his falowschip to pas.	*go*

	And furth thei go, and al anarmyt thei	*armed*
2220	Come to the King, withouten more delay,	
	The relykis brocht, as was the maner tho	*relics; then*
	When any knyghtis frome the court suld go.	*should*
	Or when the passit, or quhen thei com, thei swor [2]	
	The trouth to schaw of every adventur.	*reveal*
2225	Sir Gawan knelyng to his falowis sais,	
	"Yhe lordis, wich that in this seking gais,	*who go on this quest*
	So many noble and worthi knychtis ar yhe,	
	Methink in vayne yhour travel shuld nocht be;	*It seems to me; effort*
	For adventur is non so gret to pref,	
2230	As I suppone, nor yhe sal it esschef. [3]	
	And, if yhe lyk, as I that shal devyss	*say*
	Yhour oth to swer, into the samyne wyss,	*(see note)*
	Myne oith to kep." And that thei undertak,	
	However so that he his oith mak	

---

[1] *Heard of such a gathering made ever before*

[2] *Either when they went or when they came back, they swore*

[3] *For the enterprise is not so great a trial, / So I suppose, but that you shall accomplish it*

2235	It to conserf, and that thei have all swornn.	*To keep it*
	Than Gawan, wich that was the King beforn,	*before the King*
	On kneis swore, "I sal the suth duclar	*truth declare*
	Of everything when I agan repar	*return*
	Nor never more aghane sal I returnn	
2240	Nore in o place long for to sujornn	*one; remain*
	Whill that the knycht or verray evydens	*Until; true*
	I have, that shal be toknis of credens."	*proof of validity*
	His falouschip abasit of that thing	*was upset with*
	And als therof anoyt was the King,	*vexed*
2245	Saying, "Nece, yow haith al foly uroght	*Nephew*
	And wilfulness that haith nocht in thi thoght	
	The day of batell of Galot and me."	*battle between*
	Quod Gawan, "Now non other ways ma be."	*may*
	Tharwith he and his falowschip also	
2250	Thar halmys lasit; onto ther horss thei go,	*helmets fastened*
	Syne tuk ther lef and frome the court the fare. [1]	
	Thar names ware to long for to declar.	*There were too many names*
	Now sal we leif hyme and his cumpany	*leave*
	That in thar seking passith bissely;	*quest go diligently*
2255	And of the Lady of Melyhalt we tell,	
	With whome the knycht mot ned alway duell.	*must necessarily; dwell*
	O day she mayd hyme onto hir presens fet [2]	
	And on o sege besid hir haith hyme set.	*seat*
	"Sir, in keping I have yow halding long,"	*held*
2260	And thus sche said, "for gret trespas and wrong,	
	Magré my stewart, in worschip, and forthi	*Despite my steward; therefore*
	Yhe suld me thonk." "Madem," quod he, "and I	
	Thonk yhow so that ever, at my mycht,	*as far as I am able*
	Wharso I pass that I sal be yhour knycht."	*go*
2265	"Grant mercy, sir, bot o thing I yow pray,	*Many thanks*
	What that yhe ar yhe wold vichsauf to say."	*Who you are; grant*
	"Madem," quod he, "yhour mercy ask I, quhy	*because*

---

[1] *Then took their leave and from the court they go*

[2] *One day she had him brought into her presence*

That for to say apone no wyss may I."   *in no way*

"No! Wil yhe not? Non other ways as now   *Not otherwise for now*

2270 Yhe sal repent, and ek I mak avow   *I swear*

Oneto the thing the wich that I best love,   *Upon*

Out frome my keping sal yhe not remuf   *depart*

Befor the day of the assemblee,   *battle*

Wich that, o yher, is nerest for to bee.   *one year*

2275 And if that yow haith plessit for to say [1]

Yhe had fore me deliverit ben this day;   *as far as I am concerned*

And I sal knaw, quhether yhe wil or no,   *whether*

For I furthwith oneto the court sal go

Whar that al thithingis goith and cumyth sonn."   *tidings*

2280 "Madem," quod he, "yhour plesance mot be donne."   *will must*

With that the knycht oneto his chalmer goith   *chamber*

And the lady hir makith to be wroith   *pretended to be angry*

Aganis hyme, but suthly uas sche not,   *in truth*

For he al-out was mor into hir thoght.   *altogether*

2285 Than schapith she agane the ferd day   *she prepared for the fourth*

And richly sche gan hirself aray,   *adorn*

Syne clepit haith apone hir cusynes   *called; female relative*

And saith, "Y will oneto the court me dress.   *go*

And malice I have schawin onto yhon knycht

2290 Forquhy he wold nocht schew me quhat he hicht;   *reveal; is called*

Bot so, iwyss, it is nocht in my thocht,

For worthyar non into this erth is wrocht. [2]

Tharfor I pray and hartly I requer   *heartily I request*

Yhe mak hyme al the cumpany and chere   *befriend and entertain him*

2295 And do hyme al the worschip and the ess,   *honor; comfort*

Excep his honore, wich that may hym pless.   *Saving his honor*

And quhen I cum, deliverith hyme als fre

As he is now." "Ne have no dred," quod sche.

The lady partit and hir lef hath ton,   *leave has taken*

2300 And by hir jorné to the court is gon.   *on her journey*

The King hapnit at Logris for to bee,   *chanced*

---

[1] *And if it had pleased you to say [your name]*

[2] *For none worthier has been born on this earth*

Wich of his realme was than the chef ceté,   *the capital*
And haith hir met and intil hartly wyss   *in a heartfelt manner*
Resavit her and welcummyt oftsyss   *Received; many times*
2305 And haith hir home oneto his palice brocht,
Whar that no danté nedith to be socht,   *luxury*
And maid hir cher with al his ful entent. [1]
Eft supir oneto o chalmer ar thei went,   *chamber have they gone*
The King and sche and ek the Quen — al thre.
2310 Of hir tithandis at hir than askit hee   *news from her*
And what that hir oneto the court had brocht.
"Sir," quod sche, "I conne not al for nocht;   *(see note)*
I have o frend haith o dereyne ydoo, [2]
And I can fynd none able knycht tharto.
2315 For he the wich that in the contrar is   *in the opposition*
Is hardy, strong and of gret kyne, iwyss.   *of noble birth*
Bot it is said if I mycht have with me
Your knycht quich in the last assemblé
Was in the feld and the red armys bur,   *wore*
2320 In his manhed Y mycht my causs assur.   *courage*
And yhow, sir, richt hartly I exort   *beg*
Into this ned my myster to support."   *my plight*
"Madem, by faith oneto the Quen I aw, *the faith I owe the Queen*
That I best love, the knycht I never saw
2325 In nerness by which that I hyme knew;   *Close-up*
And ek Gawane is gan hyme for to sew   *seek*
With other fourty knychtis into cumpany."
The lady smylit at ther fantessy.   *delusion*
The Quen tharwith presumyt wel that sche
2330 Knew quhat he was and said, "Madem, if yhe *who he was*
Knowith of hyme what that he is or quhar, *who he is or where*
We yhow besech till ws for to declar."   *to us*
"Madem," quod sche, "now, be the faith that I   *by*
Aw to the King and yhow, as for no why   *Owe; reason*
2335 To court I cam but of hyme to inquere;
And sen of hyme I can no tithingis here,   *since; news hear*

---

[1] *And greeted her with all his heart*

[2] *I have a friend who has a trial by combat arranged*

Nedlyngis tomorn homwart mon I fair." [1]

"Na," quod the King, "madem, ovr son it waire.   *too soon it would be*

Yhe sal remayne her for the Qwenys sak;

2340 Syne shal yhe of our best knychtis tak."

"Sir," quod sche, "I pray yow me excuss,

Forquhy to pass nedis me behuss. [2]

Nor, sen I want the knycht which I have socht,   *since I lack*

Wtheris with me to have desir I nocht,   *Others*

2345 For I of otheris have that may suffice."

Bot yhit the King hir prayt on sich wyss   *entreated in such a way*

That sche remanit whill the thrid day,   *stayed until*

Syne tuk hir leif to pasing hom hir way.   *go on her way home*

It nedis not the festing to declar

2350 Maid oneto hir nor company nor fare.   *the people; the circumstances*

Sche had no knycht, sche had no damyseill   *damsel*

Nor thei richly rewardit war and well.   *But that they; were*

Now goith the lady homwart and sche

In her entent desyrus is to see   *heart*

2355 The flour of knychthed and of chevelry:

So was he prysit and hold to every wy.   *esteemed; (see note)*

The lady, which oneto hir palace come,

Bot of schort time remanith haith at home

When sche gart bryng, withouten recidens, [3]

2360 With grete effere this knycht to hir presens   *ceremony*

And said hyme, "Sir, so mekil have I socht*much*

And knowith that befor I knew nocht,

That if yhow lyk I wil yhour ransone mak."

"Madem, gladly, wil yhe vichsauf to tak   *if you would vouchsafe*

2365 Efter that as my powar may attenn [4]

Or that I may provid be ony menn."   *by any means*

"Now, sir," sho said, "forsuth it sal be so:

---

[1] *Necessarily tomorrow I must go home*

[2] *Since it necessarily behooves me to go*

[3] *When she had brought without delay*

[4] *Whatever afterwards I might be able to attain*

79

Yhe sal have thre and chess yhow on of tho. [1]
And if yhow lykith them for to refuss
2370   I can no mor, but yhe sal me excuss;
Yhe nedis mot susten yhour adventur   *tolerate your fate*
Contynualy inward for til endur." [2]
"Madem," quod he, "and I yhow hartly pray
What that thei say yhe wald vichsauf to say."   *(see note)*

2375   "The first," quod sche, "who hath into the chenn   *in the chain*
Of lov yhour hart, and if yhe may derenn.   *if you may say*
The next, yhour nam, the which ye sal not lye.
The thrid, if ever yhe think of chevalry
So mekil worschip to atten in feild   *much honor to attain*
2380   Apone o day in armys wnder scheld   *In one day*
As that yhe dyd the samyne day when yhe
In red armys was at the assemblee."
"Madem," quod he, "is thar non uther way
Me to redem but only thus to say
2385   Of thingis which that rynyth me to blam,   *incur blame on me*
Me to avant my lady or hir name?   *boast about*
But if that I most schawin furth that one,
What suerté schal I have for to gone   *guarantee*
At libertee out of this danger free?"
2390   "Schir, for to dred no myster is," quod shee;   *no need*
"As I am trew and fathfull woman hold,
Yhe sal go fre quhen one of thir is told."   *these*
"Madem, yhour will non uther ways I may,
I mone obey. And to the first Y say,   *must*
2395   As to declar the lady of myne hart,
My gost sal rather of my brest astart."   *escape*
(Wharby the lady fayndit al for nocht   *concealed*
The love quhich long hath ben into her thocht.)
"And of my nam, schortly for to say,
2400   It stondith so that one no wyss I may.
Bot of the thrid, madem, I se that I

---

[1] *You shall have three choices and choose one of those*
[2] *Constantly within your spirit to survive*

Mon say the thing that tuechith velany. [1]
For suth it is I trast, and God before,   *truth; trust*
In feld that I sal do of armys more

2405 Than ever I did, if I commandit bee.
And now, madem, I have my libertee,
For I have said I never thocht to say."   *said [what]*
"Now, sir," quod sche, "whenever yhe wil, ye may; *you wish [to go]*
Bot o thing is, I yhow hartly raquer,   *heartily request*

2410 Sen I have hold yhow apone such maner,
Not as my fo, that yhe uald grant me till."   *to*
"Madem," quod he, "it sal be as yhe will."
"Now, sir," quod sche, "it is nothing bot yhe *but that you*
Remann with ws wnto the assemblé,   *Remain; until*

2415 And everythyng that in yhour myster lyis *that you need*
I sall gar ordan at yhour awn devyss. [2]
And of the day I shall yow certefy   *guarantee*
Of the assemblé yhe sal not pas therby." *you shall not miss it*
"Madem," quod he, "It sal be as yhow list." *as it pleases you*

2420 "Now sir," quod sche, "and than I hald it best
That yhe remann lyk to the samyne degré *in the same condition*
As that yhe war, that non sal wit that yhe   *know*
Deliverit war. And into sacret wyss   *Freed; in a secret way*
Thus may yhe be. And now yhe sal devyss *designate*

2425 What armys that yhow lykyth I gar mak." *I have made*
"Madem," quod he, "armys al of blak."   *black*
With this, this knycht is to his chalmer gonn. *chamber*
The lady gan ful prevaly disspone   *secretly provide*
For al that longith to the knycht in feild. *pertains to*

2430 Al blak his horss, his armour, and his scheld;
That nedful is, al thing sche well previdith. *Whatever is needed*
And in hir keping thus with hir he bidith. *remains*
Suppos of love sche takyne hath the charg, *Although from*
Sche bur it clos. Therof sche uas not larg; [3]

2435 Bot wysly sche abstenit hir dissir,   *restrained*

---

[1] *Must say that thing which touches upon unknightly behavior*

[2] *I shall have prepared according to your own instructions*

[3] *She kept it secret. She was not gossipy about it.*

	For ellisquhat, sche knew, he was afyre.	*(see note)*
	Tharfor hir wit hir worschip haith defendit,	*honor*
	For in this world thar was nan mor commendit,	
	Boith of discreccioune and of womanhed,	
2440	Of governans, of nurtur, and of farhed. [1]	
	This knycht with hir thus al this whil mon duell,	*must remain*
	And furth of Arthur sumthing wil we tell —	
	That walkyng uas furth into his regiounis	*Who*
	And sojornyt in his ceteis and his townis	*cities*
2445	As he that had of uisdome sufficyans.	*enough*
	He kepit the lore of Maister Amytans	*followed the instruction*
	In ryghtwysnes, in festing and larges,	*feasting and generosity*
	In cherising cumpany and hamlynes.	*friendliness*
	For he was bissy and was deligent,	*industrious*
2450	And largly he iffith and dispent	*generously; gave and dispensed*
	Rewardis, boith oneto the pur and riche	*poor*
	And holdith fest throw al the yher eliche. [2]	
	In al the warld passing gan his name;	*spread his reputation*
	He chargit not bot of encress and famme	*cared only for*
2455	And how his puples hartis to empless.	*please*
	Thar gladnes ay was to his hart most ess.	*the greatest pleasure*
	He rakith not of riches nor tressour	*cares not for*
	Bot to dispend one worschip and honour.	*Except to dispense for*
	He ifith riches, he ifith lond and rent,	*gives*
2460	He cherissyth them with wordis eloquent	
	So that thei can them utraly propone	*utterly offer themselves*
	In his service thar lyves to dispone,	*make disposition of*
	So gladith themme his homely contynans,	*humble bearing*
	His cherisyng, his wordis of plesans,	*pleasing words*
2465	His cumpany and ek his mery chere,	*demeanor*
	His gret rewardis and his iftis sere.	*various gifts*
	Thus hath the King non uthir besynes	*concern*
	Bot cherising of knychtis and largess	
	To mak hymeself of honour be commend.	*because of honor commended*

---

[1] *Both for discretion and for womanly qualities, / For moral control, for breeding and for beauty*

[2] *And holds feasts through all [times of] the year alike*

2470	And thus the yher he dryvith to the ende.	*year he brings*

EXPLICIT SECUNDA PARS, INCIPIT TERCIA PARS. [1]

[BOOK III]

	The long dirk pasag of the uinter and the lycht	*(see note)*
	Of Phebus comprochit with his mycht,	*approaches*
	The which, ascending in his altitud,	*(see note)*
	Avodith Saturnn with his stormys rude.	*Banishes; fierce*
2475	The soft dew one fra the hevyne doune valis	*falls*
	Apone the erth, one hillis and on valis,	*vales*
	And throw the sobir and the mwst hwmouris	*gentle; moist*
	Up nurisit ar the erbis and in the flouris	*herbs*
	Natur the erth of many diverss hew	
2480	Ovrfret and cled with the tendir new. [2]	
	The birdis may them hiding in the gravis	*hide in the groves*
	Wel frome the halk, that oft ther lyf berevis.	*hawk; robs*
	And Scilla hie ascending in the ayre	*air*
	That every uight may heryng hir declar	*person may hear her*
2485	Of the sessone the passing lustynes.	*surpassing joy*
	This was the tyme that Phebus gan hym dress	*advanced*
	Into the Rame and haith his courss bygown	*Ram (i.e., Aries); orbit*
	Or that the trewis and the yher uas rown, [3]	
	Which was yset of Galiot and the King	*set by*
2490	Of thar assemblé and of thar meting.	*For; meeting [in combat]*
	Arthur haith a fiftene dais before	
	Assemblit al his barnag and more	*peers*
	That weryng wnder his subjeccioune	*were; lordship*
	Or lovith hyme or longith to his crown,	*are subject to; authority*
2495	And haith his jornay tone, withouten let,	*undertaken; delay*
	Onto the place the wich that was yset	
	Whar he hath found befor hyme mony o knycht	
	That cummyng war with al thar holl mycht	*had come; entire force*

---

[1] *The second part ends, the third part begins*

[2] *Ornamented profusely and clad in fresh new [shoots]*

[3] *Before the truce and the year had run [out]*

	Al enarmyt both with spere and scheld	*armed*
2500	And ful of lugis plantith haith the feld,	*tents*
	Hyme in the wer for to support and serf	*war; serve*
	At al ther mycht, his thonk for to disserf.	*With; thanks; deserve*
	And Gawan, which was in the seking yhit	*who was still in search*
	Of the gud knycht, of hyme haith got no wit,	*knowledge*
2505	Remembrith hyme apone the Kingis day	
	And to his falowis one this wys can say:	*companions*
	"To yhow is knowin the mater, in what wyss	
	How that the King hath with his ennemys	
	A certan day that now comprochit nere,	*approaches*
2510	And oneto ws war hevynes to here	*sorrow to hear*
	That he uar into perell or into dreid	*in*
	And we away and he of ws haith neid;	
	For we but hyme no thing may eschef,	*without him; achieve*
	And he but ws in honore well may lef.	*without us; live*
2515	For, be he lost, we may nothing withstond	
	Ourself; our honore we tyne and ek our lond.	*lose*
	Tharfor I red we pas onto the King,	*recommend; go*
	Suppos our oth it hurt into sum thing,	*Although; in some measure*
	And in the feld with hyme for til endur	
2520	Of lyf or deth and tak our adventur."	*chance*
	Tharto thei ar consentit everilkon,	*every one*
	And but dulay the have thar jorney tonne. [1]	
	When that the King them saw, in his entent	*mind*
	Was of thar com right wonder well content,	*wondrously*
2525	For he preswmyt no thing that thei wold	
	Have cummyne but one furth to ther seking hold. [2]	
	And thus the King his ost assemblit has	
	Agane the tyme, againe the day that uas	*In preparation for*
	Ystatut and ordanit for to bee,	*Decreed*
2530	And everything hath set in the dogré.	*put in order*
	And Galiot, that haith no thing forghet	*not at all forgotten*
	The termys quhich that he befor had set,	

---

[1] *And without delay they have undertaken their journey*

[2] *Have come but [that they would] remain faithful to their quest*

Assemblit has, apone his best maner,   *in the best way he can*

His folk and al his other thingis sere   *various*

2535   That to o weryour longith to provid   *for a warrior it is necessary*

And is ycome apone the tothir syde.   *the other*

Whar he befor was one than uas he two, [1]

And al his uthir artilyery also   *implements of war*

He dowblith hath, that mervell was to senn.   *doubled; see*

2540   And by the revere lychtit one the grenn   *camped in the field*

And stronghar thane ony wallit toune

His ost ybout yclosit in randoune.   *with speed*

Thus war thei cummyne apone ather syd   *either*

Befor the tyme, themself for to provid.   *prepare*

2545   Or that the trewis was complet and rwn,   *Before; truce; elapsed*

Men mycht have sen one every sid begwn

Many a fair and knychtly juperty   *encounter*

Of lusty men and of yong chevalry   *spirited; young knights*

Disyrus into armys for to pruf;   *in arms to prove themselves*

2550   Sum for wynyng, sum causith uas for luf,   *profit; love*

Sum into worschip to be exaltate,   *honor; exalted*

Sum causit was of wordis he and hate   *loud and impassioned*

That lykit not ydill for to ben —

A hundereth pair at onis one the gren.   *at once; field*

2555   Thir lusty folk thus can thar tyme dispend   *These spirited; pass*

Whill that the trewis goith to the ende.   *Until; truce*

The trewis past, the day is cummyne ononne;   *quickly*

One every syd the can them to dispone;   *they began; position*

And thai that war most sacret and most dere   *intimate; trusted*

2560   To Galiot, at hyme the can enquere,   *they inquired*

"Who sal assemble one yhour syd tomornne?   *on your side tomorrow*

Tonycht the trewis to the end is worne."

He ansuerit, "As yhit oneto this were   *in this war*

I ame avysit I wil none armys bere   *resolved*

2565   Bot if it stond of more necessitee,   *Unless there is a greater need*

Nor to the feld will pas bot for to see

Yhone knycht, the which that berith sich o fame."   *reputation*

---

[1] *Where before he had one man now he had two (i.e., his forces were double what they were before)*

85

	Than clepit he the Conquest King be name	called; by
	And hyme commandit thirti thousand tak	
2570	Againe the morne and for the feld hyme mak. [1]	
	And Gawane haith, apone the tother syde	
	Consulit his eme he schuld for them provid	Counseled his uncle
	And that he schuld none armys to hyme tak	not take up arms
	Whill Galiot will for the feld hyme mak.	Until
2575	"I grant," quod he, "wharfor yhe mone dispone	must plan
	Yhow to the feld with al my folk tomorne	[to go] to the field
	And thinkith in yhour manhed and curage	
	For to recist yhone fowis gret owtrag."	that enemy's; offense
	The nycht is gone; up goith the morow gray,	the gray morning comes
2580	The brycht sone so cherith al the day.	
	The knychtis gone to armys than in hast.	in haste
	One goith the scheildis and the helmys last.	helmets fastened
	Arthuris ost out ovr the furrde thai ryd.	ford
	And thai agane, apone the tother syd,	they in response
2585	Assemblit ar apone o lusty greyne,	pleasant field
	Into o vaill, whar sone thar mycht be seyne	In a vale; seen
	Of knychtis togedder many o pair	
	Into the feld assemblyng her and thair,	clashing
	And stedis which that haith thar master lorne;	lost
2590	The knychtis war done to the erth doune borne.	were; thrown
	Sir Esquyris, which was o manly knycht	brave
	Into hymeself, and hardy uas and wycht	In; valiant
	And intill armys gretly for to pryss,	in arms of great esteem
	Yhit he was pure, he previt wel oftsyss; [2]	
2595	And that tyme was he of the cumpanee	
	Of Galiot, bot efterwart was hee	
	With Arthur. And that day into the feild	
	He come, al armyt boith with spere and scheld,	
	With ferss desir, as he that had na dout,	no fear
2600	And is assemblit evyne apone a rowt. [3]	

---

[1] *In preparation for the morning, and to head for the field*

[2] *Although he was poor, he fought well oftentimes*

[3] *And has attacked directly into a band [of knights]*

His spere is gone; the knycht goith to the erd,   *ground*
And out onon he pullith haith o swerd.   *immediately*
That day in armys previt he rycht well   *proved*
His strenth, his manhed: Arthuris folk thai fell.
2605   Than Galys Gwynans, with o manly hart,
Which brother was of Ywane the Bastart,   *Who*
He cummyne is onone oneto the stour   *at once; battle*
For conquering in armys of honour
And cownterit with Esquyris hath so   *clashed*
2610   Than horss and man, al four, to erth thai go.   *to the ground*
And still o quhill lying at the ground   *a while; on*
With that o part of Arthuris folk thei found   *Until; they come*
Till Gwyans and haith hyme sone reskewit.   *To; rescued*
Aganis them til Esquyris thei sewyt   *In response to; they followed*
2615   Of Galiotis well thirti knychtis and mo.
Gwyans goith done and uthir seven also,   *down; seven others*
The wich war tone and Esqwyris relevit.   *taken; rescued*
Than Ywane the Anterus, aggrevit,   *vexed*
With kynnismen oneto the mellé socht.   *into the battle went*
2620   The hardy knychtis, that one thar worschip thocht,   *of their honor*
Cownterit them in myddis of the scheld   *Struck*
Whar many o knycht was born donn in the feld.   *thrown down*
Bot thei wich ware one Galiotis part   *on Galiot's side*
So wndertakand nor of so hardy hart   *bold*
2625   Ne ware thei not as was in the contrare.   *were; in the opposition*
Sir Galys Gwyans was resqwyt thare   *rescued*
With his falowis, and Esqwyris don bore.   *thrown down*
Thar al the batellis cam, withouten more,   *battalions; more ado*
On ather part, and is assemblit so   *either*
2630   Whar fyfty thousand war thei and no mo.   *more*
In o plane besyd the gret rivere
Thirty thousand one Galiotis half thei uare.   *were*
Of Arthuris ten thousand and no mo
Thei ware, and yhit thai contenit them so   *conducted themselves*
2635   And in the feld so manly haith bornn   *behaved*
That of thar fois haith the feld forswornn.   *(see note)*
The Conquest King, wich the perell knowith,
Ful manly oneto the feld he drowith.   *came*
The lord Sir Gawan, coverit with his scheld,

2640	He ruschit in myddis of the feld	
	And haith them so into his com assayt	*in his attack engaged*
	That of his manhed ware thei al affrait.	*were*
	No langer mycht thei contrar hyme endur	*against him*
	Bot fled and goith oneto discumfiture.	*defeat*
2645	And Galiot, wich haith the discumfit sen,	*who; defeat seen*
	Fulfillit ful of anger and of ten,	*wrath*
	Incontinent he send o new poware,	*Immediately; force*
	Wharwith the feldis al ovrcoverit ware	
	Of armyt stedis both in plait and maill,	*armor and chain mail*
2650	With knychtis wich war reddy to assaill.	*attack*
	Sir Gawan, seing al the gret suppris	*oppressive force*
	Of fois cummyng into sich o wys,	*in such a way*
	Togiddir al his cumpany he drew	
	And confortable wordis to them schew.	*reassuring; declared*
2655	So at the cummyng of thar ennemys	*attack*
	Thei them resauf in so manly wyss	*encounter*
	That many one felith deithis wound	*many a one feels death's*
	And wnder horss lyith sobing one the ground.	*sobbing*
	This uther cummyth into gret desir,	
2660	Fulfillit ful of matelent and ire,	*Filled; ill-will*
	So freschly, with so gret o confluens,	*charge*
	Thar strong assay hath don sich vyolens	
	And at thar come Arthuris folk so led	*(see note)*
	That thai war ay abaysit and adred.	*confused and frightened*
2665	Bot Gawan, wich that, by this uorldis fame,	
	Of manhed and of knychthed bur the name,	*was the epitome*
	Haith previt well be experiens;	*proved himself well by*
	For only intil armys his defens	
	Haith maid his falowis tak sich hardyment	*boldness*
2670	That manfully thei biding one the bent.	*fight on the field*
	Of his manhed war mervell to raherss.	*recount*
	The knychtis throw the scheldis can he perss	*through; pierce*
	That many one thar dethis haith resavit.	*received*
	None armour frome his mychty hond them savit,	
2675	Yhit ay for one ther ennemys wor thre. [1]	

---

[1] *Yet always for one of them there were three of their enemies*

Long mycht thei nocht endur in such dugree.

The press, it wos so creuell and so strong   *press of battle; was*

In gret anoy and haith continewit longe

That, magré them, thei nedis most abak, [1]

2680   The way oneto thar lugis for to tak.   *tents*

Sir Gawan thar sufferith gret myschef   *misfortune*

And wonderis in his knychthed can he pref.   *demonstrate*

His falouschip haith mervell that hym saw;

So haith his fois that of his suerd stud aw.   *stood in awe*

2685   King Arthur, that al this whill beheld

The danger and the perell of the feld,   *battlefield*

Sir Ywan with o falowschip he sende,   *sent*

Them in that ned to help and to defend,

Qwich fond them into danger and in were   *in danger and in peril*

2690   And enterit nere into thar tentis were.   *nearly*

Sir Gawan fechtand was one fut at erde   *fighting on foot on the ground*

And no defend but only in his swerde   *defense*

Aganis them both with spere and scheld.

Of Galowa the knycht goith to the erde.   *Galway*

2695   Thar was the batell furyous and woid   *fierce*

Of armyt knychtis. To the grownde thai yhud.   *went*

Sir Ywane, that was a noble knyght,

He schew his strenth, he schew thar his gret mycht,   *revealed*

In al his tyme that never of before

2700   Off armys nore of knychthed did he more.   *knightly deeds*

Sir Gawan thar reskewit he of fors,   *rescued; by force*

Magré his fois, and haith hyme set one horss   *In spite of*

That frome the first Conquest King he wann.

Bot Sir Gawan so evill was wondit than   *terribly; wounded*

2705   And in the feld supprisit was so sore   *oppressed; grievously*

That he the werss tharof was evermore.

Thar schew the lord Sir Ywan his curage,   *revealed*

His manhed, and his noble vassolage.   *prowess in battle*

And Gawan, in his doing, wald nocht irk   *be lax*

2710   So al the day enduring to the dyrk   *until the dark*

Sal them, magré of thar desyre, constren

---

[1] *That, in spite of themselves, they must necessarily retreat*

On athar half fore to depart in twen.   *On both sides; in two*
And when that Gawan of his horss uas tonn,   *from; taken*
The blud out of his noiss and mouth is gonn,   *nose*
2715 And largly so passith every wounde,   *copiously; goes from*
In swonyng thore he fell oneto the ground.   *a swoon there*
Than of the puple petee was to here   *pity; hear*
The lemytable clamour and the chere,   *sorrowful cries; display (of emotion)*
And of the King the sorow and the care,   *grief*
2720 That of his necis lyf was in disspare.   *nephew's*
"Far well," he sais, "my gladnes and my delyt,   *Farewell*
Apone knychthed far well myne appetit,   *For; farewell; inclination*
Fare well of manhed al the gret curage,   *manliness*
Yow flour of armys and of vassolage,   *prowess*
2725 Gif yow be lost." Thus til his tent hyme brocht   *If*
With wofull hart and al the surrygenis socht   *surgeons*
Wich for to cum was reddy at his neid.
Thai fond the lord was of his lyf in dreid,   *in jeopardy*
For wondit was he and ek wondit so   *wounded to such a degree*
2730 And in his syd ware brokyne ribys two.
Bot nocht forthi, the King thai maid beleif,
That at that tyme he shuld the deith eschef. [1]

Off Melyhalt the Ladyis knychtis were
Into the feld and can thir tithingis here,   *and heard these tidings*
2735 And home to thar lady ar thai went   *have they gone*
Til hir to schewing efter thar entent [2]
In every poynt how that the batell stud   *detail*
Of Galiot and of his multitud;
And how Gawan hyme in the feld hath bornn,   *fought*
2740 Throw quhoys swerd so many o knycht uas lornn,   *whose; lost*
And of the knychtly wonderis that he wrocht,   *wrought*
Syne how that he oneto his tent uas brocht.
The lady hard, that lovit Gawan so   *heard who*
She gan to wep; into hir hart uas wo.   *in her heart*

---

[1] *But they made the King believe that not on account of that / Should he achieve death (i.e., die) at that time*

[2] *To her to reveal, according to their intentions*

2745	Thir tythyngis oneto Lancelot ar gonn,	*These tidings*
	Wharof that he was wonder wobygone.	*wondrously sorrowful*
	And for the lady hastely he sent,	
	And sche til hyme, at his command, is went.	*request; has come*
	He salust hir and said, "Madem, is trew	*greeted*
2750	Thir tithingis I her report of new	*These; hear*
	Of the assemblé and meting of the ost,	
	And of Sir Gawan, wich that shuld be lost?	
	If that be swth, adew the flour of armys!	*true farewell*
	Now nevermore recoveryt be the harmys.	*rectified*
2755	In hyme was manhed, curtessy, and trouth,	*faithfulness*
	Besy travell in knychthed, ay but sleuth,[1]	
	Humylité, gentrice, and cwrag.	*gentility*
	In hyme thar was no maner of outrage.	*offense*
	Allace, knycht, allace! What shal yow say?	
2760	Yow may complen, yow may bewail the day	
	As of his deith, and gladschip aucht to ses,	*joy ought to cease*
	Baith menstrasy and festing at the des;	*minstrelsy; dais*
	For of this lond he was the holl comfort	*entire*
	In tyme of ned al knychthed to support.	
2765	Allace, madem, and I durst say at yhe	*dare say that you*
	Al yhour behest not kepit haith to me,	*promise*
	Wharof that I was in to full belef	
	Aganne this day that I schuld have my lef	*In preparation for*
	And nocht as cowart thus schamfully to ly	
2770	Excludit into cage frome chevalry,	*in prison*
	Whar othir knychtis anarmyt on thar stedis	*armed; horses*
	Hawntis ther yhouthhed into knychtly dedis."	*Spend their youth in*
	"Sir," quod sche, "I red yhow not displess,[2]	
	Yhe may in tyme herefter cum at es;	*to comfort*
2775	For the thrid day is ordanit and shal be	
	Of the ostis a new assemblé,	
	And I have gart ordan al the gere	*had prepared all the gear*
	That longith to your body for to were,	*is necessary; wage war*
	Boith horss and armour in the samyne wyss	*same manner*

---

[1] *Diligent effort in knightly deeds, always without sloth*

[2] *"Sir," said she, "I advise you not to be displeased"*

2780	Of sable, evyne aftir yhour awn devyss.	*black; instructions*
	And yhe sal her remayne oneto the day;	*here; until*
	Syne may yhe pass, fore well yhe knaw the way."	*Then*
	"I will obey, madem, to yhour entent."	*wish*
	With that sche goith and to hir rest is went.	
2785	One the morn arly up sche ross	*early; rose*
	Without delay and to the knycht sche gois	
	And twk hir lef and said that scho uald fare	*took her leave; she would go*
	Onto the court withouten any mare.	*more ado*
	Than knelit he and thankit hir oftsys	*many times*
2790	That sche so mych hath done hyme of gentriss [1]	
	And hir byhecht ever, at his myght,	*promised; as far as he could*
	To be hir awn trew and stedfast knycht.	
	Sche thonkith hyme and syne sche goith her way	
	Onto the King, withowten more delay,	
2795	Whar that in honour with King and Qwen sche sall	
	Rycht thonkfully resavit be withall.	*received; (see note)*
	Eft to Sir Gawan thai hir led, and sche	*Afterwards*
	Ryght gladly hyme desyrit for to see.	
	And sche hyme fond, and sche was glad tharfore,	*found*
2800	All uthirways than was hir told before.	*otherwise*
	The knycht, the wich into hir keping uas,	
	Sche had commandit to hir cussynece,	*commended; female relative*
	Wich cherist hyme apone hir best manere	*Who loved*
	And comfort hyme and maid hym rycht gud chere. [2]	
2805	The days goith; so passith als the nycht.	*also*
	The thrid morow, as that the sone uas lycht,	*morning; as soon as*
	The knycht onon out of his bed aross.	
	The maden sone oneto his chalmer goss	*chamber*
	And sacretly his armour one hyme spent.	*fastened*
2810	He tuk his lef and syne his way he went	*took his leave*
	Ful prevaly, rycht to the samyne grenn	*secretly; same field*
	One the revere, whar he befor had ben,	*river*
	Evyne as the day the first courss hath maad.	*Just as the day began*

---

[1] *That she had been so courteous to him*

[2] *And comforted him and treated him hospitably*

	Alone rycht thar he hovit and abaade,	*remained and waited*
2815	Behalding to the bertes whar the Qwenn	*parapet*
	Befor at the assemblé he had senn	
	Rycht so the sone schewith furth his lycht	*just as*
	And to his armour went is every wycht.	*person*
	One athir half the justing is bygon	*On both sides the jousting has begun*
2820	And many o fair and knychtly courss is rown.	*run*
	The Blak Knycht yhit hovyns on his sted;	*waits*
	Of al thar doing takith he no hed	*heed*
	Bot ay apone the besynes of thocht	*in the preoccupation*
	In beholding his ey departit nocht.	*(i.e., he stares)*
2825	To quhom the Lady of Melyhalt beheld	
	And knew hyme by his armour and his scheld,	
	Qwhat that he was. And thus sche said one hycht,	*Who; aloud*
	"Who is he yone? Who may he be, yhone knycht	*yonder; that*
	So still that hovith and sterith not his ren	*remains; rein*
2830	And seith the knychtis rynyng one the grenn?" [1]	
	Than al beholdith and in princypale	
	Sir Gawan beholdith most of all.	
	Of Melyhalt the Lady to hyme maid	*went*
	Incontinent, his couche and gart be had [2]	
2835	Before o wyndew thore, as he mycht se	*there so that*
	The knycht, the ost, and al the assemblé.	
	He lukith furth and sone the knycht hath sen;	
	And, but delay, he saith oneto the Qwen,	*without*
	"Madem, if yhe remembir, so it was	
2840	The Red Knycht into the samyne place	*same*
	That vencust al the first assemblé,	*Who vanquished*
	Whar that yone knycht hovis, hovit hee."	*abides, he abided*
	"Yha," quod the Qwen, "rycht well remembir I;	*Yes*
	Qwhat is the causs at yhe inquere and quhy?" [3]	
2845	"Madem, of this larg warld is he	
	The knycht the wich that I most desir to see	
	His strenth, his manhed, his curag, and his mycht,	

---

[1] *Though he sees the knights jousting in the field*

[2] *Immediately and caused his bed to be put*

[3] *What is the cause that you ask and the reason*

Or do in armys that longith to o knycht."   *what a knight should do*

By thus, Arthur, with consell well avysit,   *advised*
2850 Haith ordanit his batellis and devysit:[1]
The first of them led Ydrus King, and he
O worthy man uas nemmyt for to bee.   *named*
The secund led Harvy the Reveyll,
That in this world was knycht that had most feill   *knowledge*
2855 For to provid that longith to the were,   *pertains to war*
One agit knycht and well couth armys bere.   *seasoned; knew how to bear arms*

The thrid feld deliverit in the hond   *battlefield he assigned*
Of Angus, King of Ylys of Scotlande,   *To*
Wich cusing was one to King Arthur nere.   *relative; near*
2860 One hardy knycht he was, withouten were.   *without doubt*
The ferd batell led Ywons the King,   *fourth battalion*
O manly knycht he was into al thing.   *in every way*
And thus devysit ware his batellis sere   *arrayed; various forces*
In every feld fiftene thousand were.

2865 The fift batell the lord Sir Ywan lede,
Whois manhed was in every cuntré dred.   *feared*
Sone he was oneto Wryne the Kyng,   *Son; Uriens*
Forwart, stout, hardy, wyss, and yhing.   *Bold; young*
Twenty thousand in his ost thai past,   *went*
2870 Wich ordanit was for to assemblé last.   *fight*

And Galiot apone the tothir syde
Rycht wysly gan his batellis to devid.   *forces*
The first of them led Malenginys the King,
None hardyar into this erth levyng.   *in; living*
2875 He never more out of his cuntré raid,   *rode*
Nor he with hyme one hundereth knychtis hade.   *Unless*

The secund the First-Conquest King led,
That for no perell of armys uas adred.   *afraid*

---

[1] *Has arranged and made ready his troops*

94

The thrid o king clepit Walydeyne,   *called*
2880 He led, and was o manly knycht, but weyne.   *without a doubt*

The ferd, King Clamedeus has,   *fourth*
Wich that Lord of Far Ylys was.   *Who*
The fift batell, whar forty thousand were,
King Brandymagus had to led and stere,   *lead and command*
2885 O manly knycht and previt well oftsyss,   *battle-tested; often*
And in his consell wonder scharp and wyss.   *clever*
Galiot non armys bur that day,   *bore*
Nor as o knycht he wald hymeself aray,   *equip*
But as o servand in o habariowne,   *servant; coat of mail*
2890 O prekyne hat, and ek o gret trownsciownn   *(see note); club*
Intil his hond and one o cursour set,   *In; war horse*
The best that was in ony lond to get.   *to be had*
Endlong the revar men mycht behold and see   *Along the river*
Of knychtis weryne mony one assemblé   *fighting many a skirmish*
2895 And the Blak Knycht still he couth abyde   *(see note)*
Without removyng, one the river syde,   *departing*
Bot to the bartes to behold and see   *parapet*
Thar as his hart desyrit most to bee.   *Where*
And quhen the Lady of Melyhalt haith senn   *seen*
2900 The knycht so stond, sche said oneto the Qwenn,
"Madem, it is my consell at yhe send   *that you*
Oneto yone knycht, yourself for to commend,
Beseiching hyme that he wald wndertak
This day to do of armys for your sak."   *do deeds of arms; sake*
2905 The Quen ansuerit as that hir lykit nocht,   *it did not please her*
For othir thing was more into hir thocht:
"For well yhe se the perell, how disjont   *in a difficult position*
The adventur now stondith one the point   *on the brink*
Boith of my lord, his honore, and his lond,
2910 And of his men, in danger how thai stond;
Bot yhe and ek thir uthere ladice may,   *these other ladies*
If that yhow lykith, to the knycht gar say   *cause to be said*
The mesag. Is none that wil yhow let,   *hinder*
For I tharof sal nocht me entermet."   *interfere*
2915 Onto the Quen scho saith, "Her I,   *she*
If so it pless thir uthir ladice by,   *these other ladies nearby*

Am for to send oneto the knycht content."
And al the ladice can tharto assent,   *ladies*
Beseching hir the mesag to devyss,
2920   As sche that was most prudent and most wyss.
Sche grantit and o madenn haith thai tone,   *maiden; selected*
Discret, apone this mesag for till gone.   *to go*
And Sir Gawan a sqwyar bad also,   *bade*
With two speris oneto the knycht to go.   *lances*
2925   The lady than, withouten more dulay,
Haith chargit hir apone this wyss to say,   *instructed her*
"Schaw to the knycht, the ladice everilkone   *Declare; every one*
Ben in the court, excep the Quen allon,   *only*
Til hyme them haith recommandit oftsyss,   *commended many times*
2930   Beseching hyme of knychthed and gentriss   *because of; courtesy*
(Or if it hapyne evermore that he shall
Cum quhar thai may, owther an or all,   *either one or all [of them]*
In ony thing avail hyme or support,   *assist*
Or do hyme ony plesans or comfort),   *bring him any pleasure*
2935   He wold vichsaif for love of them this day   *vouchsafe*
In armys sum manhed to assay.   *valor to undertake*
And say, Sir Gawan hyme the speris sent.
Now go; this is the fek of our entent."   *tenor*
The damysell, sche hath hir palfray tone,   *taken*
2940   The sqwyar with the speris with hir gonn.
The nerest way thai pass oneto the knycht,   *most direct way; go*
Whar sche repete hir mesag haith ful rycht.
And quhen he hard and planly wnderstude   *heard*
How that the Quen not in the mesag yude,   *participated*
2945   He spak no word, bot he was not content.
Bot of Sir Gawan, glaid in his entent,   *glad in his spirit*
He askit quhar he was and of his fair.   *about his condition*
And thai to hyme the maner can duclair.   *declare*
Than the sqwyar he prayth that he wold
2950   Pass to the feld, the speris for to hold.   *Go*
He saw the knychtis semblyng her and thare,   *fighting*
The stedis rynyng with the sadillis bare.   *horses running; empty*
His spuris goith into the stedis syde,
That was ful swyft and lykit not to byd.   *to stand still*
2955   And he that was hardy, ferss, and stout,   *fierce; bold*

96

	Furth by o syd assemblyng on a rout	*fighting in a troop*
	Whar that one hundereth knychtis was and mo.	
	And with the first has recounterit so	*clashed*
	That frome the deth not helpith hym his scheld:	
2960	Boith horss and man is lying in the feld.	
	The spere is gone and al in pecis brak;	*in pieces broke*
	And he the trunscyoune in his hand hath tak	*truncheon*
	That two or thre he haith the sadillis reft	*deprived of*
	Whill in his hond schortly nothing is left.	*Until*
2965	Syne, to the squyar, of the feld is gonn.	*from*
	Fro hyme o spere into his hond haith ton	*taken*
	And to the feld returnyt he agayne.	
	The first he met, he goith one the plan,	*onto the ground*
	And ek the next, and syne the thrid also.	
2970	Nor in his hond, nore in his strak was ho.	*striking was there a halt*
	His ennemys that ueryng in affray	*were terrified*
	Befor his strok and makith roum alway.	*give way constantly*
	And in sich wyss ay in the feld he urocht,	
	Whill that his speris gon uar al to nocht.	
2975	Wharof Sir Gawan berith uitnesing	*bears witness*
	Throw al this world that thar uas non levyng,	*none living*
	In so schort tyme so mych of armys wrocht.	*did such deeds of arms*
	His speris gone, out of the feld he socht	*made his way*
	And passit is oneto the revere syde,	*has gone*
2980	Rycht thore as he was wont for to abyde	*where he usually remained*
	And so beholdyne in the samyne plann	*looking*
	As to the feld hyme lykit nocht agann. [1]	
	Sir Gawan saw and saith onto the Quen,	
	"Madem, yhone knycht disponit not, I weynn,	*plans; suspect*
2985	To help ws more, fore he so is avysit.	*has decided*
	As I presume, he thinkith hyme dispisit	*thinks himself despised*
	Of the mesag that we gart to hyme mak.	*had delivered to him*
	Yhowreself yhe have so specialy outtak,	*excluded*
	He thinkith evill contempnit for to bee,	*cruelly slighted*
2990	Considering how that the necessitee	
	Most prinspaly to yhowr supporting lyis.	*concerns support for you*

---

[1] *As it did not please him [to go] back to the field*

	Tharfor my consell is, yhow to devyss	*declare*
	And ek yhowreself in yhowr trespas accuss	*of your fault*
	And ask hyme mercy and yhour gilt excuss.	
2995	For well it oucht o prince or o king	*befits*
	Til honore and til cheriss in al thing	
	O worthi man that is in knychthed previt.	*proven*
	For throw the body of o man eschevit	*achieved*
	Mony o wondir, mony one adventure	
3000	That mervell war til any creature.	*it were to*
	And als ofttyme is boith hard and sen,	*heard and seen*
	Quhar fourty thousand haith discumfit ben	*defeated*
	Uith five thousand and only be o knycht.	*because of one*
	For throw his strenth, his uorschip and his mycht,	*through*
3005	His falowschip sich comfort of hym tais	*companions; takes*
	That thai ne dreid the danger of thar fays.	*foes*
	And thus, madem, I wot withouten were,	*know without a doubt*
	If that yhone knycht this day will persyvere	
	With his manhed for helping of the King,	
3010	We sal have causs to dred into no thing.	*fear*
	Our folk of hyme thai sal sich comfort tak	
	And so adred thar ennemys sal mak	*terrified*
	That sur I am, onys or the nycht,	*at some time before*
	Of forss yhone folk sal tak one them the flycht. [1]	
3015	Wharffor, madem, that yhe have gilt to mend,	*since you*
	My consell is oneto yhon knycht ye send."	
	"Sir," quod sche, "quhat plessith yhow to do	
	Yhe may devyss and I consent tharto."	*arrange*
	Than was the Lady of Melyhalt content	
3020	And to Sir Gawan into contynent	*(see note)*
	Sche clepit the maid, wich that passit ar,	*called; who went before*
	And he hir bad the mesag thus duclar.	*bade; declare*
	"Say the knycht the Quen hir recommendith [2]	
	And sal correk in quhat that sche offendith	*correct*
3025	At his awn will, howso hyme list devyss [3]	*humble manner*

---

[1] *Necessarily that army will take to flight*

[2] *Tell the knight the Queen commends herself [to him]*

[3] *According to his own wish, however it pleases him to arrange it*

	And hyme exortith in most humyll wyss,	*exhorts; humble manner*
	As ever he will, whar that sche can or may	
	Or powar haith hir charg be ony way,	
	And for his worschip and his hie manhede	
3030	And for hir luf to helpen in that ned	
	The Kingis honore, his land fore to preserf,	*preserve*
	That he hir thonk forever may deserf."	*thanks*
	And four squyaris chargit he also	*commanded*
	With thre horss and speris ten to go	
3035	Furth to the knycht, hyme prayng for his sak	*begging*
	At his raquest thame in his ned to tak.	*them [the lances]*

	The maden furth with the sqwyaris is went	
	Oneto the knycht and schawith ther entent.	*reveals*
	The mesag hard and ek the present senn,	*heard; gift seen*
3040	He answerit and askith of the Qwen.	
	"Sir," quod sche, "sche into yhone bartiis lyis,	*on that parapet*
	Whar that this day yhour dedis sal devyss,	*shall observe*
	Yhowr manhed, yhour worschip and affere,	*deportment*
	How yhe contenn and how yhe armys bere,	*conduct yourself*
3045	The Quen hirself and many o lady to	*too*
	Sal jugis be and uitnes how yhe do."	*judges*
	Than he, whois hart stant in o new aray,	*in a new condition*
	Saith, "Damyceyll, onto my lady say	*Damsel*
	However that hir lykith that it bee,	
3050	Als far as wit or powar is in me,	
	I am hir knycht; I sal at hir command	
	Do at I may, withouten more demand.	*that [which]; demurring*
	And to Sir Gawan, for his gret gentriss,	*courtesy*
	Me recommend and thonk a thousand syss.	*commend; times*
3055	With that, o sper he takith in his hond	
	And so into his sterapis can he stond,	*stirrups*
	That to Sir Gawan semyth that the knycht	
	Encresyng gon o larg fut one hycht.	*Grew a full foot in height*
	And to the ladice saith he, and the Qwen,	*ladies*
3060	"Yhon is the knycht that ever I have sen	
	In al my tyme most knychtly of affere	*bearing*
	And in hymeself gon farest armys bere."	*bore arms the best*

99

	The knycht that haith remembrit in his thocht	
	The Qwenys chargis and how sche hym besocht,	*commands; beseeched*
3065	Curag can encresing to his hart.	*increased*
	His curser lap and gan onon to start;	*charger reared; race forward*
	And he the sqwaris haith reqwyrit so	
	That thai with hyme oneto the feld wald go.	
	Than goith he one, withowten mor abaid,	*delay*
3070	And ovr the revar to the feld he raid.	*river; rode*
	Don goith his spere onone into the rest,	*(see note)*
	And in he goith withouten mor arest	*delay*
	Tharas he saw most perell and most dred	*peril; risk*
	In al the feld and most of held had ned,	*(see note)*
3075	Whar semblyt was the First-Conquest King	*assembled [for battle]*
	With mony o knycht that was in his leding.	*under his command*
	The first he met, doune goith boith horss and man;	
	The sper was holl, and to the next he rann	
	That helpit hyme his hawbrek nor his scheld,	*[neither] his mail*
3080	Bot throuch and throuch haith persit in the feld.	
	Sir Kay, the wich haith this encontyr sen,	*encounter seen*
	His horss he strekith ovr the larg gren	*urges on*
	And Syr Sygramors ek the Desyrand,	
	With Sir Gresown cummyth at thar honde,	*close by them*
3085	Son of the duk and alsua Sir Ywan	*also*
	The Bastart, and Sir Brandellis onan,	*at once*
	And Gaherss, wich that brothir was	
	To Gawan. Thir sex in a rass	*These six in a charge*
	Deliverly com prekand ovr the feldis	*Quickly; riding*
3090	With speris straucht and coverit with thar scheldis,	*extended*
	Sum for love, sum honor to purchess	*win*
	And aftir them one hundereth knychtis was,	
	In samyne will, thar manhed to assay.	*With the same wish; prove*
	On his five falowis clepit than Sir Kay	*called*
3095	And saith them, "Siris, thar has yhonder ben	*yonder*
	A courss that nevermore farar was sen	*passage at arms; fairer; seen*
	Maid be o knycht, and we ar cummyn ilkon	*Made by; each one*
	Only ws one worschip to dispone.	*plan [on winning]*
	And never we in al our dais mycht	
3100	Have bet axampil than iffith ws yone knycht	*example; gives*
	Of well doing. And her I hecht for me	*vow*

	Ner hyme al day, if that I may, to bee	*Near*
	And folow hyme at al mycht I sall,	*to the best of my ability*
	Bot deth or uthir adventur me fall. [1]	
3105	With that, thir sex, al in one assent,	*these six; in agreement*
	With fresch curag into the feld is went.	
	The Blak Knychtis spere in pecis gonne,	
	Frome o sqwyar onne uthir haith he tonne,	*taken*
	And to the feld onone he goith ful rycht.	*immediately; directly*
3110	Thir sex with hyme ay holdith at thar mycht. [2]	
	And than bygan his wonderis in the feld.	
	Thar was no helme, no hawbryk, nore no scheld,	
	Nor yhit no knycht so hardy, ferss nore stout,	*fierce; bold*
	No yhit no maner armour mycht hald owt	
3115	His strenth, nore was of powar to withstond.	*nor was strong enough*
	So mych of armys dyde he with his honde	
	That every wight ferleit of his deid	*person wondered at his deeds*
	And al his fois stondith ful of dreid.	*foes; fear*
	So besely he can his tyme dispend	*diligently*
3120	That of the speris wich Sir Gawan send,	*sent*
	Holl of them all thar was not levit onne;	*Unbroken; left*
	Throw wich but mercy to the deyth is gon	*without mercy*
	Ful many o knycht and many o weriour	
	That couth susten ful hardely o stour. [3]	
3125	And of his horss supprisit ded ar two,	*struck dead*
	One of his awn, of Gawanis one also;	
	And he one fut was fechtand one the gren,	*on foot; fighting*
	When that Sir Kay haith with his falowis senn.	*companions seen*
	The sqwyar with his horss than to hym brocht.	
3130	Magré his fois, he to his courseir socht	*horse made his way*
	Deliverly, as of o mychty hart,	*Quickly*
	Without steropis into his sadill start,	*leapt*
	That every wycht beholding mervel has	*person*
	Of his strenth and deliver besynes.	*nimble effort*
3135	Sir Kay, seing his horss, and how that thai	

---

[1] *Unless death or another chance [which would prevent me] befall me*

[2] *These six constantly remain by him as far as they are able*

[3] *Who knew how to fight a battle quite valiantly*

War cled into Sir Gawanis aray,   *dressed in*
Askith at the squyar if he knewith   *Asks of*
What that he was, this knycht. And he hyme schewith   *declares*
He wist nothing quhat that he was, nore hee   *knew not at all who*
3140 Befor that day hyme never saw with ee.   *eye*
Than askith he how and one quhat wyss   *in what manner*
On Gawanis horss makith hyme sich service.   *does him such*
The sqwar saith, "Forsuth Y wot no more;   *squire; In truth; know*
My lord ws bad, I not the causs quharfore."   *bade us; know not*
3145 The Blak Knycht, horsit, to the feld can sew   *sallied forth*
Als fresch as he was in the morow new.   *morning*
The sex falowis folowit hyme ilkone   *six companions; each one*
And al in front onto the feld ar gonn.
Rycht freschly one thar ennemys thai foght
3150 And many o fair poynt of armys uroght.   *(see note)*

Than hapnyt to King Malangins ost
By Ydras King discumfit was and lost   *defeated*
And fled and to the Conquest King ar gonne;
Thar boith the batellis assemblit into one.   *forces joined*
3155 King Malengynis into his hart was wo,   *sorrowful*
For of hymeself no better knycht mycht go.
Thar forty thousand war thai for fiftene.   *were they as opposed to*
Than mycht the feld rycht perellus be sen
Of armyt knychtis gaping one the ground,   *(see note to line 1090)*
3160 Sum deith and sum with mony a grevous wond;   *dead*
For Arthuris knychtis that manly war and gud,
Suppos that uthir was o multitude,   *Although*
Resavit tham well at the speris end.   *Received*
Bot one such wyss thai may not lang defend.   *long hold out*
3165 The Blak Knycht saw the danger of the feld
And al his doingis knowith quho beheld   *who*
And ek remembrith into his entent   *mind*
Of the mesag that sche haith to hyme sent.
Than curag, strenth encresing with manhed,   *increase*
3170 Ful lyk o knycht oneto the feld he raid,   *rode*
Thinking to do his ladice love to have,   *act in order; lady's*
Or than his deth befor hir to resave.   *then; receive*
Thar he begynyth in his ferss curag   *fierce*

102

	Of armys, as o lyoune in his **rag**.	*lion; violent anger*
3175	Than mervell was his doing to behold.	
	Thar was no knycht so strong nor yhit so bold	
	That in the feld befor his suerd he met	
	Nor he so hard his strok apone hyme set	*That he did not*
	That ded or wondit to the erth he socht,	*dead; made his way*
3180	For thar was not bot wonderis that he wrocht.	
	And magré of his fois everilkone,	*every one*
	Into the feld ofttymys hyme alonn	*In*
	Throuch and throuch he passith to and fro.	*goes*
	For in the ward it was the maner tho	*(see note)*
3185	That non o knycht shuld be the brydill tak	*by*
	Hyme to orest nore cum behynd his bak	*halt*
	Nor mo than on at onys one o knycht	*one at a time*
	Shuld strik, for that tyme worschip stud so rycht.	*honor*
	Yhit was the feld rycht perellus and strong	*fierce*
3190	Till Arthuris folk set thai contenyt longe.	*although they endured*
	Bot in sich wyss this Blak Knycht can conten	*bore himself*
	That thai, the wich that hath his manhed senn,	
	Sich hardyment haith takyne in his ded,	*boldness; taken*
	Them thocht thai had no maner causs of dred	*It seemed to them*
3195	Als long as he mycht owthir ryd or go,	*either ride or walk*
	At every ned he them recomfort so.	*aided*
	Sir Kay haith with his falowis al the day	*companions*
	Folowit hyme al that he can or may,	*knows how or is able to*
	And wondir well thai have in armys previt	*proven themselves*
3200	And with thar manhed oft thar folk relevit.	*assisted*
	Bot well thai faucht in diverss placis sere,	*fought; various*
	With multitud ther folk confusit were [1]	
	That long in sich wyss mycht thai nocht contenn.	*endure*
	Sir Kay, that hath Sir Gawans squyaris sen,	*seen*
3205	He clepit hyme and haith hyme prayt so	*called; entreated*
	That to Sir Harvy the Revell wil he go	
	And say to hyme, "Ws think hyme evil avysit, [2]	

---

[1] *With the large number [of enemies] their army was overwhelmed*

[2] *And say to him [Harvy], "It seems to us that he is ill advised"*

	For her throuch hyme he sufferit be supprisit [1]	
	The best knycht that ever armys bur;	*bore arms*
3210	And if it so befell of adventur,	*by chance*
	In his defalt, that he be ded or lamyt,	*Because of his absence*
	This warld sal have hyme utraly defamyt.	*[hyme=Harvy]; disgraced*
	And her ar of the Round Table also	
	A falouschip that sall in well and wo	
3215	Abid with hyme and furth for to endur	*hereafter endure*
	Of lyf or deth, this day, thar adventur.	*their fate*
	And if so fal discumfyt at thai bee,	*it befalls defeated that*
	The King may say that wonder evill haith he	
	Contenit hyme and kepit his honore,	*Borne himself and guarded*
3220	Thus for to tyne of chevalry the flour."	*lose*
	The sqwar hard and furth his way raid;	*squire heard; rode*
	In termys schort he al his mesag said.	*In a few words*
	Sir Harvy saith, "Y wytness God that I	
	Never in my days comytit tratory;	*committed treachery*
3225	And if I now begyne into myne eld,	*in my old age*
	In evill tyme fyrst com I to this feld.	*came*
	Bot, if God will, I sal me son discharg.	*acquit*
	Say to Sir Kay I sal not ber the charg;	*accusation*
	He sal no mater have me to rapref.	*legal issue; charge against*
3230	I sal amend this mys if that I lef."	*fault; live*
	The sqwyar went and tellit to Sir Kay.	
	And Sir Harvy, in al the hast he may,	*as fast as he can*
	Assemblyt hath his ostis and ononn	*at once*
	In gret desyre on to the feld is gon	
3235	Befor his folk and haldith furth his way.	*went forth on his way*
	Don goith his sper, and evyne before Sir Kay	*Down; right before*
	So hard o knycht he strykith in his ten	*anger*
	That horss and he lay boith apone the gren.	
	Sir Gawan saw the counter that he maad	*encounter*
3240	And leuch for al the sarues that he had.	*laughed; (see note)*
	That day Sir Harvy prevyt in the feld	*proved himself*
	Of armys more than longith to his eld;	*is expected of; age*

---

[1] *Because here, through his (i.e., Harvy's own) fault, he allowed to be oppressed*

	For he was more than fyfty yher of ag,	*years*
	Set he was ferss and yong in his curag.	*Although; fierce*
3245	And fro that he assemblyt his bataill	*force*
	Doune goith the folk of Galotis al haill.	*completely*
	For to withstond thai war of no poware	*might*
	And yhit of folk ten thousand mo thei uare.	*more were they*

	Kyng Walydone, that sauch on such o wyss	*saw*
3250	His falowis dangerit with thar ennemys,	*endangered by*
	With al his folk, being fress and new,	*fresh*
	Goith to the feld onon, them to resskew.	*rescue*
	Thar was the feld rycht perellus aganne;	
	Of Arthuris folk ful many on uar slan.	*many a one was slain*

3255	Bot Angus, quhich that lykith not to bid	*remain inactive*
	And saw the perell one the tothir sid,	*other*
	His sted he strok and with his ost is gon	
	Whar was most ned; and thar the feld has ton.	*taken*

| | Kyng Clamedyus makith non abaid, | *delay* |
| 3260 | Bot with his ost oneto the sid he raid. | *rode* |

	And Ywons King, that haith his cummyn sen,	*arrival seen*
	Encounterit hyme in myddis of the grenn.	
	The aucht batellis assemblyt one this wiss;	*eight*
	On ather half the clamore and the cryiss	*cries*
3265	Was lametable and petws for til her	*lamentable; pitiable to hear*
	Of knychtis wich in diverss placis sere	*various*
	Wondit war and fallyng to and fro;	*Wounded*
	Yhit Galyotis folk war twenty thousand mo.	

	The Blak Knycht than onto hymeself he said,	
3270	"Remembir the how yhow haith ben araid,	*afflicted*
	Ay sen the hour that yow was makid knycht,	*Ever since*
	With love agane quhois powar and whois mycht	*against whose*
	Yow haith no strenth; yow may it not endur,	
	Nor yhit non uthir erthly creatur.	

3275	And bot two thingis ar the to amend,[1]	
	Thi ladice mercy or thi lyvys end.	*lady's; life's*
	And well yhow wot that onto hir presens,	*know*
	Til hir estat nor til hir excellens,	*rank*
	Thi febilness nevermore is able	
3280	For to attan, sche is so honorable.	*attain*
	And sen no way yow may so hie extend,	*aim*
	My verray consell is that yow pretend	*true; attempt*
	This day — sen yow becummyne art hir knycht	*since you have become*
	Of hir comand and fechtit in hir sycht —	*fight; sight*
3285	And well yow schaw, sen yow may do no mor,[2]	
	That of resone sche sal the thank tharfore,	*So that reasonably; you*
	Of every poynt of cowardy yow scham	*cowardice; be ashamed*
	And intil armys purchess the sum nam."[3]	
	With that of love into o new desir	
3290	His spere he straucht and swift as any vyre[4]	
	With al his forss the nerest feld he soght,	
	His ful strenth in armys thar he uroght,	
	Into the feld rusching to and fro.	
	Doune goith the man, doune goith the horss also;	
3295	Sum throw the scheld is persit to the hart,	*pierced*
	Sum throw the hed — he may it not astart.	*escape*
	His bludy suerd he dreuch, that carvit so	*drew; cut*
	Fro sum the hed and sum the arm in two;	
	Sum in the feld fellit is in swonn;	*swoon*
3300	Throw sum his suerd goith to the sadill doune.	
	His fois waren abasit of his dedis,	*afraid of*
	His mortell strok so gretly for to dred is.	*deadly*
	Whar thai hyme saw, within a lytall space	*time*
	For dreid of ded, thai levyng hyme the place,	*fear of death; leave*
3305	That many o strok ful oft he haith forlornn.	*wasted*
	The spedy horss away the knycht hath bornn.	
	Into his wyrking nevermore he sest,	*In his activity; ceased*

---

[1] *And there are only two things which can cure you*

[2] *That you make a good showing, since you may do no more*

[3] *And in arms win yourself some reputation*

[4] *His lance he lowered and swift as any cross-bow bolt*

Nor non abaid he makith nor arest.   *delay; pause*

His falowis so in his knychthed assuryd,   *trusted*

3310 Thai ar recomfort, thar manhed is recoveryt,   *reassured; restored*

And one thar fois ful fersly thai soght.   *fiercely; attacked*

Thar goith the lyf of many o knycht to nocht.[1]

So was the batell wonderful to tell,

Of knychtis to se the multitud that fell

3315 That pety was til ony knycht to senn   *pity; for any; see*

The knychtis lying gaping on the gren.   *(see note to l. 1090)*

The Blak Knycht ay continewit so fast

Whill many one discumfit at the last   *defeated*

Are fled and planly of the feld thei pas.   *from the field; go*

3320 And Galyot haith wondyr, for he was

Of mor powar, and askit at them qwhy   *larger force; of*

As cowartis thai fled sa schamfully.   *cowards*

Than saith o knycht, sor wondit in the brayne,   *seriously wounded*

"Who lykith, he may retwrn agayne

3325 Frome qwhens we come, mervalis for to see   *whence*

That in his tyme never sich sauch hee."   *saw*

"Marvell," quod he, "that dar I boldly say

Thay may be callit and quhat thai ar, I pray."[2]

"Schir, in the feld forsuth thar is o knycht   *in truth*

3330 That only throw his body and his mycht

Vencussith all that thar may non susten   *Vanquishes; abide*

His strokis, thai ar so fureows and ken.   *sharp*

He farith as o lyone or o beyre,   *bear*

Wod in his rag, for sich is his affere.   *Mad; wrath; conduct*

3335 Nor he the knycht into the armys red   *in*

Wich at the first assemblé in this sted   *battle; place*

Vencussith all and had the holl renown,   *all the glory*

He may to this be no comparysoune;

Fore never he sesith sen the day uas gonn   *ceases since*

3340 Bot evermore continewit into one."   *continued steadfastly*

Quod Galiot, "In nome of God and we   *name*

---

[1] *There the life of many a knight perishes*

[2] *They may be called, and what they are I ask [you to tell me]*

Al, be tyme, the suthfastness sal see."   *in time; truth*

Than he in armys that he had is gon
And to the feld with hyme agane hath ton   *taken*
3345   Al the flearis and found yne sich aray   *those who fled; (see note)*
His folk that ner discumfyt al war thay.   *nearly defeated*
Bot quhen thai saw cummyne ovr the plan   *coming*
Thar lord, thai tuk sich hardement agann   *courage*
That thar essenyeis lowd thai gon to cry.   *battle-cries*
3350   He chargit tham to go, that ware hyme by,
Straucht to the feld with al thar holl forss;   *Straight; entire*
And thai, the wich that sparit not the horss,
All redy war to fillyng his command   *fulfill*
And freschly went withowten more demand.   *question*
3355   Throw qwich thar folk recoveryt haith thar place,
For al the feld preswmyt that thar was
O new ost, one such o wyss thai soght,   *attacked*
Whar Arthuris folk had passith al to nocht.[1]
Ne war that thai the better war ilkonne[2]
3360   And at thai can them utraly disponne   *that; utterly decided*
Rathar to dee than flee, in thar entent,   *die; heart*
And of the Blak Knycht haith sich hardyment,   *encouragement*
For at al perell, al harmys and myschef,   *Because; trouble*
In tyme of ned he can tham al ralef.   *rescue*

3365   Thar was the batell dangerus and strong;   *fierce*
Gret was the pres, bath perellus and throng.   *battle; crowded*
The Blak Knycht is born onto the ground;
His horss hyme falyth, that fellith dethis wound.   *fails; feels*
The six falowis that falowit hyme al day,   *companions; followed*
3370   Sich was the press that to the erth go thay.
And thar in myd among his ennemys   *in the midst of*
He was about enclosit one sich wyss
That quhare he was non of his falowis knew
Nor mycht nocht cum to help hyme nore reskew.   *rescue*

---

[1] *That Arthur's army would have perished*

[2] *Were it not that they [Arthur's troops] were better, each one*

108

3375	And thus among his ennemys allon	*alone*
	His nakid suerd out, of his hond, haith ton;	*with his hand; taken*
	And thar he previt his vertew and his strenth,	
	For thar was none within the suerdis lenth	*sword's length*
	That came bot he goith to confusioune.	*without being killed*
3380	Thar was no helme, thar was no habirioune	*helmet; coat of mail*
	That may resist his suerd, he smytith so.	*strikes*
	One every syd he helpith to and fro	
	That al about the compas thai mycht ken	*all around they might see*
	The ded horss lyith uirslyng with the men.	*struggling*
3385	Thai hyme assalyeing both with scheld and spere;	*attack*
	And he agane, as at the stok the bere	*in response; (see note)*
	Snybbith the hardy houndis that ar ken,	*Checks; fierce*
	So farith he; for never mycht be sen	*seen*
	His suerd to rest that in the gret rout	*throng*
3390	He rowmyth all the compas hyme about.	*clears all the circumference*
	And Galiot, beholding his manhed,	
	Within hisself wonderith of his ded	*deeds*
	How that the body only of o knycht	*one*
	Haith sich o strenth, haith sich affere and mycht.	*ability*
3395	Than said he thus, "I wald not that throw me	*because of me*
	Or for my causs that such o knycht suld dee,	*on my account; die*
	To conquer all this world that is so larg."	
	His horss than can he with his spuris charg	*spurs urge on*
	A gret trunsioune into his hond hath ton	*club; hand; taken*
3400	And in the thikest of the press is gonn	
	And al his folk chargit he to sess.	*commanded; cease*
	At his command thai levyng al the press;	*leave all the battle*
	And quhen he had departit all the rout	*separated; forces*
	He said, "Sir knycht, havith now no dout."	*fear*
3405	Wich answerit, "I have no causs to dred."	*Who*
	"Yis," quod he, "sa ever God me sped,	*so; God help me*
	Bot apone fut quhill ye ar fechtand here	*on foot; fighting*
	And yhow defendith apone sich manere	
	So hardely and ek so lyk o knycht	
3410	I sal myself with al my holl mycht	
	Be yhour defens and uarand fra al harmys.	*protector from*
	Bot had yhe left of worschip intil armys,	*neglected honor in*

What I have don I wold apone no wyss.   *in no way*

Bot sen yhe ar of knychthed so to prys   *since; of such worth*

3415 Yhe salt no maner causs have for to dred.

And set yhour horss be falit at this ned,   *although; has failed*

Displess yhow not, forquhy ye sal not want   *because; lack*

Als many as yhow lykith for to hawnt.   *As many as it pleases you to use*

And I myself, I sal yhowr sqwyar bee,

3420 And, if God will, never more sal wee

Depart." With that anon he can to lycht   *Separate; dismounted*

Doune frome his horss and gaf hyme to the knycht.

The lord he thonkit and the horss hath ton,   *thanked; taken*

And als so fresch oneto the feld is gon   *fresh*

3425 As at no strokis he that day had ben.   *As if in no combat*

His falowis glad one horss that hath hym sen,

To Galiot one uthir horss thai broght;

And he goith one and frome the feld he socht   *gets on; went*

And to the plan quhar that his ostis were.

3430 And Brandymagus chargit he to stere   *direct himself*

Efter hyme within a lytill space,   *short time*

And ten thousand he takyne with hym hass.

Towart the feld onon he can to rid   *he rode*

And chargit them befor the ost to byd.   *ordered; wait*

3435 Wp goith the trumpetis and the claryownis,

Hornys, bugillis blawing furth thar sownis,

That al the cuntré resownit hath about.   *resounded*

Than Arthuris folk uar in dispar and dout   *fear*

That hard the noys and saw the multitud   *heard the noise*

3440 Of fresch folk: thai cam as thai war wod.   *mad*

Bot he that was withowten any dred,

In sabill cled, and saw the gret ned   *black dressed*

Assemblyt al his falowis and arayd.   *marshalled*

And thus to them in manly termes said:

3445 "What that ye ar I knaw not yhour estat;   *rank*

Bot of manhed and worschip, well I wat,   *courage and honor; know*

Out throuch this warld yhe aw to be commendit,   *ought*

This day ye have so knychtly yhow defendit.

And now yhe see how that, aganis the nycht,   *just before the night*

3450 Yhour ennemys pretendit, with thar myght   *intended*

Of multitud and with thar new ost

And with thar buglis and thar wyndis bost   *(see note)*

Freschly cummyng into sich aray,   *in such array*

To ifyne yhow one owtray or affray.   *give; offense; fright*

3455   And now almost cummyne is the nycht,

Quharfor yhour strenth, yhour curag and yhour mycht

Yhe occupye into so manly wyss

That the worschip of knychthed and empryss   *chivalric enterprise*

That yhe have wonyng and the gret renown   *won*

3460   Be not ylost, be not ylaid doune.

For one hour the sufferyng of distress,

Gret harm it war yhe tyne the hie encress   *if you should lose*

Of uorschip servit al this day before.   *honor earned*

And to yhow al my consell is, tharfore,

3465   With manly curag but radour yhe pretend   *courage without fear you attempt*

To met tham scharply at the speris end

So that thei feil the cold speris poynt

Outthrow thar scheldis in thar hartis poynt   *stab*

So sal thai fynd we ar nothing affrayt,   *frightened*

3470   Wharthrouch we sall the well less be assayt. [1]

If that we met them scharply in the berd, [2]

The formest sal mak al the laif afferd."   *first; remainder afraid*

And with o voyss thai cry al, "Sir knycht   *one voice*

Apone yhour manhed and yhour gret mycht

3475   We sal abid for no man shall eschef   *stand fast; flee*

Frome yhow this day, his manhed for to pref."   *prove*

And to his ost the lord Sir Ywane said,

"Yhe comfort yow, yhe be nothing affrayd.

Ws ned no more to dreding of suppriss: *fear unexpected attack*

3480   We se the strenth of al our ennemys."

Thus he said, for he wend thai uar no mo,   *thought*

Bot Sir Gawan knew well it uas not so;

For al the ostis mycht he se al day

And the gret host he saw quhar that it lay.   *where*

---

[1] *Through which we shall be much the less attacked*

[2] *If we met them openly and resolutely*

3485 And Galiot, he can his folk exort,   *exhort*
     Beseching them to be of good comfort
     And sich enconter . . .   *such a battle*

[The manuscript ends at this point. Lines 299–313 indicate the general content of the entire romance and thus give some indication of how it would have concluded.]

Notes

2   *Set* is an astronomical term implying that the winter is no longer ascendent, but has passed.

3   *Illumynare* is an aureate term for the sun.

12   The *kalendis* (kalends) was the first day of a month in the Roman calendar (and the word from which "calendar" is derived).

18   The verb *deuit* (manuscript reading: "devit") is a form of "douen," which means "to have worth or validity; be useful, profitable, helpful, or effective; avail" (MED).

24   *Phebus* (Apollo) is the god of the sun.

28   The form *carving* reflects the common practice of this manuscript of using *-ing* where one would expect to find *-en* or *-in*, as in infinitives or plural forms of verbs. Here "carving" is the infinitive following "cann," which gives a past sense to the verb, "did carve" or "carved," (as also in line 36, "cann constrein," and many other places in the text). The subject of "cann carving" is the "suerd" of the following line, and "hart" is the object: "The terrible sword of love's intense desire did carve my sorrowful heart in two."

38–40 The motif of the helpless lover, frustrated by the knowledge that his beloved knows nothing of his plight, is commonplace in courtly literature. See, for example, Chaucer's *Troilus and Criseyde*, I, 806–812.

48   In the manuscript there is a line over the *o*, which is usually used for an abbreviation of *n* or *m*. Here it seems not to be significant (unless the scribe intended an abbreviation of *gh*. The same word with the same line occurs again in line 258.

51   *Pryapus* (Priapus) is the Greek god of fertility, sometimes associated with medieval love gardens. See Chaucer's Merchant's Tale, where Priapus is called "god of gardens" (IV, 2034–35).

56   I follow Skeat in emending the manuscript reading "closit" to "clos it."

57   Skeat is probably correct in noting that the manuscript reading *Alphest* is erroneously written for "Alcest." Alcestis was a faithful wife who chose to die so that her husband Admetus could live. She was then rescued from the underworld by Hercules. Gower tells her story in Book VII of the *Confessio Amantis*, but the suggestion that she was turned into a flower is not found there. Nor is it found in the Classical sources of the legend such as Euripides' *Alcestis*. In the Prologue to *The Legend of Good Women*, Chaucer refers to "the quene Alceste, / That turned was into a dayesye" (511–12). Perhaps this is the source of the identification here of Alceste with a "flour."

74   I follow Skeat and Gray in emending "besor" to "be sor." "Gan" in this line is an auxiliary to "occupy" in the following line and gives a past sense to that verb.

81 ff.   Bird debates and instructions of lovers by birds are conventional devices in late medieval English poetry. See, for example, Chaucer's *Parliament of Fowls* and Thomas Clanvowe's "Boke of Cupid" ("The Cuckoo and the Nightingale").

109   *Althir* is a genitive plural of "al" (all). Literally the line translates: "The last he calls the best of all of the two (i.e., he calls the latter the better of the two)." The works of the Roman poet Ovid (Publius Ovidius Naso [43 B.C.–17 or 18 A.D.]) were well known, particularly his *Metamorphoses* and his books about love. He is called by Chaucer "Venus clerk Ovide" in the *House of Fame* (1487). In the *Art of Love* (*Ars amatoria*), Ovid expresses the preference for keeping love secret that is referred to here: "Cytherea [Venus], especially, forbids that her mysteries should be revealed. I give thee warning, no babbling knaves should ever draw near her altars. . . . The beasts of the field abandon themselves, in any place and in the sight of all, to the delights of love, and often at the spectacle a young girl will turn away her head; but for our loves we must have a secret bower, closed doors, and we must needs cover with vesture the secret places of our body. . . . Let us, on the other hand, speak sparingly of our real amours, and hide our secret pleasures beneath an impenetrable veil" (*The Art of Love and Other Love Books of Ovid* [New York: The Universal Library, 1959], pp. 160–161).

112–14   The sense of these lines seems to be: Although you presume or believe that you will test yourself in his (Love's) service, to see whether you like it or not (literally, "whether it will run or walk"), do not presume it (that you will try love out and decide if you like it), for it will not be so.

115   *Thine* is the genitive of the pronoun "thou." Thus the opening of the line means "Entirely in spite of yourself" (or, loosely, "No matter what you want").

138   *Be maner oft endit.* That is, in courtly verse.

143   Skeat notes that *at lyte* (literally "in little") is here used as an expletive.

171   Gray glosses *wyss* as "wise man." Skeat translates the line: "At command of a wise (god from) whose vision." As Skeat's translation implies, a preposition must be supplied or must be assumed to be implied by the case of the noun "visioune" in order to make sense of the line.

177–89   The poet's elaborate humility trope is part of the poem's wit. The device is common and ranges in its application from the pious sincerity of Chaucer's Parson (*CT*, X, 55–57) to the inflated modesty of his Franklin (*CT*, V, 716–28), or the youthful uncertainty of the Squire (*CT*, V, 34–41).

202   Lancelot's father, Ban, is king of *Albanak* (Malory's Benwick), generally said to be in Brittany.

204   A *clerk* in this context is someone who can read and write.

211   The term *romans* was originally applied to the language of France, as distinguished from Latin. (The term "romance language" was later used to describe any of the languages derived from the Latin of the Romans.) The word "romance" came to be transferred from the language itself to a story told in French. Then it came to be applied to the types of stories told in French, no matter what language they were written in.

214   Skeat translates the line: "I will not waste my efforts thereupon." Gray glosses "depend" as "expend, spend." The original reading may well have been "despend" rather than the manuscript reading "depend."

214–98   The author uses this elaborate instance of *occupatio* (the saying of what you say you are not going to say) to recount the material from his French source that he is not dealing with at length in his poem. This was a common rhetorical device. It appears, for example, in Chaucer's Knight's Tale (I, 2919–66) and, on a much smaller scale, in the Squire's Tale (V, 67–72).

226   Gray translates *to the stak* as "to the hilt." Skeat translates "iwondit to the stak" as "very deeply wounded." In his glossary Skeat lists various conjectures to explain the phrase "to the stak." Among others, he quotes the Scottish phrase "to the steeks," meaning "completely" and refers to the idea that Gray picks up on, namely that "stak" may be a form of "stock" ("hilt"). MED cites the phrase "driven to the stak" (where "stak" is "a post to which someone is tied for execution, punishment, or restraint" as meaning "driven to the last extremity." A similar meaning might apply here. But perhaps, since the next line refers to the piercing of the heart, an anatomical image is intended. MED cites one meaning of "stok n. (1)" as "a main vein or artery."

247–48   Skeat and Gray agree that the manuscript wrongly transposes these lines.

252   The prepositional phrase *of desir* seems not to be adjectival modifying "armys" but rather adverbial, meaning something like "eagerly."

255   *The Lady of Nohalt* (Nohaut in the Vulgate *Lancelot*) appealed to Arthur for a champion to aid her against the King of Northumberland, who was besieging her castle. Lancelot, who had just been knighted by Arthur, asked to be allowed to assist her; and Arthur could not refuse. Because Lancelot engaged in a fierce combat on his journey, the Lady of Nohalt delayed the fight with the King of Northumberland's champion until his wounds were healed. In the meantime, since no news had been received at court, Kay asked to be sent to complete the mission begun by Lancelot. When he arrived at the Lady of Nohalt's castle and found Lancelot ready to fight for the Lady, he was willing to fight Lancelot for the right to complete the mission. The Lady of Nohalt, however, diplomatically avoided such a fight by asking the King of Northumberland to send two champions so that both Lancelot and Kay could fight for her. In the ensuing combats both of Arthur's knights were victorious.

258   In the manuscript there is a line over the *o* in *throue*. Either this is a meaningless stroke or it is used to indicate the omission of *gh*. It surely does not signify here the omission of an *m* or *n*, as it usually does.

278   In the Vulgate *Lancelot*, while Lancelot is staring so intensely at Guinevere that he is unaware of what is going on around him, his horse wanders into danger-

ously deep water. Ywain leads him to a ford so he is out of danger. There Dagonet (Fr. "Daguenet") finds him and leads him, still gazing on the Queen and unaware of everything else, back to the court. In Malory, as in the French tradition, Dagonet is Arthur's fool as well as a knight.

291   The manuscript reads "to his his"; I follow Gray and Skeat in emending to "to hir his."

302   *Galiot* is referred to in Malory as "Galahalt" (or some variation thereof, such as "Galahaut" or "Galahaud"). He is sometimes referred to in French texts as the son of "la bele Jaiande," the wife of Brunor. The similarity between her name and the English word "giant" may have caused some confusion, as in the English Prose *Merlin*, where Galehaut is referred to as "the son of the Geaunt" (EETS o.s. 36, p. 601).

309   *Venus, siting hie abuf.* Venus is the goddess of love and the deity usually addressed by courtly lovers as she, from her seat in the third sphere, watches over their woes. See, for example, Chaucer's *Troilus and Criseyde*, III, 1–49, his Complaint of Venus and Complaint of Mars, and the Knight's Tale, I, 1918–66; Henryson's *Testament of Cresseid*, lines 8–28; and Gower's *Confessio Amantis*, I, 124–202, and VIII, 2171–2940.

318 ff.   The poet alludes to an unnamed Latin poet. Perhaps he has in mind a specific person like Ovid, who as a poet who wrote about love might be an appropriate figure to refer to and an obvious author for readers to think of in this context. Or perhaps he deliberately leaves the poet unnamed to create a mythic figure like the Lollius to whom Chaucer refers in *Troilus and Criseyde*, I, 394, or the "man of gret auctorite" at the end of *The House of Fame*.

334   *Endit* could mean one of two things in this context. Either it is a form of the verb "to end" and means that "this [prologue] ends [at this point]" or it is a noun meaning "composition" or "poem," in which case the meaning is that the great poet to whom the author refers has his thanks for any pleasant phrase that he writes and also for "this [entire] poem."

335–42 The Titans were pre-Olympian gods and were the children of Uranus and Gaia (Heaven and Earth). Among them was Hyperion, father of Helios (the Sun) to whom the name "Titan" is often applied in later poetry, as it is here. In this astrological reckoning of time, Titan (the sun) is twenty days into Aries. Since the sun enters Aries on March 12, the time is the very beginning of April. (See also the note to lines 2486–87.) Chaucer uses a similar device for telling the time in the General Prologue to *The Canterbury Tales*, lines 1–8.

345   For *anerding*, Stevenson reads "awerding," which is clearly not the reading of the manuscript. Skeat reads "auerding" and glosses "auerding to" as "belonging to (?)." Gray reads "anerding" and defines it as a Scottish word meaning /"adhering." The confusion between *u* and *n* results from the fact that the two minims which comprise the letter could be read either way. Gray's reading seems correct. The *Dictionary of the Older Scottish Tongue* defines the verb "enherde" and its variant "anherd" as "to adhere." The OED lists "anerd" as another variant.

347   *The Arthurian Handbook*, by Norris J. Lacy and Geoffrey Ashe (New York: Garland, 1988), identifies *Carlisle* as the "city of Cumbria, of Roman origin, that survived for some time after the separation of Britain from the empire. The first syllable of its old name, *Luguvallum*, suggests a connection with the god Lugh. In the course of time the name was shortened and the Welsh *caer*, "city," was prefixed. . . . It figures in English tales with Gawain as hero. It is also the place where, in Malory, Lancelot rescues Guinevere when she is about to be burnt at the stake" (p. 323).

357   *Camelot* as the legendary site of Arthur's court first appears in Chrétien's *Le Chavalier de la Charrette* (line 34). On the origin of the name see William C. Hale, "Camelot," *Avalon to Camelot* 2.2 (1986), 40–41. On the possible site of the central fortification of the historical figure behind the Arthurian legends, see Leslie Alcock, *Was This Camelot? Excavations at Cadbury Castle 1966–70* (New York: Stein and Day, 1972).

374   The statement that Arthur *thoght* in the same manner (*apone the samyne wyss*) suggests a recurrence of the dream.

376   In his glossary under *liging*, Skeat notes that "the sense requires *lay*, i.e. the 3rd *p. s. pt. t. indic.*, but properly the word is the present participle, *lying*." However, it may be that the *-ing* is written for the ending normally appearing as *-en*, as is a common practice in this manuscript. Thus "liging" would be a plural form. The shift from singular to plural might reflect the difference between the *stomach* falling out and the *guts* lying on the ground.

390   The notion that dreams *are thingis that askith no credens* is similar to the opinion expressed by Pandarus in Chaucer's *Troilus and Criseyde*: "A straw for alle swevenes significaunce! / God helpe me so, I counte hem nought a bene!" (V, 362–63), and by Pertelote in the Nun's Priest's Tale: "Ne do no fors of dremes" (VII, 2941). According to Macrobius (*Commentary on the Dream of Scipio*, trans. William Harris Stahl [1952; rpt. New York: Columbia University Press, 1990]), one of the standard medieval authorities on dreams, there are certain types of dreams, the nightmare and the apparition, which "are not worth interpreting since they have no prophetic significance" (p. 88). However, there are other types which Macrobius considers meaningful: the "oracular" dream "in which a parent, or a pious or revered man, or a priest, or even a god clearly reveals what will or will not transpire, and what action to take or avoid"; the "prophetic vision," which "actually comes true"; and the "enigmatic dream," which conceals with strange shapes and veils with ambiguity the true meaning of the information being offered, and requires an interpretation for its understanding" (p. 90). The last is the sort of dream that Arthur has.

        A summary of medieval dream lore can be found in the "Proem" to Chaucer's *House of Fame*. For further information on medieval beliefs about dreams, see chapters 8 and 9 ("Mediaeval Dream-Lore" and "Chauntecleer and Pertelote on Dreams") in Walter Clyde Curry's *Chaucer and the Mediaeval Sciences* (1926; rpt. New York: Barnes and Noble, 1960), and Stephen F. Kruger's *Dreaming in the Middle Ages* (Cambridge: Cambridge University Press, 1992).

393   *Superfleuytee* (or superfluity) is an excess of one of the bodily humors, which was believed to be one of the causes of dreams. In Chaucer's "The Nun's Priest's Tale," Pertelote tells Chauntecleer that his dream "Cometh of the greet superfluytee / Of youre rede colera" (VII, 2927–28).

401   *Clergy* here suggests not only clerics but also, and more importantly in this context, "learned men."

417   In order for the clerks to provide an astrological interpretation of the dream they must know the time ("the houre") and date ("the nyght") when it occurred.

433   Stevenson read "fete" for the manuscript "set." Skeat and Gray both suggest emending "set" to "fet" (fetched or got). However, it seems that the manuscript reading needs no emendation. The suggestion is that the scholars "arranged" or "set out" all the books they would need for their work.

434–36   A similar but longer list of authorities on astronomy occurs in Book 7 of Gower's *Confession Amantis*. George G. Fox, in *The Mediaeval Sciences in the Works of John Gower* (1931; rpt. New York: Haskell House, 1966), pp. 81–83, comments on Gower's list: "The astrological lore of Abraham [who is not mentioned in *Lancelot of the Laik*] and Moses may, Gower says, never have been committed to writing. Nimrod, or as Gower [as well as the author of *Lancelot of the Laik*] calls him, Nembrot, is the mighty hunter of the Bible, the son of Canaan, the son of Shem, the son of Noah. This is the genealogy given by Michael Scot . . . . Two manuscripts have been found which, although not by Nimrod himself, purport to be based on his teachings. Arachel refers probably to Arzachel (Al-Zarkali), whose astronomical tables were in common use." In *Lancelot of the Laik*, Danghelome is a bastardized form of Ptolemy (whose name appears in Gower as "Danz Tholome"). Ptolemy was most famous for a book called *The System of Mathematics*, which was known in the Middle Ages as the *Almageste* (from its Arabic title, *al-Kitab-al-Midjisti*, meaning "the greatest book"), a work which is, as its translator G. J. Toomer says (in *Ptolemy's Almagest* [New York: Springer, 1984], p. 1), "a complete exposition of mathematical astronomy as the Greeks understood the term." *Herynes* is, as Skeat notes, written for "Herymes" (Hermes). William Cecil Dampier in *A History of Science* (4th ed; Cambridge: Cambridge Up, 1949), p. 50, observes that "there are . . . writings, probably of the third century, assigned to "Hermes Trismegistor," the Greek equivalent of the Egyptian god Thoth. They are chiefly concerned with Platonic and Stoic philosophy, but they also contain much astrology as well as alchemy, and were afterwards well known in Latin translations."

438   The *disposicioune* is the "character or position (of a planet) in the horoscope as influencing persons or events" (MED).

472   I follow Skeat and Gray in emending manuscript "shat" to "shal."

519   *Fyne* in this line is coordinate with "adew" in line 518.

536   The line completing the couplet (and rhyming with "also") is apparently missing here, though there is no gap in the manuscript. Skeat constructs the line: "In to the feld can rusching to and fro," in imitation of line 3293.

538   Edward, Second Duke of York, in *The Master of the Game*, ed. Wm. A. and F. Baillie-Groham (New York: Duffield, 1919), says of the greyhound: "a good

greyhound should go so fast that if he be well slipped he should overtake any beast . . . ." Line 538 echoes this idea.

554 To *holde* lands from someone is to receive them from a feudal lord. The implication is that Arthur would become a vassal to Galiot and thus owe him obligations ("tribut and rent") as overlord and ultimate owner of Arthur's lands.

559 Skeat and Gray read "Shir"; but Stevenson's edition follows the manuscript in reading "Schir."

599 Ackerman in *An Index of the Arthurian Names in Middle English* (Stanford: Stanford University Press, 1952) identifies *Galygantynis of Walys* as "Seneschal to Galehaut." However, this is a different person. Galygantynis is clearly a knight of Arthur's court. Even in the Vulgate *Lancelot*, there are two different characters with similar names: Galeguinant, one of Galahot's knights whom Sommer identifies as "le senescal Galahot" (Index, p. 39), and Galegantins li Galois (i.e., the Welshman), one of Arthur's knights.

600-1 These lines seem to echo the description of Chaucer's Knight who had "ridden, no man ferre, / As wel in cristendom as in hethenesse" and of whom we are told "At many a noble armee hadde he be" (General Prologue, 48–49, 60).

621 *Lest* is a variant of "list" (to want or desire). The phrase translates literally, "This I want to say" and seems to be used as a way of emphasizing the previous statement. The phrase "ayan the morn" means "against the coming of the morning" or "towards the morning."

675—76 The use of anaphora, the repetition of a word or words at the beginning of successive clauses or sentences, in these lines and also in line 1289 has a Chaucerian ring. Compare these instances with the line from the Knight's Tale, "Up roos the sonne, and up roos Emelye" (I, 2273).

699 Skeat notes that "the metre of Lancelot's lament is that of Chaucer's 'Cuckoo and Nightingale,' and was very possibly copied from it." That poem was once thought to be by Chaucer and only appears in manuscripts which contain other works by him. But in his volume of *Chaucerian and Other Pieces* (1897), which is a supplement to the *Complete Works of Geoffrey Chaucer*, Skeat himself observes that the author of this poem, "the true title" of which he gives as "The Book of Cupid, God of Love," is not Chaucer but probably Thomas Clanvowe,

"a well known personage at the courts of Richard II and Henry IV" (pp. lvii–lviii).

735–36   It is possible that the type of carts described here was some sort of armored vehicle with iron wheels and bars for defense against enemy weapons. In *English Weapons & Warfare 449–1660* (Englewood Cliffs, N. J.: Prentice Hall, 1979), A. V. B. Norman and Don Pottinger describe such vehicles from the time of Henry VIII: "There are a number of references to armoured cars, and one drawing shows an English army accompanied by them. These were box-like structures on wheels with a battlemented top like a tiny castle. They were propelled by a horse or horses placed between the wheels and protected by the sides of the cart. . . . The immediate inspiration for these probably came from the Scots, who used them in the campaign of 1523, but ultimately they derive from the armoured wagons of the Hussite Wars in Bohemia (1420–1434)" (p. 163).

753   On the *Kyng An Hundereth Knychtis*, see the note to line 806.

771   The *Dictionary of Middle English Musical Terms* defines *trumpet* as "perhaps a short cylindrical bore instrument with a wide flared bell . . . . (The ME. term may simply designate a small species of either the straight or the folded trumpet . . .)" and a "clarioun" as an instrument "of the trumpet class; before 1400 with probable reference to a straight trumpet . . . , afterwards to the folded trumpet." "Trumpet" is a diminutive from "trompe" or "trump," "a name applied to a wind-instrument with a long slender pipe, which was made of wood, horn, or metal, and which terminated in a fairly large, funnel-shaped bell . . .; after c1400, frequently an instrument folded in the shape of the letter *S*."

806   *Maleginis* is identified in the French source with the King of a Hundred Knights and is said to be the seneschal of Galiot ("la premiere bataille ot malaguins ses senescaus che fu li rois des C cheualiers qui moult estoit preus & hardis" [the first troop was commanded by Malaguins, his (i.e., Galiot's) seneschal, who was the King of One Hundred Knights who was very valiant and bold"] (see H. Oskar Sommer's edition of *The Vulgate Version of the Arthurian Romances*, III, 236). The author of the English poem does not make a specific connection between the two in any of the places where he mentions Maleginis (see also line 2873, "Malenginys"; line 3151, "Malangins"; line 3155, "Malengynis"; line 753, "Kyng An Hundereth Knychtis"; line 1545, "King of Hundereth Knychtis"; line 1554, "King of Hunder Knyghtis").

809   Because of the way the second letter in the word is written in the manuscript, it is impossible to be sure whether the fourth word in this line should be read *berde* or *borde*. Stevenson and Skeat read "borde," but Skeat adds a note: "or 'berde.'" Skeat, who places a semicolon at the end of line 808, takes "borde" as a verb and translates "In the midst they encounter . . . ." Gray, who has no punctuation at the end of line 808 and who reads "berde," glosses the phrase "in the berde" as "in the front, face to face." Gray's reading seems less forced.

817   The line translates: "When he saw their latter battalion move out . . . ." In his note to the line, Skeat translates "latter" as "last." While it is possible that this is the sense, it seems more likely that the literal meaning is intended, perhaps as a way of showing the superior tactics of Gawain, who was advised on the disposition of his troops by Arthur. Instead of having one large charge by the mass of the army (the "rout") and just one battalion in reserve, Gawain has his smaller force attack in five waves, each time sending in fresh troops to support and boost the spirits of their comrades.

820   *Strokis.* Skeat suggested the need for the insertion of the word "strokis" in this line. Both the meter and the sense suggest that something has been left out, and "strokis" seems satisfactory on both counts; thus I have followed his emendation (though Skeat's translation "His enemies began his mortal strokes to feel" seems not quite accurate because it would be unusual for "feel" to be spelled with the double *l*. The line might better be translated: "His deadly strokes felled his enemies").

823   The manuscript reading "into on hour" seems strange and even inappropriate in this context, as if it sets a time limit on Gawain's ability to conduct himself well. It is more likely that the original reading was something like "into o shour" ("in a battle"). It makes much more sense to say that he conducts himself well in battle; and this formula is fairly common. See, for example, lines 1107–8 where virtually the same phrase, with the substitution of "stour," another word meaning "battle" or "combat," occurs.

895   At the beginning of the line a space for an illuminated letter (obviously a *T*) has been left. (A similar thing occurs in line 1083, where a space has been left for an *A*.)

911   The manuscript reads "presonerere" because of the use of an abbreviation for *er* followed by the letters *er*.

918   Skeat is probably correct in noting that *wight* is an "unusual, and perhaps wrong," form of "with."

923   The phrase "mak the ransone" means something like "set the ransom [at an amount]."

925   There are a couple of ways this line might be interpreted. If "on" is taken as part of "her" it could mean "Because I have been told about this ['her-on'] by word of mouth." But the construction "on be" meaning "by" appears again in line 964. So it seems preferable to read "her" as the verb "to hear" and translate the line as: "Because I hear [it] told ['be-told,' though the words are separated in the manuscript] by word of mouth."

960   The manuscript reads "behold." I follow Skeat and Gray in emending to "be hold."

963   Skeat is probably correct in identifying *sutly* here as a variant form of "sothly" ("truly").

979   *Commandit* is governed by *haith* in line 977.

1007   The manuscript reads "abertes." I follow Skeat and Gray in emending to "a bertes."

1009–10 Skeat translates: "His spirit started (owing to the) love (which) anon hath caught him."

1026   *Mayne* might be a variant of "mene" ("means" or "way"); or it might be a variant of "main" (force), the sense being that he is unable to come (to his lady's favor) by force.

1028   The ME verb "sterfen" or "sterven," which becomes the Modern English "starve," meant "to die" by any means and not just by hunger. Thus a knight could "sterf" in battle.

1047   The duties of the herald originally seem to have concerned the conduct of tournaments but later also included such things as serving as messengers and marshalling troops in battle. They also recorded and reported deeds done in tournament or battle. Thus it seems perfectly appropriate for a herald to remind

Lancelot to pay heed to his honor. By the fourteenth century knowledge of the heraldic devices of knights and noblemen, which was crucial to identifying knights in armor, became the herald's prime concern. On the history and functions of heralds, see Anthony Richard Wagner, *Heralds and Heraldry in the Middle Ages* (2nd ed.; London: Oxford University Press, 1960), and Chapter VII of Maurice Keen's *Chivalry* (New Haven: Yale University Press, 1984).

1053   *Screwis* (Modern English "shrews") means "rogues," "villains," or "ill-natured persons." In ME the term is more often applied to men than to women.

1056   The *ventail* is either "a piece of armour protecting the neck, upon which the helmet fitted" or "the lower movable part of the front of the helmet, as distinct from the vizor; latterly, the whole movable part including the vizor" or "one of the vents or air-holes in this" (OED).

1064   As is explained below (lines 1546–47) this king is so named because he is the first that Galyot conquered.

1066   *The tother* is from "thet other" or "that other"; it is formed in a manner similar to "the tone" (from "thet one" or "that one"), i.e., "the *t* of *thet* being attached to *an, on* [or *other*], when *the* became the general form of the definite article" (OED). ("The tother" is also found in lines 2571 and 2584, and the variant spelling "the tothir" in line 2536.)

1070   A *hawbrek* is a coat or tunic of chain mail.

1077   The manuscript reads "sched." Both Skeat and Gray emend to "scheld," which is obviously the correct reading.

1090   *Gaping* might refer to wounded knights and mean "gasping in pain," but more likely it refers to the open mouths of the dead bodies.

1092   A *vyre* is a quarrel or bolt for a cross-bow.

1152–53 Generally, the places where I have placed a blank line between blocks of text are places where the manuscript indicates a division by a large capital letter. However, in order to facilitate reading, here and after lines 1806, 1934, 1940, 1944, 1998, 2130, 2140, 2150, and 2252, I have added a blank line where no large capital appears.

1215   Skeat suggests that the manuscript reading of "them" might be a mistake for "then" but does not emend the text. Though the "Thir" at the beginning of the next line makes "them" seem redundant, the occurrence of a similar phrase in line 1552 (where the "them" again seems redundant and where Skeat again believes that "then" might be the correct reading), suggests the possibility of an idiomatic usage.

1221–22 The prefix "to-" serves as an intensive and is used with the words "hurt," "schent" and "rent" to indicate the severity with which Lancelot has been wounded, disfigured, and cut up.

1233   Skeat and Gray emend "alyt" to "a lyt."

1243   The phrase *the more* is a survival of the instrumental form as in the phrase "the more, the merrier." The sense is that Lancelot will blame all others "by that much more."

1253   Gray offers no glosses for *appelit* or for *thret*. Skeat translates this and the following line, "But what if he be appealed to and threatened / and (meanwhile) his heart be elsewhere set to love." *Thret* is better read as from the verb "threte" meaning "to dispute, contend; to quarrel, wrangle" (OED). The sense seems to be: "But what if he is appealed to and [his love] disputed [by someone else], while his heart is fixed on love elsewhere [with the one contending for his affection]."

1302   The *seven science* (or branches of knowledge) are the seven areas of study in the medieval curriculum comprising the *trivium* (grammar, logic, and rhetoric) and the *quadrivium* (arithmetic, geometry, astronomy, and music).

1304   Bertram Vogel's article on "Secular Politics and the Date of 'Lancelot of the Laik,'" *Studies in Philology* 40.1 (Jan. 1943) observes that the wise man who advises Arthur is unnamed in the French source but that "Actually, the name *Amytans* is found elsewhere in the Old French story, in the slightly different form *Amustans*. Indeed, this character found in another section of the tale is also an advisor of King Arthur. He does not, however, give political advice, but denounces Arthur for his illicit relations with the second or 'false' Guinevere. What the Scottish poet has done, then, is apparent: he has converted a holy man who, in the Old French romance, gives Arthur exclusively moral advice into a political adviser . . ." (pp. 4–5). In a note to line 1608, Skeat observes that "for many of the precepts given by Amytans the author must have been indebted to Gower [*Confessio Amantis*, Book 7], or, at any rate, to the author of the *Secreta Secretorum*."

1318   Gray glosses *careldis* as "carols, merry-makings." Skeat suggests that it is the plural of "careld, a merry-making, revel"; but he adds a question mark to this gloss. In a note he translates the line: "nigh of thy revels (i.e. because of thy revels) in the gulf it falls." This is a forced reading of the phrase. *Ney of* seems not to be indicating causality but rather location. The phrase also appears to be part of the metaphor, which is explained in lines 1320 and following ("That is to say . . ."). The line seems to have been corrupted. The original sense may be something like "[Which] is near to [i.e., not far off the shore from] your [city of] Carduel" in which case the text should read "Ney of thi Carduel is."

1343   Skeat suggests that the word "diverss" is needed before "peplis" to complete the meter of the line and cites line 731 as an example of a similar construction.

1357   The concept of a spiritual *raknyng* (an accounting or reckoning) is similar to that found in *Everyman*, in which because of the sinfulness of the human race, God determines that He "will, in all the haste, / Have a reckoning of every man's person" (lines 45–46). When Death announces God's decision, he tells Everyman to bring "thy book of count" to the reckoning (line 104).

1365 ff. It is not clear what Biblical passage the author is referring to in these lines. The author, who admits in lines 1438–39 that he is no confessor, may be mistaken about the source of the quotation. Perhaps he is thinking of Proverbs 14:31 ("He that oppresseth the poor upbraideth his Maker") or Proverbs 17:5 ("He that despiseth the poor, reproacheth the Maker"); but these are not the words of Daniel. Similarly in lines 1378–80, when the author attributes to "Salomon" the sentiment "Wo be to hyme that is byleft alone, / He haith no help" he is apparently misattributing the line from Ecclesiastes 4:10, "woe to him that is alone, for when he falleth, he hath none to lift him up."

1378–79 See the note to lines 1365 ff.

1404   Gray emends "amendit" to "amend it."

1414   Sins committed *of fre will* are sins of commission as opposed to those done *of neglygens* or by omission. Morton Bloomfield (*The Seven Deadly Sins* [1952; East

Lansing: Michigan State University Press, 1967], p. 126) observes that Vincent of Beauvais's *Speculum naturale* "discusses sins of omission and commission." See also Reginald Pecock's *The Donet* ([1921; rpt. New York: Kraus Reprint, 1971] EETS o.s. 156), which observes that sins can be the "leevingis or vnfulfill-ingis of eny poynt comaundid . . . or ellis doingis of the contrarye to eny poynt comaundid" (p. 96).

1430   In addition to the five outer wits or senses, medieval theory recognized inner wits, one of which is the *wit memoratyve*. John of Trevisa (in *On the Properties of Things: John of Trevisa's Translation of Bartholomæus Anglicus De Proprietatibus Rerum* [Oxford: Clarendon Press, 1975] I, 98) says: "The innere witte is departid athre by thre regiouns of the brayn, for in the brayn beth thre smale celles. The formest hatte *ymaginatiua*, therin thingis that the vttir witte apprehendith withoute beth i-ordeyned and iput togedres withinne . . . . The middil chambre hatte *logica* therin the vertu estimatiue is maister. The thridde and the laste is *memoratiua*, the vertu of mynde. That vertu holdith and kepith in the tresour of the mynde thingis that beth apprehendid and iknowe bi the ymaginatif and *racio*."

1437   The *holl romans* or "whole romance" of which the author speaks is his French source, the Vulgate *Lancelot*. The author has catalogued above (lines 214–298) those parts of the source that he has chosen not to retell.

1448   *Thy*. The manuscript clearly reads "my" and not "thy"; and both Skeat and Gray follow the manuscript. However, the emendation to "thy" seems necessary. According to the Vulgate *Lancelot*, Arthur's father Uther Pendragon ("Uter-pandragon") had helped Hoel (or Aramont) of Lesser Britain against his enemy Claudas. In return Hoel agreed to become Uther's vassal. Together Hoel and Uther desolated Claudas's lands. After the death of Hoel and Uther, Claudas regained control of his lands and began to wage war on Ban, who had been a vassal of Hoel. After Uther's death those who owed allegiance to him then became vassals of Arthur. When Arthur was fighting rebellious barons, he appealed to Ban for assistance and Ban responded, as was fitting for a vassal to do. When Claudas attacked Ban, the latter appealed to Arthur for help but Arthur did not respond because of his difficulties at home: "li rois bans auoit plusours fois enuoie pour secours au roi artu. Mail li rois artus auoit tant a faire de maintes pars quil ne se pooit mie legierement entremetre dautrui besoigne" (Sommer, III, p. 5). It is this failure to assist a vassal (one in his service) who had faithfully assisted him that Amytans suggests Arthur has forgotten to confess. The corresponding passage in the Vulgate *Lancelot* supports the emendation. Arthur is asked: "es tu confes del grant pechie que tu as del roi ban de benoic qui mors fu en ton ["thi" in English] seruice" (Sommer, III, p. 217).

1474   I follow Skeat and Gray in emending manuscript "assit" to "assist."

1485   The land which God promised to his people is the land of Canaan, called the Promised Land because God promised to give it to Abraham and his descendants (see Genesis 12:7 and 28:13).

1500   *Rent* in this context seems to mean "the right to receive rents from tennants" (MED) rather than a payment made by Arthur to those who serve him. The term can also be used to mean the homage due to or from a lord. (See David Lyle Jeffrey, "The Friar's Rent," *JEGP* 70 [1971], 600–06.)

1507   A *fee* is "an estate in land (in England always a heritable estate), held on condition of homage or service to a superior lord, by whom it is granted and in whom the ownership remains" (OED).

1517   The author seems to be presenting *multitude* (a term which often means "army" or "host") as an alternative to *confluens* ("a rushing together"). Thus the best translation for these terms might be something like "pitched battle" and "charge."

1541   Skeat's translation of the line — "Except wise conduct falleth to a king" — seems a forced reading. Perhaps a better translation is achieved by punctuating the Middle English line with a colon after "not" (which Skeat does not do): "Thus it does not fail: a king without moral control, both the realm and he go to ruin."

1545   On the *King of Hundereth Knychtis*, see note to line 806.

1546   Gray notes that she is emending *Kinghe* to "king he"; Skeat emends to "king" and explains the spelling as resulting from confusion with the word "knight" even though, as he believes, another spelling with *h* ("Kinghis") occurs in line 2527. In both cases, it seems that the scribe has merely run two words together and no emendation or further explanation is required to make sense of the lines.

1547   The phrase *of one* or "of ane" is used in Scottish in the sense of "of all," as, for example, in *Rauf Coilyear*, line 576 ("And in ane rob him arrayit richest of ane").

1552   On *them thei boith*, where the "them" seems redundant and Skeat suggests the possibility of emending to "then," see the note to line 1215.

1608   Skeat suggests that the *And* at the beginning of the line is redundant in modern English. However, the word seems to have the force of "In either case."

1624   Skeat glosses *medyre* as "mediator" but follows his gloss with a question mark and says "I am not at all sure of this word." Gray notes: "Word almost undecipherable; 'medyre' is Professor Skeat's reading. Possibly 'mesyre,' a forced form of 'measure' for sake of rhyme." The word is in fact relatively clear in the manuscript except for the letter which Stevenson and Skeat read as *d* and which Gray suggests might be an *s*, which is partially obscured because it is written over the downward stroke of the elongated *s* from the line above. The letter does appear to be a *d*, but the word "medyre" is not recorded in the MED, the OED, or the *Dictionary of the Older Scottish Tongue*. Assuming that the text is not corrupt and that the obscured letter is a *d*, the sense seems more likely to be "moderation" than "mediator."

1629   The manuscript reads "w justly." Skeat is surely correct in emending to "wnjustly."

1666   The rhyme and an empty space in the manuscript suggest that a line has been omitted here.

1668   I follow Skeat and Gray in emending "behold" to "be hold."

1687   *Cuntreis* might mean "countrysides" (to contrast with "tounis") or "counties."

1689   A *bachelor* is "a young knight, not old enough, or having too few vassals, to display his own banner, and who therefore followed the banner of another" (OED).

1700   The *most philosephur* or greatest philosopher is Aristotle, purported author of the *Secreta Secretorum*, which advises: "a kyng owith not to shewe him ouer oftene to his peple, ne ouer oft haunte the company of his sugetis, and specially of chorlis and ruralle folke, for bi ouyr moche homelynes [too much familiarity] he shalle be the lasse honourid" (*Three Prose Versions of the Secreta Secretorum*, ed. Robert Steele, EETS e.s. 74 [1898; rpt. Millwood, NY: Kraus Reprint, 1973] pp. 12–13).

1728   The sense of the line is either that the greatest gifts and affections should be given after the knight *berith uitnesing* (bears witness) to his worthiness by his deeds or that the greatest gifts and affection should be given after the knight bears witness to the truth of the advice by having used well the earlier gifts of horse and treasure.

1729   *Tennandis* or "tennants" are those who hold land from a feudal lord. The OED, citing this line, defines a *vavasour* as "a feudal tenant ranking immediately below a baron."

1730   A hackney is "a small saddle horse, often one let for hire" (MED); a palfrey is a fine riding horse; and a courser is a war horse or charger.

1737   In the manuscript there is a line over the *a* in "stable," but it appears to have no significance.

1788   The manuscript reads "to lede"; the "to" seems in this context to make sense only as a prefix used as an intensive with "lede" (lead). Thus my reading of "to-lede."

1802   I take *them* to refer to princes, the plural being implied by the phrase "no prince" in line 1799. The sense is that except for virtue and honor which abide with princes, the world divides up the remainder (*laif*) when they are dead and buried. The lack of strict agreement according to modern rules is not uncommon in Middle English and is exemplified again in the verb "abidith," which is technically singular even though both "vertew" and "worschip" are subjects.

1818   The line contains a paradox: "The riches best kept are those well dispensed." The explanation is provided by the instruction given above in lines 1765–1778.

1856   Wearing the *palm* (palm leaf) was a sign of victory.

1864   The phrase *takith larges in his awn kynd* can be translated as "practice generosity according to its own [true] nature." "Take" in the phrase "take largess" seems to be used much as it is in "take pity."

1899   Skeat sees *Ye* as the equivalent of "The," which he says means "The one, He." However, the shift to direct address to God does not present any problems of interpretation and seems an effective rhetorical device.

1903–4   I take *blyndis* to be a variant of "blindness." (The MED does not record this form but gives "bleinasse" as a variant.) The sense of the lines is: In this [the oppression of his people which is punished by God] is the blindness of kings [because they do not foresee the ultimate rather than the immediate punishment by God] and the downfall of princes and of kingdoms.

1956 ff.   There is a shift from the plural *kingis* in line 1956, which states a wish that all kings would act in the way outlined in the following lines, to the singular *he* in the elaboration of the specific circumstances.

1983   The manuscript reads "that," which is the reading found in all earlier editions. I have emended to *thai* because the sense seems to demand the change. The word "that" in the manuscript could be the result of scribal confusion caused by "that" in the line above.

2047   The notion of the lion as the king of the beasts, which is still current today, can be found in the *Etymologies* of Isidore of Seville. Isidore says that "Leonis vocabulum ex Græca origine inflexum est in Latinum. . . . Leo autem Græce, Latine *rex* interpretatur, eo quod princeps sit omnium bestiarum" (*Patrologia Latina*, 82, p. 434). John of Trevisa (in *On the Properties of Things: John of Trevisa's Translation of Bartholomæus Anglicus De Proprietatibus Rerum* [London: Oxford University Press, 1975]) echoes this notion in what is virtually a restatement of the passage from Isidore: "*Leo* in grew hatte *rex* in latyn, kyng in englisshe, and hatte *leo* 'king' for he is kyng and prince of alle bestes, as Ysidorus seith" (II, p. 1214).

2035   *Hee*, that is the lion who represents God, is in the water of the sin of the clerks interpreting the dream, not, of course, of His own sin.

2036   Skeat suggests that the correct reading might be "see" instead of "bee," though he does not emend his text. "Bee" makes sense if we read it with an understood main verb from several lines above: "On account of which [being in the water of sin] it is impossible to be [standing in pure religion]." Standing in the cleanliness of religion rather than in the murky water of sin would have allowed them to see clearly.

2064   The *qualyté* of the year refers to the effect of a particular astrological sign. As Walter Clyde Curry notes, in *Chaucer and the Mediaeval Sciences* (1926; rpt. New York: Barnes and Noble, 1960), "in astro-medical lore the Zodiacal signs have certain 'qualities' or 'virtues' assigned to them: Aries, Leo, and Sagittarius are fiery; Taurus, Virgo, and Capricorn are earthy; Gemini, Libra, and Aquarius are airy; Cancer, Scorpio, and Pisces are watery" (p. 7).

2065–67   On *disposicioune* see the note to line 438. A medieval doctor was expected to have a knowledge of astrology. Chaucer's Doctour of Phisik, for example, "was grounded in astronomye" (*Canterbury Tales*, General Prologue, 414). This was important because the heavens were believed to control the elements which made up all things, including the human body. Much of medieval medical theory was founded on the notion that an excess of one of the four bodily *hwmowris* (or "humors") was the cause of disease. The four humors were thought to be combinations of the basic attributes (heat, cold, moistness, and dryness) of the four elements of earth (cold and dry), air (hot and moist), fire (hot and dry), and water (cold and moist). The attributes combined to form the humors of blood (which was hot and moist), phlegm (cold and moist), yellow bile or cholera (hot and dry), and black bile or melancholia (cold and dry). The proportion of the humors in the body produced the *compleccyoune* ("complexion") or the temperament. Thus a person could be sanguine, phlegmatic, choleric, or melancholy. The dominance of one of these humors predisposed a person to certain diseases and also to certain emotional states.

2068   The phrase *wnder reull* probably means "under the control [of God]," though it might also mean "according to [medical] procedures."

2153   *Cardole* (or Carduel) is a city in Wales which is identified in several medieval romances as one of the places where Arthur holds court.

2180   *Travell* (travail) and *ess* (comfort) are a contrasting pair such as is commonly used in Middle English to denote completeness. Thus when Arthur says his knights would not leave him for "travell nor for ess," he means they would not leave him for any reason.

2212   The line might be interpreted to mean either "The more who go, the less they achieve" or "The more who go, the fewer are those who succeed."

2221–24   James Bentley observes that "from the time of St. Augustine until just before the reformation a relic remained a powerful sanction when any person was required to take an oath. Fear of the consequences of offending the saint in Heaven after swearing on his earthly remains could keep the most powerful from breaking their vows." And he notes that "the first reference to taking an oath in the presence of a relic is to be found in the writings of St. Augustine. Augustine recounts that the people of Milan brought home to a thief the evil fruits of his larceny by making him swear before a saint not to steal again. Presumably the Bishop of Milan (later St. Ambrose) supported this, but we cannot be certain. The first theologian actually to declare in writing his approval of the practice was Augustine himself. A couple more centuries elapsed before the Popes began to approve" (*Restless Bones: The Story of Relics*, [London: Constable, 1985], pp. 79–80).

2232–33   Gawain encourages the knights to swear (*Yhour oth to swer*) to keep the same oath that he will swear to (*Myne oith to kep*).

2301   *Logris* or Logres is sometimes used to refer to Arthur's kingdom, as, e.g., in *Sir Gawain and the Green Knight*, line 691 ("ryalme of Logres") and in Malory (I, 444 of Vinaver's edition) ("realme of Logrys"). Here, however, it clearly refers to the capital city of Arthur's realm. Geoffrey of Monmouth, in *The Historia Regum Britanniæ*, ed. Acton Griscom (London: Longmans Green, 1929), p. 253, traces the name to Locrine, one of the sons of Brutus, the legendary founder of Britain: "Locrinus qui primogenitus fuerat possedit partem insule quæ postea de nomine suo appellata est loegria" (Locrine, who was the first-born, possessed the part of the island which afterwards from his name is called Logris").

2312   Skeat and Gray emend *conne* to "come." This is the easier reading to explain: the lady says she does not come to court for no reason (i.e., she comes for a reason, which she gives in the next line). The manuscript reading is, however, possible. She says "I know [that I come] not for nothing," by which she might mean that she knows that her quest will meet with success at Arthur's court.

2356   Gray glosses *wy* as "person," taking it as a variant of "wye"; Skeat glosses as "reason," taking it as a variant of "why." Gray's interpretation seems preferable in the context of knightly reputation.

2374	Skeat and Gray both suggest that the first "say" in the line might be a scribal error and that the proper reading might be "bee."

2386   To boast of one's lady is blameworthy because the code of courtly love, in which the lovers were not married, demanded secrecy. In the Middle English poem *Sir Launfal*, Launfal's fairy lover makes this clear: "But o thing, Syr Knyght, I warne the, / That thou make no bost of me / For no kennes mede" (lines 361–63); the breaking of the injunction is temporarily disastrous for Launfal.

2395   A space is left at the beginning of this line for an illuminated letter. Skeat supplies *I*, Gray *A*, which seems to make better sense.

2436   *Ellisquhat* means "otherwise." That Lancelot is "ellisquhat . . . afyre" means that he is burning with love for someone else.

2471   Skeat notes that "The line is too long, and the sense imperfect; but there is no doubt about the reading of the MS." He suggests emending "pasag" to "pasith."

2473   The *altitud* is "the elevation or angular height of a celestial body above the horizon" (MED).

2474   Saturn was traditionally associated with cold and stormy weather, as in Chaucer's Knight's Tale, I, 2443–76. In the *Tetrabiblos* (ed. and trans. F. E. Robbins [Cambridge: Harvard University Press, 1940]), Ptolemy observes that "because two of the four humours are fertile and active, the hot and the moist (for all things are brought together and increased by them), and two are destructive and passive, the dry and the cold, through which all things, again, are separated and destroyed, the ancients accepted two of the planets, Jupiter and Venus, together with the moon, as beneficent because of their tempered nature and because they abound in the hot and the moist, and Saturn and Mars as producing effects of the opposite nature, one [Saturn] because of his excessive cold and the other for his excessive dryness; the sun and Mercury, however, they thought to have both powers, because they have a common nature, and to join their influences with those of the other planets, with whichever of them they are associated" (p. 39).

2475   Skeat suggests that the manuscript reading *valis* should be "falis." However, one of the meanings of the verb "vailen" or "valen" is "to fall."

2483 Gray glosses *Scilla* as "a bird, a lark." The term comes from Scylla, daughter of Nisus of Megara. Her story is told by Ovid in the *Metamorphoses*, Book 8. For love of Minos of Crete, she cut off a lock of purple hair from her father's head. Nisus's life and the fate of his city depended on that lock of hair. When Minos, appalled by her betrayal of father and country, rejected her and sailed off, Scylla leapt into the sea and clung to his ship. Her father, who had been turned into an osprey, attacked her, whereupon she was turned into a bird called "ciris." The exact translation of "ciris" is uncertain; Lewis and Short, in their *Latin Dictionary*, define it merely as "a bird . . . into which Scylla, the daughter of Nisus, was changed."

2486–87 These lines echo a similar astrological dating in the opening of Chaucer's *Canterbury Tales*: "the yonge sonne / Hath in the Ram his half cours yronne" (lines 7–8). In Chaucer's lines the sun is halfway through or in the latter half of Aries. Since the sun is in Aries from March 12 to April 11, Chaucer opens his poem near the beginning of April. In *Lancelot of the Laik*, the sun (Phebus) is said to be beginning its course in Aries. The time would thus be near March 12. However, the precise date seems less important than the indication that the year has passed and spring — and the time for battle — has arrived.

2527 See the note to line 1546.

2574 I follow Skeat in emending the manuscript reading "Wihill" to "Whill."

2575 The *he* in this line does not appear in the manuscript. Skeat, Gray, and Stevenson are surely correct in supplying it.

2589 I follow Skeat in emending "borne" to "lorne."

2591 Galiot's knight *Sir Esquyris* is a minor figure who appears only in this scene in the extant text. Perhaps the most significant thing about him is that despite his poverty he fought well. Since he later becomes one of Arthur's knights, as lines 2596–97 make clear, he is a perfect example of why Arthur should follow the advice of Amytans (in lines 1696–98) that he show his favor not only to the rich but to the poor worthy man as well.

2605 Arthur's knight *Galys Gwynans* appears in no other Middle English text.

2606 *Ywane the Bastart* or Ywain the Bastard, a different character from Sir Ywain, is the illegitimate son of Urien begotten on his steward's wife. He appears again in lines 3085–86. It may also be that this is the Ywain referred to as "Ywons the King" in line 2861 and as "Ywons King" in line 3261.

2618 *Ywane the Anterus* is identified by Ackerman in *An Index of the Arthurian Names in Middle English* (Stanford: Stanford University Press, 1952) as Ywain, the legitimate son of Urien rather than Ywain the Bastard, perhaps because the latter appears just twelve lines above as "Ywane the Bastart." However, as Ackerman notes, Ywain the Bastard is often called Ywain les Avoutres because "Avoutres represents the Latin *adulter*." In Malory, the name also appears as Auenturous. Apparently there is some confusion between "Avoutres" and "Auenturous." Thus "Ywane the Anterus" might well be "Ywane les Avoutres" or Ywain the Bastard.

2630–35 Skeat explains the arithmetical discrepancy in these lines by saying "It would appear that Galiot had 40,000, of whom 10,000 were held *in reserve*; so that in line 2632 only 30,000 are mentioned."

2636 *Forswornn* is the past participle of "forsweren," which usually means "to break an oath" or "to leave (a country) under oath not to return, go into banishment" (MED). Such meanings are clearly not applicable here. The sense suggests that the word must mean something like "cleared" the field. Perhaps this is a reasonable extension of the notion of banishment or exile sometimes implied by the word.

2663 *Led* is the past participle of the verb "leien," used here in the sense of "struck down" or "humbled."

2687 *Ywan* is, as is mentioned in the text (lines 2865–67), son of Urien. In Malory, his mother is Morgan le Fay. He is the hero of Chrétien's *Yvain* and one of the heroes of the Middle English *Ywain and Gawain*. "Sir Ywan" also appears in line 2707.

2693–94 Skeat suggests emending the manuscript reading "erde" to "felde." This emendation would preserve the rhyme scheme. However, there appear to be two or more lines missing from the text, probably inadvertently omitted by the scribe, since the second line does not seem to follow naturally from the first.

2712   I follow Skeat and Gray in inserting "to" between "fore" and "depart."

2744   I follow Skeat in emending the manuscript reading "in in" to "into."

2762   The *des* (dais) is a raised platform where those of the highest rank would sit. This arrangement is very different from the equality among knights suggested by the Round Table.

2796   The word *withall*, which literally means something like "moreover," or "at the same time," or "likewise," is often difficult to translate directly into a modern equivalent. Sometimes, as here, it seems merely to have a kind of intensive force.

2820   The *t* in "knychtly" does not appear in the manuscript.

2833   The second *l* in "Melyhalt" does not appear in the manuscript.

2851   *Ydrus* (or *Ydras* in line 3152) is probably the Idrus whom Malory identifies as son of Ywain and as one of the knights who fought with Arthur against Emperor Lucius.

2853   *Harvy the Reveyll* appears in Malory, as "Heruys de Reuel," a knight who does "merveylous dedys of armes" in Arthur's battle against Nero, brother of King Royns, and is recommended by King Pellinore as one of the older knights to be made a Knight of the Round Table to fill the seats of those killed in battle.

2858   *Angus*, King of Scotland, appears as Auguselus in Geoffrey of Monmouth and is identified in Layamon's *Brut* as brother to Lot and Urien. Originally opposed to Arthur, Angus becomes his ally.

2861   On *Ywons the King* see note to line 2606.

2865   I follow Skeat in emending the manuscript reading "first" to "fift," which is obviously the correct reading. The same error occurs in line 2883, where I again follow Skeat in emending to "fift."

2865–67 On *Ywan* or Ywain, son of Urien, see the note to line 2687.

2873   On *Malenginys*, see the note to line 806.

2879   *Walydeyne*, the leader of one of Galiot's forces, appears again in line 3249 ("Walydone," which I have normalized from the manuscript reading "Valydone").

2881   *King Clamedeus*, one of Galiot's knights, is "Lord of Far Ylys." The Far Isles, sometimes called the "Oute Isles," may refer to the Scilly Isles or the Hebrides. Ackerman, in *An Index of the Arthurian Names in Middle English* (Stanford: Stanford University Press, 1952), notes that the name "was used by early historians to designate many islands such as Orkney, Wight, etc." (p. 184).

2883   See note to line 2865.

2884   *Brandymagus* is Malory's Bagdemagus, King of Gore. In Malory, he is the father of the wicked knight Meleagant, who kidnaps Guinevere. On the name, see the section on "Baudemaguz" in Roger Sherman Loomis's *Arthurian Tradition and Chrétien de Troyes* (New York: Columbia University Press, 1949), pp. 240–250.

2890   The *Dictionary of the Older Scottish Tongue*, citing this line, defines a *prekyne hat* as "a (presum. lightweight) head-piece for riding, perh. of the sallet or basinet variety." The term is derived from a Middle English word ("priken" or "preken") meaning "to ride"; see line 3089 below for an example of the verb in this romance.

2895   In this line *couth* is used much the way "can" or "gan" is frequently used, as an auxiliary verb indicating the past tense (and here perhaps adding emphasis). Thus "he couth abyde" might be translated "he *did* remain."

2984   The word "not" does not appear in the manuscript; but, as Skeat suggests, it "seems required." Gray also adds "not" to the line.

3020   *Into contynent* is the equivalent of "incontynent," which means "immediately."

3041   The second *sche* in this line does not appear in the manuscript. Skeat is surely correct in supplying it. Gray suggests not supplying the second "sche," but changing "Whar that" in the next line to "Wha that"; this seems a less satisfactory emendation.

3071   A *rest* is "a projection attached to the right side of the breastplate to receive the butt end of the lance when couched for the charge" (MED).

3074   Skeat and Gray emend *held* to "help." However, the emendation does not seem necessary. Though "held(e)," meaning "favor" or "grace," is usually used in a religious context, the extension of the meaning to "aid" or "assistance" seems natural enough.

3083   *Syr Sygramors* (Malory's Sagramore le Desyrus) is called "the Desyrand" in the sense of desirous of or eager for battle, that is, bold.

3084   *Gresown* is a name otherwise unknown in Middle English Arthurian romance. Robert W. Ackermann, in *An Index of the Arthurian Names in Middle English* (Stanford: Stanford University Press, 1952), suggests that the name might be "a corrupt form of Gryflet." Though Ackermann offers no explanation for the conjecture, it must be based on the fact that in the corresponding passage in the Vulgate *Lancelot* "Gifles" (Middle English Gryflet) appears with Kay, Sagramore, and Ywain (see Sommer, III, p. 239).

3087   *Gaherss* is Malory's Gaheris, son of Lot and Morgawse and brother to Gawain, Agravain, and Gareth.

3150   The sense seems to be: "And many a fine point in the art of combat they performed."

3151   On *Malangins* or *Malengynis* (in line 3155), see note to line 806.

3184   Skeat glosses *ward* as "world" and observes that "the omission of the *l* is common." Gray glosses the word as "a division of an army, an army."

3204   Skeat gives the manuscript reading of "qsquyaris." I follow Gray in omitting the initial *q*.

3240   Skeat glosses *sarues* as "service." However, it seems more likely that it is a plural form of "sorwe," here meaning "injuries." The suggestion is that Sir Gawain laughs at the sufferings of his enemy at the hand of the older knight.

3249   On *Walydone*, see the note to line 2879.

3259   On *King Clamedyus* see the note to line 2881.

3261   On *Ywons King* see the note to line 2606.

3318   I follow Skeat in emending the manuscript reading "Whilk" to "Whill."

3345   Skeat adds the word "in" after the manuscript reading "foundyne," though, as he notes, the word is required by the sense and not the meter. Thus Gray is probably right when she suggests that the correct reading is "found in" (or perhaps it should be "found yne") rather than "foundyne."

3373   I follow Skeat and Gray in adding *his* to this line.

3386   The reference here is to the practice of bear-baiting, "the sport of setting dogs to attack a bear ['bere'] chained to a stake ['stok']" (OED).

3435–36 On *trumpetis* and *claryownis* see the note to line 771. *Hornys* were "wind instruments which have as a distinguishing feature a tube gradually tapering outward from the mouthpiece to the opening rather than terminating in the flared bell of instruments of the trumpet class." *Bugillis* or "bugles" were wind instruments "of straight or semi-circular design, consisting of a hollow tube, usually of horn, which tapered gradually from the bell to the mouthpiece" and which were "used for sounding military or heraldic signals, alarms, announcements or assemblies" (quotations are from Henry Holland Carter, *A Dictionary of Middle English Musical Terms* [Bloomington: Indiana University Press, 1961]).

3452   The *Dictionary of Middle English Musical Terms*, citing this line, defines *wind*: "In reference to the playing of a wind instrument: the breath, or breath control." However, the "wyndis bost" or "boast of wind" surely refers not only to the musical calls to battle but also to what Lancelot sees as the insubstantiality of the enemy's martial claims.

3487   The last partial line survives as a catch phrase at the bottom of folio 42v of the manuscript.

Sir Tristrem

Introduction

The story of Tristan and Isolt, one of the most popular tales of the Middle Ages, has its roots in early Celtic literature and legend. The name Tristan (Drystan or Trystan, as it appears in the Celtic sources) is apparently Pictish in origin but was "borrowed fairly early by the Welsh and perhaps by the Irish" (see the note on the name in *Trioedd Ynys Prydein: The Welsh Triads*, ed. Rachel Bromwich [2nd ed.; Cardiff: University of Wales Press, 1978], p. 329). There is also early evidence of localization of the Tristan story in Cornwall, where the Tristan Stone was found near Castle Dore in Cornwall, a place associated with King Mark. The stone contains "the earliest inscribed evidence for the name" though "whether or not the man so named can really have been the prototype of the romance hero is an open question" (Rachel Bromwich, "The *Tristan* of the Welsh," in *The Arthur of the Welsh: The Arthurian Legend in Medieval Welsh Literature*, ed. Rachel Bromwich, A. O. H. Jarman, and Brynley F. Roberts [Cardiff: University of Wales Press, 1991], p. 221). Nevertheless, it seems that "the Continental poets, and Béroul in particular, evidently derived their principal knowledge of the Tristan story from a Cornish source" (Bromwich, "The *Tristan* of the Welsh," p. 220).

Later literary versions of the legend have traditionally been divided by scholars into two branches, each deriving ultimately from an earlier "*Ur-Tristan*," an original or parent version of the story. The two branches have been referred to as the common and the courtly because of the manner in which they treat the story. The former tradition is represented by Eilhart von Oberge's *Tristrant* and Béroul's *Roman de Tristran*, both written in the latter half of the twelfth century. The earliest example of the courtly tradition is found in the *Tristan* of the Anglo-Norman poet Thomas, which survives only in fragments estimated to comprise about one-sixth of the poem. The plot of Thomas's poem can be reconstructed, however, because of the works which were based on it. It was translated by a Brother Robert into the Old Norse *Tristrams saga ok Isöndar* for King Hákon Hákonarson of Norway in 1226; and some years earlier (c. 1210) it was reworked into the masterpiece of medieval Tristan stories, Gottfried von Strassburg's *Tristan*. The Middle English *Sir Tristrem*, written late in the thirteenth century, has also traditionally been considered a poor adaptation of Thomas's poem (though, on this question, see below in this introduction).

143

There also exist a number of medieval prose versions of the Tristan legend. In these, as in Malory's treatment of the story, Tristan is presented as one of the greatest knights of Arthur's court. In the verse romances, however, there is little (in Béroul) or no (in Thomas) mention of Arthur. Because of Malory and his influence on Tennyson, this prose tradition has been an extremely important influence on modern Tristan stories in England and America, where it is common to link Tristan to Camelot. However, the tradition represented by Thomas has also been influential in the English-speaking world. Algernon Charles Swinburne, seeking to avoid the moralizing of Tennyson, looked to the Middle English *Sir Tristrem*, along with other medieval versions of the story, as a source for his *Tristram of Lyonesse*. In addition, the great French medievalist Joseph Bédier reconstructed Thomas's poem (using its Old Norse, German and Middle English descendants) in a modern French version. This was translated into English in 1903 by Hilaire Belloc. This version of the legend became widely known and influenced the resurgence of interest in the Tristan story that occurred in the early twentieth century in England and America.

The Middle English poem *Sir Tristrem* survives only in the great anthology of Middle English literature known as the Auchinleck Manuscript. The manuscript received its name from Alexander Boswell of Auchinleck (the father of James Boswell, Samuel Johnson's biographer), who "rescued it in 1740 from a professor of Aberdeen University who had been tearing out leaves to make covers for notebooks" (Arthur Johnston, *Enchanted Ground: The Study of Medieval Romance in the Eighteenth Century* [London: The Athlone Press, 1964], p. 179). Boswell gave the manuscript to the Advocates' Library in Edinburgh. It remained there until 1925 when it was given to the newly established National Library of Scotland, where it is currently located and designated Advocates' MS 19.2.1.

Originally this vellum manuscript, compiled about 1330–1340, contained "considerably more than 386 leaves, of which there survive 331 leaves and 14 stubs in the main part" as well as ten other leaves identified as having belonged to the manuscript but now in three different libraries (Edinburgh University Library, University of London Library, and St. Andrews University Library) (*The Auchinleck Manuscript: National Library of Scotland Advocates' MS. 19.2.1*, introduction by Derek Pearsall and I. C. Cunningham, p. xi). The significance of the Auchinleck manuscript is not only in the sheer number of religious poems and romances that it contains but also in the fact that many of the works collected in it are unique. In his introduction to the facsimile edition, Derek Pearsall notes that of the eighteen romances, which account for three quarters of the manuscript, "eight are in unique copies, and all the remainder, except *Floris* . . ., are here in their earliest copies" (p. viii). One of the romances which appears only in the Auchinleck manuscript is *Sir Tristrem*.

Introduction

Walter Scott, the poem's first editor, believed that *Sir Tristrem* was written by Thomas of Erceldoune and therefore assumed it was in a Scottish dialect. When George P. McNeill edited the poem, he did so for the Scottish Text Society and defended its Scottish origin. While Angus McIntosh's 1989 article "Is *Sir Tristrem* an English or a Scottish Poem?" argues effectively that the forms some earlier scholars had cited as evidence of Scottish origin support no such conclusion, the poem's dialect still needs further study. McIntosh believes that the poem is in a northern, not a Scottish, dialect. To be sure there are northern forms. For example, there are words which retain the OE long *a*, such as "stan" (lines 115, 270, etc.) The forms "ta" and "tan" appear for "take" and "taken" (lines 607, 2767; 111, 753, 895, etc.). However, in his investigation, McIntosh was virtually assuming a northern (either northern English or Scottish) origin of the poem.

Yet, as Bertram Vogel pointed out in his article on the dialect of *Sir Tristrem* in 1940, there are actually far more non-northern forms in the poem than there are northern. On page 542 of his article, Vogel summarizes these forms. His evidence includes, for example, the fact that Old English *hw* is always *wh*, never Nth. *qu(h)* [see, for example, "who," line 4; "when," line 101; and "while," line 209]; the fact that "the pronoun for the third person feminine singular is either *sche* [see lines 79, 99, etc.] or *hye* [see lines 101, 103, etc]. Nth. *scho* is not used"; the fact that "for the genitive and the objective cases of the pronoun for the third person plural, non-Nth. *h*-forms are regularly used" [see lines 15, 112, etc. [for genitive case] and lines 41, 144, etc. for objective case]; the fact that "non-Nth. *miche, michel* are used in 15 instances; Nth *mikel* is not found;" etc.

McIntosh, who does not cite Vogel, assumes that these forms are scribal, as do some earlier scholars; but this remains an assumption. The preponderance of non-Northern forms must be given due weight in a discussion of the dialect of the poem; and Vogel is certainly correct in asserting that we should not assume *Sir Tristrem* is northern. Rhyme words, often prized as linguistic evidence since they are more likely to be authorial, appear in both southeastern and northern forms. Perhaps it is impossible to decide absolutely; but the question of the poem's dialect is worth further consideration. It may even be that additional literary-critical study of *Sir Tristrem* will shed some light on the question.

Though Scott's edition of *Sir Tristrem* was popular and Swinburne looked to the medieval poem as inspiration for his *Tristram of Lyonesse*, twentieth-century critical judgment has generally been less than favorable. This is due in large part to the pronouncements of Joseph Bédier in his edition of the Anglo-Norman poet Thomas's *Roman de Tristan*. Bédier reacted with considerable pique to the fact that the English poem was of little use in reconstructing Thomas's fragmentary French text: "Par son extrême brièveté, par les contraintes de versification qu'il s'est imposées, par son style tourmenté, il s'est interdit de jamais traduire son modèle, et nous ne lui devrons jamais de retrouver une phrase authentique de Thomas" (2, 88).

The influence of Bédier can be seen even in the account of the poem given by Helaine Newstead in the first volume of *A Manual of the Writings in Middle English 1050–1500* (New Haven: The Connecticut Academy of Arts and Sciences, 1967). Newstead speaks of "the drastic condensation of the story and the elimination of the debates and soliloquies characteristic of the original" which result in "a much coarsened version of its subtle and moving original, significant chiefly because it preserves, however inadequately, the lost episodes of its source" (p. 79).

Although T. C. Rumble argued in 1959 that the changes made by the English poet were designed to make the story "more consistent with . . . the tastes of the English audience for which his version was intended" and Cedric Pickford in 1973 claimed that the poem is "an interesting social document" and also "a fresh retelling of a great story, presented simply and directly" (p. 228), recent opinion seems unchanged by their studies. Susan Crane argues that "an audience capable of enjoying the length and thematic complexity of *Beues of Hamtoun*, *Guy of Warwick*, and *Amis and Amiloun* cannot be invoked to explain the extraordinary reductions and simplifications of *Sir Tristrem*" (pp. 192–93). Crane concludes that in the English poem "the Tristan story has lost the significance developed for it by Thomas, and it has not gained a new one" (p. 195).

The criticisms of the poem and even the defenses in terms of a less sophisticated audience and a simple and direct retelling all point to certain undeniable characteristics of the poem. There is an abbreviation of the episodes found in the Thomas version, the "extrême brièveté" that Bédier disapproved of, and there is a less than courtly cast to much of the material. That this version, different from the standard Tristan story, may be objected to is something that the author himself recognized:

> Tho Tomas asked ay
> Of Tristrem, trewe fere [true companion],
> To wite [know] the right way
> The styes [ins and outs of his story] for to lere [learn].
> Of a prince proude in play [battle]
> Listneth, lordinges dere [noble lords].
> Whoso better can say,
> His owhen he may here
> As hende [politely, courtly].
> Of thing that is him dere
> Ich man preise at ende. (lines 397–407)

It may even be that the author concedes that his version is not as courtly as the original when he says others may tell their versions "As hende." McNeill suggests that this means the others should wait and thus tell their stories politely in their turn. But it may mean that others can tell of Tristan in a more polite (i.e., courtly) manner.

However one reads this phrase, there is ample evidence in the poem to suggest that *Sir Tristrem* is not merely a poorly constructed abridgement of Thomas's courtly version or a coarsened version for a less sophisticated English audience but rather a deliberate parody of the received version.[1]

When one looks at *Sir Tristrem* as a parody rather than as a poem poorly imitating the masterly psychological and courtly performance of Thomas, some scenes become wonderfully comic. For example, when Tristrem and Ysonde drink the love potion, the tragically romantic moment is comically undercut by having the ill-trained hound Hodain lap the cup:

> An hounde ther was biside
> That was ycleped [called] Hodain;
> The coupe he licked that tide
> Tho [When] doun it sett Bringwain. (1673–76)

Rumble sees this scene as "an obvious attempt to give some rational explanation for the unusual faithfulness of Tristrem's dog" (p. 225). Such an explanation, however, hardly seems necessary; and the scene is more farcical than expository — especially in the light of the poet's comment a few lines later. After describing Tristrem's delight in being able to spend his time making love with Ysonde night and day (lines 1684–90), the author notes that "Thai loved with al her [their] might / And Hodain dede also" (lines 1693–94). This scene is particularly telling, first of all in the use of the word "play" twice [lines 1686 and 1690] to describe the cause of Tristrem's delight. No courtly euphemism is used to elevate the action. The word, used frequent-

---

[1]It should be noted that a similar process of parody has been suggested, although not universally accepted, as being found in the Old Icelandic version of the Old Norse *Tristrams saga*. Early critical opinion considered the Icelandic version a "boorish account of Tristram's noble passion [which] has very properly been called a rustic version in distinction from Robert's court translation" (Henry Goddard Leach, *Angevin Britain and Scandinavia* [1921; rpt. New York: Kraus Reprint, 1975], p. 186). This opinion, which parallels that of early critics of *Sir Tristrem*, was challenged by Paul Schach who saw the Icelandic redaction as "a 'deliberate reply' to the Norwegian version" ("The *Saga af Tristram ok Isodd*: Summary or Satire," *Modern Language Quarterly* 21 [1960], 352). A later article, however, questions Schach's conclusion that the Icelandic work contains deliberate parody (see M. F. Thomas, "The Briar and the Vine: Tristan Goes North," *Arthurian Literature* 3 [1983], 53–90).

ly in the text to describe the lovers' activity, almost takes on the connotation of the modern phrase "to fool around." But even more important is the blatant absurdity of including Hodain in the sentence about the ardor of their love.

This very uncourtly love-play seems to be the dominant and determining activity of the lovers. After Tristrem slays the giant Urgan and is reconciled with Mark, they return to their love-play: "Thai playden al bituene, / Tho tuo" (lines 2439–40). When Mark is again incensed by their actions, he banishes them to the forest as his revenge upon them: "Ful wele awreken to ben" (2446). The poet emphasizes the absurdity of the punishment by telling his audience that they were never happier: "Blither, withouten wene, / Never ere nar thay" (lines 2452–53); and this idea is repeated in lines 2463–64. Their joy comes from the fact that "For love ich other bihalt, / Her non might of other fille" (2496–97). When Mark and his knights find the lovers sleeping with a sword between them, they decide that "Thai no hede nought of swiche play" because "trewe love it is" (lines 2549 and 2552). As soon as Tristrem and Ysonde are back at court, however, they "Stalked to her [their] play" (2578). While this scene follows the outline of the action in the analogous *Tristrams saga* (translated from the Norse by Paul Schach as *The Saga of Tristram and Isönd* and used here for comparison since Thomas's version is so fragmentary), it is precisely those qualities objected to by some earlier critics, the compression of the action and the uncourtly nature of the references to the love-play, that give it its value as parody. There is a wide stylistic gulf between the English poem's account of the resumption of love-play:

> So bifel bidene
> Opon a somers day
> Tristrem and the Quen
> Stalked to her play (lines 2575–78)

and the account found in the saga:

> Tristram could by no means restrain his will and desire and
> therefore he made use of every opportunity he could find.
> It happened one day that he and Isönd were sitting together
> in an orchard, and Tristram held the queen in his arms. (p.
> 104)

The very fact that there is no contrast similar to that between "trewe love" and the "play" to which the lovers must "stalk" but only Tristram's unrestrainable will and desire ("fysn ok vilja" [p. 81 of Kölbing's edition of the saga]) makes the saga passage thematically quite different.

Introduction

Even Tristrem's heroic deeds are subordinated to his desire for physical contact with Ysonde. Just before Tristrem goes to Wales and kills the giant Urgan, the author explains:

> For [Because] he ne may Ysonde kisse,
> Fight he sought aywhare [everywhere]. (lines 2298–99)

Thus his battle becomes a kind of sublimation of his desire.

Parody can be seen in other aspects of the poem as well. When Tristrem brings Ganhardin to the territory of the giant Beliagog in order to see the statues in the hall of images, Beliagog, whose leg Tristrem has cut off earlier, enters "on a stilt [peg leg]" (line 2956). The scene has a comic effect lacking in the Norse version, where Tristram makes a wooden leg for the giant immediately after the combat so the giant can follow and serve him (p. 116) but is not mentioned in the chapter that parallels the Middle English lines under discussion. Later, when Ganhardin sees the image of the fierce giant Beliagog in the hall of images, he bangs his head on the wall of the cave as he turns to flee from the statue. Then, the author comments,

> Ganhardin schamed sore [was very ashamed];
> His heved ran on blod [was covered with blood]. (lines 2982–83)

Again, in the Norse text, there is a parallel scene. Kardin (Ganhardin's name in the saga) sees the giant and "was so frightened that he almost lost his wits . . . . And because of this fear and the fragrance [described earlier in the same chapter as "the sweet fragrance of balsam and of all the sweetest herbs there"] that filled the room, he was affected so strangely that he fell into a swoon" (128).

The unheroic bleeding head is paralleled by an earlier episode. In the crucial encounter with Morgan, who has usurped Tristrem's patrimony, Morgan insults Tristrem's parents:

> Thi fader thi moder gan hide [cohabit with secretly]; (lines 861–62)
> In horedom [fornication] he hir band [had intercourse with].

Tristrem's initial response is to slap him and give him a nosebleed

> On his brest adoun
> Of [from] his nose ran the blod. (lines 870–71)

Though he goes on to slay Morgan, the initial response seems comically inappropriate. One might compare the action here with the encounter between Sir Gawain and

Sir Tristrem

Sir Gayous in the *Alliterative Morte Arthure* (lines 1346–54 in Larry Benson-Edward Foster edition in *King Arthur's Death* [Kalamazoo: Western Michigan University Press, 1994]). Gayous says that the Britons are "braggers of old" and calls Gawain a "boy" (knave). In response:

> Then greved Sir Gawain at his grete wordes
> Graithes toward the gome with grouchand herte;
> With his steele brande he strikes off his heved . . . . (lines 1352–54)

The flyting or exchange of insults is a convention that has its origin in early Germanic heroic poetry, but it does not usually take the "your mother was a whore" form that it has in *Sir Tristrem*; and the slap in the face and resulting nosebleed seem deliberately inappropriate to a society so conscious of honor that insults demand an immediate response like Gawain's beheading of Gayous.

Even the fight with the dragon loses some of the heroic quality it has in the saga where the confrontation is presented as a fierce and fearless attack by Tristram:

> He struck his horse with his spurs and thrust his lance
> forward with such fearful force and fury into the dragon's
> mouth that all of its teeth that the spear struck flew far out
> of its head. The iron lance head ran right through the heart
> and came out through the belly, so that Tristram buried
> part of the shaft in his neck and body. But the fire that the
> dragon flung out killed and dispatched his horse. Tristram
> nimbly sprang from its back, drew his sword, made at the
> dragon and cut it asunder at the middle. (p. 56)

By contrast, in the English poem Tristrem charges with his lance "As a lothely lioun," and strikes with a "spere feloun" [deadly spear] (lines 1444 and 1446), but the heroic imagery is undercut when the blow "no vailed o botoun" [availed not a bit, literally, not a button] (line 1448). The commonplace, almost colloquial, expression seems intentionally at odds with the lofty claims of the preceding lines. When the dragon slays Tristrem's horse, the hero does attack and slay the monster with his sword — but only after rushing behind a tree and saying a prayer that he will not be killed (lines 1459–63). Then when he strikes the dragon, he first cuts off its lower jaw so that fire rushes out and shamefully disfigures Tristrem's shining armor (lines 1473–74). The poet presents the threat as one to Tristrem's noble appearance rather than as one to life and limb.

Tristrem's courtly knowledge and skill, as well his accomplishments as a lover and a hero, are also parodied in the Middle English poem. In a couple of places, his accomplishments seem obnoxious smugness. In her book on *Hunting in Middle English Literature* (Woodbridge, Suffolk: The Boydell Press, 1993), Anne Rooney notes that in contrast to the Tristan stories by Gottfried and Brother Robert, the author of *Sir Tristrem* "pays no attention to the hunters' interest in the terminology of the hunt. Instead, he concentrates on Tristrem's dismay at their treatment of the carcasses, their willingness to learn the new techniques and their delight in the lesson" (p. 92). In fact, Tristrem's dismay is less than courteous: he tells the hunters that they slaughter animals foolishly ("folily ye hem spille," line 462). Similarly when he heard a harper composing a lay at Mark's court he berated ("aresound," line 552) the fellow minstrel and boasted of his ability to construct a better one (lines 555–56).

Another of Tristrem's courtly achievements, his skill at chess, is presented in a distinctly parodic manner in the English poem. In the saga, after a deal is concluded for the purchase of hawks, Tristram plays chess with one of the merchants "for a high wager" (p. 21). The merchants, impressed with his skill and his accomplishments, believe that "if they were able to abduct him, they would stand to gain greatly from his abilities and great knowledge; and also, if they wished to sell him, that they would receive much money for him" (p. 22). So they sail off while he is engrossed in his game.

In *Sir Tristrem*, the contest is presented very differently. For one thing, the details of the wager are spelled out. Tristrem bets twenty shillings against a hawk. Then the poet comments that:

> He dede als so the wise:
> He gaf has he gan winne
> In raf [winnings]. (lines 326–28)

These lines seem to suggest that Tristrem plays cleverly by letting his opponent win sometimes. If this interpretation is correct, Tristrem becomes a chess hustler. The outcome seems to support this reading: "Tristrem wan that day / Of him an hundred pounde" (lines 340–41). When they sail off with him, the act is called a "tresoun" — and that immediately after a line saying that "Tristrem wan that [what] ther was layd [wagered]," as if the two actions were linked (lines 342–43).

The practical, almost mercenary, interest in specific amounts of money and the emphasis on the winnings rather than on the skill of Tristrem undercuts the romantic story. Similarly mercenary is the scene in which Tristrem, put ashore by the mariners, encounters two pilgrims. In the saga Tristrem uses his wits ("he answered them craftily," p. 25) and suggests he has friends nearby but has become separated from them while hunting; then, upon learning that the pilgrims are heading for "Tintajol," he claims to have business there and accompanies them, gleaning news of the region

151

as they travel. In the Middle English poem, however, it is not Tristrem's wits but his offer of ten shillings to each of the pilgrims that gets him to Tintagel. Later when Rohand enters the realm he encounters the same two pilgrims and also offers them each ten shillings to bring him to court. An incident which does not appear in the saga, this is clearly designed to parody the romance world where events happen by chance or providence rather than, as in the real world, because of practical transactions.

In the saga, Róaldur (as Rohand is called there) does give Mark's porter an unspecified "gift" (p. 31) to gain access to the court. The English poet not only makes the gift a "ring" but also has Rohand offer a bribe at yet another level, to the "huscher" (the "usher" or door-keeper) to gain access to the king's hall. When Rohand sees his ward after the third bribe, Tristrem, contrary to the text of the saga in which Tristram immediately recognizes Róaldur, fails to recognize him because of his clothes, made ragged as he searched through seven kingdoms for his ward. In this scene, the author presents Tristrem as a little too spoiled and pompous. He says of his hero:

> He no trowed it never in lede [would never have believed it]
> That Rohand robes were torn,
> That he wered swiche a wede [wore such clothing]. (lines 651–53)

In his edition of Thomas's fragments, Bédier, echoing Kölbing, observes that the author "raconte à l'ordinaire comme si ses auditeurs savaient déjà dans le moindre détail ce qu'il raconte" (I, 87). I believe this to be true. The author of *Sir Tristrem* does seem to expect his audience to know the story as well as some of the conventions of romance. It is precisely this knowledge that makes effective the parody of romance conventions which runs throughout the poem.

As a parody, *Sir Tristrem* must be considered alongside works with similar intent, such as Guillaume le Clerc's *Romance of Fergus* and Chaucer's Tale of Sir Thopas, rather than as a poor imitation of Thomas's poem. In this light, it becomes a poem of much more interest and merit than it has previously been given credit for.

Selected Bibliography

Manuscript

The Auchinleck MS (Advocates 19.2.1), fols. 281a–299b, in the National Library of Scotland, c. 1330.

Introduction

The MS is reproduced in facsimile: *The Auchinleck Manuscript: National Library of Scotland Advocates' MS. 19.2.1.* Introduction by Derek Pearsall and I. C. Cunningham. London: The Scolar Press in association with The National Library of Scotland, 1979.

Previous Editions

Sir Tristrem; A Metrical Romance of the Thirteenth Century; by Thomas of Erceldoune, Called The Rhymer. Ed. Walter Scott. 3d ed.; Edinburgh: Archibald Constable and Co., 1811. (Scott's edition first appeared in 1804.)

Sir Tristrem: Mit Einleitung, Anmerkungen und Glossar. Ed. Eugen Kölbing. Heilbronn: Gebr. Henninger, 1882.

Sir Tristrem. Ed. George P. McNeill. Scottish Text Society 8. Edinburgh: William Blackwood and Sons, 1886.

Translation

Sir Tristrem. In *The Chief Middle English Poets: Selected Poems Newly Rendered and Edited, with Notes and Bibliographical References.* Ed. and trans. Jessie Weston. 1914. Rpt. New York: Phaeton Press, 1968. Pp. 141–73.

Analogues

Tristrams Saga ok Isondar: Mit Literarhistorischen Einleitung, Deutscher Uebersetzung und Anmerkungen. Ed. Eugen Kölbing. Heilbronn: Gebr. Henniger, 1878.

The Saga of Tristram and Isönd. Trans. Paul Schach. Lincoln: University of Nebraska Press, 1973.

Thomas. *Le Roman de Tristan: Poème du XIIe siècle.* 2 vols. Ed. Joseph Bédier. Société des Anciens Textes Français. Paris: Firmin Didot, 1902.

Sir Tristrem

Criticism

Crane, Susan. *Insular Romance: Politics, Faith and Culture in Anglo-Norman and Middle English Literature*. Berkeley: University of California Press, 1986. Pp. 190–96. Crane suggests that *Sir Tristrem* shares with other insular romances a "tendency to portray lovers' commitment coexisting easily with other kinds of devotion" (p. 194). Nevertheless, she believes that while Tristrem's "exemplary ability or breeding or bearing substitute for Thomas's exploration of fatal love as the significance of the Tristan story," the English version of the story "has lost the significance developed for it by Thomas, and it has not gained a new one" (p 195).

McIntosh, Angus. "Is *Sir Tristrem* an English or a Scottish Poem?" In *In Other Words: Transcultural Studies in Philology, Translation, and Lexicology Presented to Hans Heinrich Meier on the Occasion of His Sixty-Fifth Birthday*. Dordecht, Holland: Foris Publications, 1989. Pp. 85–95. McIntosh examines the linguistic and other evidence for the provenance of *Sir Tristrem* and concludes that "it is unlikely to have been further north in England than Yorkshire"(p. 92). A useful appendix to his article lists forms appearing in the poem but not recorded in any work known to be written in a Scottish dialect.

Pickford, Cedric E. "*Sir Tristrem*, Sir Walter Scott and Thomas." In *Studies in Medieval Literature and Languages in Memory of Frederick Whitehead*. Ed. W. Rothwell, W. R. J. Barron, David Blamires, and Lewis Thorpe. Manchester: Manchester University Press, 1973. Pp. 219-28. Pickford believes that *Sir Tristrem* has suffered "from the critical judgements of Continental scholars" (p. 225) like Bédier for whom "less meant worse" (p. 226) but that actually the English poem may be seen both as "an interesting social document" and also "a fresh retelling of a great story, presented simply and directly" (p. 228).

Rumble, T. C. "The Middle English *Sir Tristrem*: Towards a Reappraisal." *Comparative Literature* 11 (1959), 221–28. Rumble argues that "the cumulative force" of the changes made by the author of *Sir Tristrem* suggest that poem is not a "garbling" of its source as some critics have claimed but an attempt to make the material "more consistent with . . . the tastes of the English audience for which his version was intended." He calls on future scholarship to evaluate the poem "in terms of its own intrinsic worth" (p. 228).

Vogel, Bertram. "The Dialect of *Sir Tristrem*." *JEGP* 40 (1941), 538–44. Vogel offers significant evidence that *Sir Tristrem* is not "unequivocally Northern" and argues that there is more evidence for a southeast-Midland origin. He concludes that "it may well be that, after all, the author of *Sir Tristrem* was, in reality, a cosmopolitan Londoner who perhaps spent part of his youth in the North, but who, at any rate, was familiar not only with the Northern dialect, but also with Northern literary tradition" (pp. 543-44).

Sir Tristrem

	I was at Ertheldoun	
	With Tomas spak Y thare;	*spoke*
	Ther herd Y rede in roune	*recounted in a poem*
	Who Tristrem gat and bare,	*Who conceived and bore Tristrem*
5	Who was king with croun,	*crown*
	And who him forsterd yare,	*willingly*
	And who was bold baroun,	
	As thair elders ware.	*were*
	Bi yere	*From year to year*
10	Tomas telles in toun	*town*
	This aventours as thai ware.	*These events*

	This semly somers day,	*beautiful*
	In winter it is nought sen;	
	This greves wexen al gray,	*These thickets become*
15	That in her time were grene.	*their*
	So dos this world, Y say,	
	Ywis and nought at wene,	*Indeed and without a doubt*
	The gode ben al oway	*The good have all passed away*
	That our elders have bene.	
20	To abide,	*continue*
	Of a knight is that Y mene,	*what I speak*
	His name, it sprong wel wide.	*spread*

	Wald Rouland thole no wrong,	*Would; suffer*
	Thei Morgan lord wes;	*Though*
25	He brak his castels strong,	*[He = Rouland]*
	His bold borwes he ches,	*castles he occupied*
	His men he slough among	*slew*
	And reped him mani a res.	*dealt him many an attack*
	The wer lasted so long	*war*
30	Til Morgan asked pes	*peace*

156

	Thurch pine.	*Because of the suffering*
	For sothe withouten les,	*Truly; lying*
	His liif he wende to tine.	*His life he expected to lose*
	Thus the batayl, it bigan	
35	(Witeth wele it was so)	*Know*
	Bituene the Douk Morgan	
	And Rouland that was thro,	*valiant*
	That never thai no lan	*ceased*
	The pouer to wirche wo.	*(see note)*
40	Thai spilden mani a man	*killed*
	Bituen hemselven to	*Between the two of them*
	In prise.	*battle*
	That on was Douk Morgan,	*one*
	That other Rouland Rise.	
45	The knightes that were wise,	
	A forward fast thai bond	*firm agreement they made*
	That ich a man schul joien his	*each person; enjoy*
	And seven yer to stond;	
	The Douke and Rouland Riis	
50	Therto thai bed her hond	*offered their hands*
	To heighe and holden priis	*To improve and preserve renown*
	And foren till Inglond	*journeyed to*
	To lende.	*arrive*
	Markes king thai fond	
55	With knightes mani and hende.	*courtly*
	To Marke the King thai went	
	With knightes proude in pres	*valiant in battle*
	And teld him to thende	*the end*
	His aventours as it wes.	*circumstances*
60	He preyd hem as his frende	
	To duelle with him in pes.	*dwell; peace*
	The knightes, thai were hende	*courtly*
	And dede withouten les	*And did so truly*
	In lede.	*Among the people*
65	A turnament thai ches	*decided upon*
	With knightes stithe on stede.	*stalwart; horses*

Glad a man was he
The turnament dede crie   *was announced*
That maidens might him se
70 And over the walles to lye.   *lean*
Thai asked who was fre   *noble [enough]*
To win the maistrie;   *victory*
Thai seyd that best was he,
The child of Ermonie,   *(see note)*
75 In tour.   *tower*
Forthi chosen was he   *Therefore*
To maiden Blauncheflour.   *For*

The maiden of heighe kinne   *noble*
Sche cald hir maisters thre:
80 " . . .

   . . . .
Bot yive it be thurch ginne.   *if; through cunning*
A selly man is he;   *remarkable*
Thurch min hert withinne   *Through*
85 Ywounded hath he me
So sone: *quickly*
Of bale bot he me blinne,[1]
Mine liif days ben al done."   *The days of my life*

He was gode and hende,   *courtly*
90 Stalworth, wise and wight;   *valiant*
Into this londes ende
Y not non better knight,   *do not know*
Trewer non to frende
And Rouland Riis he hight.   *is called*
95 To batayl gan he wende,   *he went*
Was wounded in that fight
Ful felle.   *cruelly*
Blauncheflour the bright,   *beautiful*
The tale than herd sche telle.

---

[1] *Unless he cause my torment to cease*

100	Sche seyd "wayleway"	
	When hye herd it was so.	*she heard*
	To hir maistresse sche gan say	*governess*
	That hye was boun to go	*she; prepared*
	To the knight ther he lay.	*where*
105	Sche swouned and hir was wo,	*was sorrowful*
	So comfort he that may,	
	A knave child gat thai tuo	*male; those two*
	So dere;	
	And seththen men cleped him so:	*afterwards; called*
110	Tristrem the trewe fere.	*true companion*

	The trewes that thai hadde tan	*truce; agreed upon*
	And stabled in her thought	*ratified; their*
	Than brak the Douk Morgan;	
	He no wald held it nought.	*would not keep it*
115	Rohand, trewe so stan,	*free from deceit as a stone*
	A letter he ther wrought	
	And sent to Rouland onan,	*at once*
	As man of socour sought	
	In kare	*trouble*
120	To help what he mought	*might*
	Or lesen al that ther ware.	*lose everything*

	Rouland Riis in tene	*distress*
	Tok leve at Markes King . . .	*from*

[Lines 124–35 are missing in the manuscript.]

	" . . . Or thou wilt wende with me."	*go*
	"Mi duelling is hir ille;	*My remaining is bad for her*
	Bihold and tow may se.	*you*
	Mi rede is taken thertille,	*I have decided about that*
140	That fare Y wille with the	*you*
	And finde	
	Thi fair folk and thi fre	
	O lond ther is thi kinde."	*where; kindred*

	Thai busked and maked hem boun;	*prepared; themselves ready*

159

145	Nas ther no leng abade.	*There was no long delay*
	Thai lefted goinfainoun	*raised the banner (see note)*
	And out of haven thai rade	*harbor; sailed*
	Til thai com til a toun,	*Until; to*
	A castel Rohant had made.	
150	Her sailes thai leten doun,	*Their; lowered*
	And knight overbord thai strade	*strode*
	Al cladde.	*armed*
	The knightes that wer fade,	*eager for battle*
	Thai dede as Rohand bade.	
155	Rohand, right he radde:	*advised*
	"This maiden schal ben oure,	*ours*
	Rouland Riis to wedde,	
	At weld in castel tour,	*To govern*
	To bring hir to his bedde	
160	That brightest is in bour.	*fairest; chamber*
	Nas never non fairer fedde	*There was none; alive*
	Than maiden Blauncheflour	
	Al blithe."	*lovely*
	After that michel anour,	*great honor*
165	Parting com ther swithe.	*quickly*
	In hird nas nought to hele [1]	
	That Morgan telles in toun,	
	Mekeliche he gan mele,	*Humbly; talk*
	Among his men to roun;	*speak*
170	He bad his knightes lele	*loyal*
	Com to his somoun	*summons*
	With hors and wepenes fele	*deadly*
	And rered goinfaynoun,	*raised banner (see note to line 146)*
	That bold.	*valiant [knight]*
175	He rode so king with croun	*as; crown*
	To win al that he wold.	*wanted*
	Of folk the feld was brade,	*people; full*

---

[1] *Among the people it was not hidden (i.e., it was no secret; it was well known).*

Ther Morgan men gan bide; — *Where Morgan's men awaited battle*
Tho Rouland to hem rade, — *When; rode*
180 Ogain him gun thai ride; — *Against*
Swiche meting nas never made — *Such an encounter*
With sorwe on ich a side. — *grief; on each side*
Therof was Rouland glade;
Ful fast he feld her pride, — *overcame*
185 With paine.
Morgan scaped that tide — *escaped; time*
That he nas nought slain. — *So that he was not*

Morganes folk cam newe — *again*
On Rouland Riis the gode.
190 On helmes gun thai hewe,
Thurch brinies brast the blod;[1]
Sone to deth ther drewe
Mani a frely fode. — *noble young warrior*
Of Rouland was to rewe — *Roland was in a pitiable condition*
195 To grounde when he yode, — *went*
That bold. — *valiant [man]*
His sone him after stode,
And dere his deth he sold. — *dearly; exacted payment for*

Rewthe mow ye here — *Something pitiful you may hear*
200 Of Rouland Riis the knight.
Thre hundred he slough there — *slew*
With his swerd bright;
Of al tho that ther were
Might non him felle in fight, — *kill*
205 Bot on with tresoun there — *Except that someone; treachery*
Thurch the bodi him pight — *stabbed*
With gile.
To deth he him dight. — *put*
Allas that ich while! — *that very time*

210 His hors o feld him bare — *onto the ground*

---

[1] *Through coats of mail the blood spewed*

Alle ded hom in his way;
Gret wonder hadde he thought thare
That folk of ferly play.   *terrible*
The tiding com with care   *sorrow*
215 To Blauncheflour, that may.   *maiden*
For hir me reweth sare: *I am very sorry*
On childbed ther sche lay
Was born
Of hir Tristrem that day,
220 Ac hye no bade nought that morn.   *But she didn't live through*

A ring of riche hewe
Than hadde that levedi fre;   *noble lady*
Sche toke it Rouhand trewe.   *entrusted*
Hir sone sche bad it be: *[For] her son*
225 "Mi brother wele it knewe;   *intimately*
Mi fader gaf it me.   *gave*
King Markes may rewe   *grieve*
The ring than he it se   *when*
And moun.   *remember*
230 As Rouland loved the,
Thou kepe it to his sone."   *for his son*

The folk stode unfain   *sorrowful*
Bifor that levedi fre.   *noble lady*
"Rouland, mi lord, is slain;
235 He speketh no more with me.
That levedi, nought to lain,   *lady; lie*
For sothe ded is sche.   *Truly*
Who may be ogain?   *Who can come back to life*
As God wil, it schal be
240 Unblithe."   *Sorrowful*
Sorwe it was to se
That levedi swelted swithe.   *lady to have died [too] soon*

Geten and born was so   *Conceived*
The child was fair and white.   *child [who] was*
245 Nas never Rohand so wo;   *sad*

162

He nist it whom to wite. [1]
To childbed ded he go   *(see note)*
His owhen wiif al so tite,   *wife; quickly*
And seyd he hadde children to;   *two*
250   On hem was his delite,
Bi Crist!
In court men cleped him so: *called*
Tho "Tram" bifor the "Trist."   *The*

Douk Morgan was blithe
255   Tho Rouland Riis was doun;   *When*
He sent his sond swithe   *messenger quickly*
And bad al schuld be boun   *ready*
And to his lores lithe,   *listen to his decrees*
Redi to his somoun.   *summons*
260   Durst non ogain him kithe,   *None dared oppose him*
Bot yalt him tour and toun   *yielded to him tower and town*
So sone.   *Immediately*
No was no king with croun
So richeliche hadde ydone.   *powerfully*

265   Who gaf broche and beighe?   *brooch and ring*
Who bot Douke Morgan?
Cruwel was and heighe,   *Cruel; proud*
Ogaines him stode no man.   *Against*
To conseil he calleth neighe
270   Rohand trewe so stan,   *true as stone*
And ever he dede as the sleighe   *the clever man*
And held his hert in an,   *(see note)*
That wise.   *wise [man]*
It brast thurch blod and ban [2]
275   Yif hope no ware to rise.   *If; were not*

Now hath Rohand in ore   *security from danger*
Tristrem and is ful blithe.

---

[1] *He did not know whom to blame for it*

[2] *It [his heart] would have burst through blood and bone*

	The child he set to lore	*placed under instruction*
	And lernd him al so swithe;	*taught; swiftly*
280	In bok, while he was thore,	*there*
	He stodieth ever, that stithe.	*bold [man]*
	Tho that bi him wore	*Those; by; were*
	Of him weren ful blithe,	
	That bold.	*courageous [man]*
285	His craftes gan he kithe	*He revealed his skills*
	Ogaines hem when he wold.	*To them*

	Fiftene yere he gan him fede,	*raise*
	Sir Rohand the trewe.	
	He taught him ich a lede	*each song*
290	Of ich maner of glewe	*every style of music*
	And everich playing thede,	*(see note)*
	Old lawes and newe.	
	On hunting oft he yede;	*went*
	To swiche a lawe he drewe	
295	Al thus.	
	More he couthe of veneri	*knew of hunting*
	Than couthe Manerious.	

	Ther com a schip of Norway	
	To Sir Rohandes hold	*stronghold*
300	With haukes white and gray	
	And panes fair yfold.	*garments*
	Tristrem herd it say	
	On his playing he wold	
	Tuenti schilling to lay.	*Twenty; bet*
305	Sir Rouhand him told	
	And taught;	
	For hauke, silver he yold,	*put up*
	The fairest men him raught.	*brought to him*

	A cheker he fond bi a cheire;	*chessboard*
310	He asked who wold play.	
	The mariner spac bonair:	*spoke courteously*
	"Child, what wiltow lay	*Young man; bet*
	Ogain an hauke of noble air?"	*Against a hawk of noble breed*

"Tuenti schillinges, to say.
315   Whether so mates other fair   *Whoever checkmates the other*
Bere hem bothe oway."
With wille
The mariner swore his faye: *faith*
"For sothe, ich held thertille."   *truth; thereto*

320   Now bothe her wedde lys,   *put up their stakes*
And play thai biginne;
Ysett he hath the long asise   *(see note)*
And endred beth therinne.   *began*
The play biginneth to arise.   *to become more intense*
325   Tristrem deleth atuinne;   *(see note)*
He dede als so the wise:
He gaf has he gan winne
In raf.   *winnings*
Of playe ar he wald blinne,   *before; cease*
330   Sex haukes he gat and gaf.   *won; gave*

Rohand toke leve to ga;   *go*
His sones he cleped oway.   *called*
The fairest hauke he gan ta   *take*
That Tristrem wan that day;
335   With him he left ma   *more*
Pans for to play.   *Money*
The mariner swore also
That pans wold he lay   *money; wager*
An stounde.   *In his turn*
340   Tristrem wan that day   *won*
Of him an hundred pounde.

Tristrem wan that ther was layd.   *bet*
A tresoun ther was made: *committed*
No lenger than the maister seyd,
345   Of gate nas ther no bade.   *There was no delay of departure*
As thai best sat and pleyd,   *those best [of men]*
Out of haven thai rade   *port; sailed*
Opon the se so gray,   *sea*
Fram the brimes brade   *broad waves*

350	Gun flete.	*Sailed*
	Of lod thai were wel glade,	*journey*
	And Tristrem sore wepe.	
	His maister than thai fand	
	A bot and an are	*boat; oar*
355	Hye seyden, "Yond is the land,	*They*
	And here schaltow to bare.	*you shall [go] into the waves*
	Chese on aither hand	*Choose*
	Whether the lever ware	*you would rather*
	Sink or stille stand;	
360	The child schal with ous fare	*travel*
	On flod."	*On the sea*
	Tristrem wepe ful sare;	*wept grievously*
	Thai lough and thought it gode.	*laughed; amusing*
	Niyen woukes and mare	*Nine weeks and more*
365	The mariners flet on flod,	*sailed on the sea*
	Til anker hem brast and are	*anchor; broke; oar*
	And stormes hem bistode.	*oppressed them*
	Her sorwen and her care	*Their sorrows*
	Thai witt that frely fode;	*blamed upon that noble young man*
370	Thai nisten hou to fare,	*did not know how to navigate*
	The wawes were so wode	*waves; tumultuous*
	With winde.	
	O lond thai wold he yede	*they wished he might go*
	Yif thai wist ani to finde.	*If; knew how*
375	A lond thai neighed neighe,	*approached*
	A forest as it ware,	
	With hilles that were heighe	*high*
	And holtes that weren hare.	*forests; dark*
	O lond thai sett that sleighe	*put ashore; clever [person]*
380	With al his wining yare,	*winnings willingly*
	With broche and riche beighe,	*brooch; ring*
	A lof of brede yete mare,	*bread in addition*
	That milde.	*noble person*
	Weder thai hadde to fare,	*Regardless of where*
385	A lond thai left that childe.	*On land*

	Winde thai had as thai wolde;	*wished*
	A lond bilaft he;	*On land he was left behind*
	His hert bigan to cold	*to grow cold*
	Tho he no might hem nought se.	*When; see them no longer*
390	To Crist his bodi he yald,	*entrusted*
	That don was on the Tre:	*put*
	"Lord, mi liif me bihold,	*protect*
	In world Thou wisse me	*guide*
	At wille;	
395	Astow art Lord so fre,	*As you; generous*
	Thou lete me never spille."	*perish*
	Tho Tomas asked ay	*Then; (see note)*
	Of Tristrem, trewe fere,	*true companion*
	To wite the right way	*know*
400	The styes for to lere. [1]	
	Of a prince proude in play	*battle*
	Listneth, lordinges dere.	*noble lords*
	Whoso better can say,	*(see note)*
	His owhen he may here	
405	As hende.	*politely, courtly*
	Of thing that is him dere	
	Ich man preise at ende.	
	In o robe Tristrem was boun	*dressed*
	That he fram schip hadde brought	
410	Was of a blihand broun,	*brown silk*
	The richest that was wrought,	
	As Tomas telleth in toun.	*(see note)*
	He no wist what he mought	*knew not; might [do]*
	Bot semly sett him doun	*graciously*
415	And ete ay til him gode thought;	*ate; until*
	Ful sone	*quickly*
	The forest forth he sought	
	When he so hadde done.	

---

[1] *To learn the ins and outs of [his] story*

	He toke his lod unlight;	*journey*
420	His penis with him he bare.	*money; carried*
	The hilles were on hight;	*high*
	He clombe tho holtes hare.	*climbed those gray wooded hills*
	Of o gate he hadde sight	*path*
	That he fond ful yare.	*eagerly*
425	The path he toke ful right;	
	To palmers mett he thare	*Two pilgrims*
	On hand.	
	He asked hem whennes thai ware.	*whence*
	Thai seyd, "Of Yngland."	
430	For drede thai wald him slo	*slay*
	He temed him to the king.	*(see note)*
	He bede hem pens mo,	*offered them more money*
	Aither ten schilling,	*Each*
	Yif thai wald with him go	*If*
435	And to the court him bring.	
	"Yis," thai sworen tho	*Yes; then*
	Bi the Lord over al thing	
	Ful sone.	
	Ful wel biset his thing	*[are] arranged his affairs*
440	That rathe hath his bone.	*quickly; request*
	The forest was fair and wide,	
	With wilde bestes ysprad.	*teeming*
	The court was ner biside;	
	The palmers thider him lad.	*pilgrims; led*
445	Tristrem hunters seighe ride;	*saw*
	Les of houndes thai ledde.	*A leash (see note)*
	Thai token in that tide	*time*
	Of fat hertes yfedde	
	In feld.	
450	In blehand was he cledde.	*silk; clad*
	The hunters him biheld.	
	Bestes thai brac and bare;	*cut up*
	In quarters thai hem wrought,	
	Martirs as it ware	*(see note)*

455	That husbond men had bought.	
	Tristrem tho spac thare	*then spoke*
	And seyd wonder him thought:	*it seemed to him*
	"Ne seighe Y never are	*saw; before*
	So wilde best ywrought	*In such a way a wild beast dressed*
460	At wille.	*By choice*
	Other," he seyd, "Y can nought	*Either; I have no knowledge*
	Or folily ye hem spille."	*foolishly; slaughter*
	Up stode a serjaunt bold	
	And spac Tristrem ogain:	*replied to Tristrem*
465	"We and our elders old	
	Thus than have we sain;	*seen [it done]*
	Other thou hast ous told.	*Otherwise*
	Yond lith a best unflain;	*unskinned*
	Atire it as thou wold	*Dress*
470	And we wil se ful fain	*gladly*
	In feld."	
	In lede is nought to lain,	*(see note)*
	The hunters him biheld.	*watched him*
	Tristrem schare the brest;	*cut*
475	The tong sat next the pride;	*tongue set; spleen*
	The heminges swithe on est	*(see note); quickly with pleasure*
	He schar and layd biside.	*cut*
	The breche adoun he threst;	*hind quarters*
	He ritt and gan to right;	*cut; apportion*
480	Boldliche ther nest	*next*
	Carf he of that hide	*Carved; off*
	Bidene.	*Quickly*
	The bestes he graithed that tide,	*prepared; time*
	As mani seththen has ben.	*many a one since*
485	The spaude was the first brede;	*(see note)*
	The erber dight he yare.	*first stomach; prepared; readily*
	To the stifles he yede	*(see note); went*
	And even ato hem schare;	*in two cut them*
	He right al the rede,	*set out; fourth stomach*
490	The wombe oway he bare,	*bowels*

169

	The noubles he gaf to mede.	*(see note); as a reward*
	That seighen that ther ware	*That they who were there saw*
	Al so.	
	The rigge he croised mare,	*The back he cut crosswise*
495	The chine he smot atuo.	*The backbone he chopped in two*
	The forster for his rightes	*forester*
	The left schulder gaf he,	
	With hert, liver and lightes	*lungs*
	And blod tille his quirré;	*(see note)*
500	Houndes on hyde he dightes;	*puts*
	Alle he lete hem se.	
	The raven he gave his giftes,	*(see note)*
	Sat on the fourched tre	*forked*
	On rowe.	*In order*
505	"Hunters, whare be ye?	
	The tokening schuld ye blowe."	*signal*
	He tight the mawe on tinde	*stretched the viscera on a tine*
	And eke the gargiloun;	*gullet*
	Thai blewen the right kinde	
510	And radde the right roun.	*played; note*
	Thai wist the king to finde	*knew how*
	And senten forth to toun	
	And teld him under linde	*told; under a tree*
	The best, hou it was boun	*beast; prepared*
515	And brought.	
	Marke, the king with croun,	
	Seyd that feir him thought.	*it seemed good to him*
	The tokening when thai blewe,	*signal*
	Ther wondred mani a man;	
520	The costom thai nought knewe;	
	Forthi fro bord thai ran.	*Therefore; table*
	No wist thai nought hou newe	*knew*
	Thai hadde hunters than.	
	It is a maner of glewe	*sport*
525	To teche hem that no can	*those who do not know*
	Swiche thing.	*Such*

170

	Alle blithe weren thai than	
	That yede bifor the king.	*went*
	The king seyd, "Where were thou born?	
530	What hattou, bel amye?"	*What is your name, fair friend*
	Tristrem spac biforn:	*(see note)*
	"Sir, in Hermonie.	
	Mi fader me hath forlorn,	*lost*
	Sir Rohand, sikerly	*surely*
535	The best blower of horn	
	And king of venery	*hunting*
	For thought."	*(see note)*
	The lasse gaf Mark forthi,	*Mark could not care less about that*
	For Rohand he no knewe nought.	
540	The king no seyd no more	
	Bot wesche and yede to mete.	*washed; went to [his] meal*
	Bred thai pard and schare —	*cut the crust off and sliced*
	Ynough thai hadde at ete.	*to eat*
	Whether hem lever ware	*Whether they preferred*
545	Win or ale to gete,	
	Aske and have it yare,	*readily*
	In coupes or hornes grete	*cups; great*
	Was brought.	
	Ther, while thai wold, thai sete	*as long as they wanted*
550	And risen when hem gode thought.	*it seemed good to them*
	An harpour made a lay	
	That Tristrem aresound he.	*berated*
	The harpour yede oway,	*went away (i.e., gave way to Tristrem)*
	"Who better can, lat se."	*let's see*
555	"Bot Y the mendi may,	*Unless I can surpass you*
	Wrong than wite Y the."	*Wrongly then I blame you*
	The harpour gan to say,	
	"The maistri give Y the	*victory I give to you*
	Ful sket."	*quickly*
560	Bifor the kinges kne	
	Tristrem is cald to set.	*sit*

Blithe weren thai alle
And merkes gun thai minne,   *distinctive features; take note of*
Token leve in the halle   *(see note)*
565   Who might the child winne.
Mark gan Tristrem calle,
Was comen of riche kinne;   *[Who] was born*
He gaf him robe of palle   *fine cloth*
And pane of riche skinne   *cloak*
570   Ful sket.   *quickly*
His chaumber he lith inne
And harpeth notes swete.

Now Tristrem lat we thare;   *we cease to speak of*
With Marke he is ful dere.
575   Rohand reweth sare   *grieves greatly*
That he no might of him here;   *hear*
Over londes he gan fare   *travel*
With sorwe and reweful chere,   *doleful spirit*
Seven kingriche and mare   *kingdoms*
580   Tristrem to finde there
And sought.
His robes riven were;   *tattered*
Therfore no leved he nought.[1]

Nought no semed it so
585   Rohand, that noble knight.
He no wist whider to go,   *knew where*
So was he brought o might;   *deprived of strength*
To swinke men wold him to   *Men wanted to take him to work*
For mete and robes right.   *Just for food and clothes*
590   With other werkmen mo   *more*
He bileft al night   *remained*
In land.
Of the palmers he hadde a sight   *pilgrims*
That Tristrem first fand.   *encountered*

---

[1] *He did not stop [searching] because of that*

595	His asking is ever newe	*constant*
	In travail and in pes.	*trouble; peace*
	The palmer seyd he him knewe	*pilgrim*
	And wiste wele what he wes:	*knew; who he was*
	"His robe is of an hewe	*of a solid color*
600	Blihand withouten les;	*Silk in truth*
	His name is Tristrem trewe;	
	Bifor him scheres the mes	*carves the meal*
	The king.	
	Y brought him ther he ches;	*where he chose [to go]*
605	He gave me ten schilling."	

	"So michel wil Y give the,"	*much*
	Quath Rohand, "will ye ta,	*take [it]*
	The court ye lat me se."	
	The palmers seyd, "Ya."	*pilgrims*
610	Blithe therof was he	
	And redily gaf him sa	*willingly*
	Of wel gode moné	*money*
	Ten schilinges and ma	*more*
	Of gayn.	
615	Rohand was ful thra	*eager*
	Of Tristrem for to frain.	*ask*

	In Tristrem is his delit,	*delight*
	And of him speketh he ay.	*always*
	The porter gan him wite	*blame*
620	And seyd, "Cherl, go oway,	
	Other Y schal the smite!	*Or*
	What dostow here al day?"	
	A ring he raught him tite —	*gave; quickly*
	The porter seyd nought nay —	
625	In hand.	
	He was ful wise, Y say,	
	That first gave gift in land.	

	Rohand tho tok he	*then*
	And at the gate in lete.	*let [him] in*
630	The ring was fair to se;	

	The gift was wel swete.	*pleasing*
	The huscher bad him fle:	*door-keeper*
	"Cherl, oway wel sket,	*quickly*
	Or broken thine heved schal be	*head*
635	And thou feld under fet	
	To grounde."	
	Rohand bad him lete	*asked him to cease [his threats]*
	And help him at that stounde.	*[him = Rohand]; time*

	The pouer man of mold	*mortal man*
640	Tok forth another ring;	
	The huscher he gaf the gold,	*door-keeper*
	It semed to a king,	*It seemed worthy of a king*
	Formest tho in fold.	*The greatest then on earth*
	He lete him in thring.	*push forward*
645	To Tristrem trewe in hold	
	He hete he wold him bring	*promised*
	And brought.	
	Tristrem knewe him no thing,	
	And ferly Rohand thought.	*it seemed surprising to Rohand*

650	Thei men Tristrem had sworn,	*Though; to Tristrem*
	He no trowed it never in lede	*would never have believed it*
	That Rohand robes were torn,	*Rohand's*
	That he wered swiche a wede.	*wore such clothing*
	He frained him biforn,[1]	
655	"Child, so God the rede,	*Young man, may God advise you*
	How were thou fram Rohand lorn?	*separated*
	Monestow never in lede?"	*Do you remember*
	Nought lain	*Truly*
	He kneled better spede	*kneeled right away*
660	And kist Rohand ful fain.	*gladly*

	"Fader, no wretthe the nought;	*do not become angry*
	Ful welcom er ye.	*are*
	Bi God that man hath bought,	*redeemed*

---

[1] *He [Rohand] asked him [Tristrem] directly*

174

	No thing no knewe Y the.	*I didn't know you at all*
665	With sorwe thou hast me sought;	
	To wite it wo is me!"	*It grieves me to know it*
	To Mark the word he brought:	
	"Wil ye mi fader se	
	With sight?	*With your own eyes*
670	Graithed Y wil he be,	*Equipped I want him to be*
	And seththen schewe him as knight."	*then*

	Tristrem to Mark it seyd,	*told*
	His aventours, as it were,	*adventures*
	Hou he with schipmen pleyd,	
675	Of lond hou thai him bere,	*From; carried*
	Hou stormes hem bistayd,	*beset them*
	Til anker hem brast and are.	*anchor; oar*
	"Thai yolden me that Y layd;	*returned to me what I bet*
	With al mi wining yare	*readily*
680	In hand,	
	Y clambe the holtes hare	*climbed the grey wooded hills*
	Til Y thine hunters fand."	*encountered*

	A bath thai brought Rohand inne;	
	A barbour was redi thare.	*barber*
685	Al rowe it was, his chinne;	*shaggy-haired*
	His heved was white of hare.	*head*
	A scarlet with riche skinne	*(see note)*
	Ybrought him was ful yare,	*quickly*
	Rohand of noble kinne.	
690	That robe ful fair he bare,	*wore*
	That bold.	*valiant man*
	Who that had seyn him thare	*seen*
	A prince him might han told.	*reckoned*

	Fair his tale bigan	
695	Rohand, thei he com lat;	*although he came recently*
	Tristrem, that honour can,	*who knows how to treat with honor*
	To halle led him the gate.	*led him on the way*
	Ich man seyd than	
	Nas non swiche, as thai wate,	*There was none such as far as they knew*

700	As was the pouer man	*poor*
	That thai bete fram the gat	*beat; gate*
	With care.	*Unfortunately*
	Nas non that wald him hate,	
	Bot welcom was he thare.	
705	Water thai asked swithe,	
	Cloth and bord was drain	*spread*
	With mete and drink lithe	*pleasant*
	And serjaunce that were bayn	*serving men; eager*
	To serve Tristrem swithe	
710	And Sir Rohand, ful fayn	*gladly*
	Whasche when thai wald rise;	*Wash*
	The king ros him ogain	*rose to greet him*
	That tide.	
	In lede is nought to layn,	
715	He sett him bi his side.	
	Rohand, that was thare,	
	To Mark his tale bigan:	
	"Wist ye what Tristrem ware,	*If you knew*
	Miche gode ye wold him an.	*grant*
720	Your owhen soster him bare."	
	The King lithed him than.	*listened to*
	"I nam sibbe him na mare;	*I am not related*
	Ich aught to ben his man,	*be his servant*
	Sir King.	
725	Know it yive ye can,	*if*
	Sche taught me this ring	*entrusted to me*
	"When Rouland Riis the bold,	
	Douke Morgan gan mete."	*encounter*
	The tale when Rohand told,	
730	For sorwe he gan grete.	*weep*
	The King biheld that old,	*old [man]*
	Hou his wonges were wete.	*cheeks*
	To Mark the ring he yold —	*gave*
	He knewe it al so sket	

735	Gan loke. [1]	
	He kist Tristrem ful skete	
	And for his nevou toke.	*nephew*
	Tho thai kisten him alle,	
	Bothe levedi and knight	*lady*
740	And serjaunce in the halle	*serving-men*
	And maidens that were bright.	*beautiful*
	Tristrem gan Rohand calle	
	And freined him with sight,	*asked; (see note)*
	"Sir, hou may this falle?	
745	Hou may Y prove it right?	
	Nought lain	*Truly*
	Tel me, for Godes might,	
	Hou was mi fader slayn."	
	Rohand told anon	
750	His aventours al bidene,	*adventures completely*
	Hou the batayle bigan,	*fighting*
	The werres hadden yben,	*battles*
	His moder hou hye was tan	*she was taken*
	And geten hem bituene.	*(see note)*
755	"Slawe was Rouland than	*Slain*
	And ded Blaunche the Schene.	*dead; Beautiful*
	Naught les,	
	For dout of Morgan kene	*fear; cruel*
	Mi sone Y seyd thou wes."	
760	Tristrem, al in heighe,	*haste*
	Bifor the king cam he.	
	"Into Ermonie,	
	Sir, now longeth me;	*I want [to go]*
	Thider fare wil Y.	
765	Mi leve Y take of the	
	To fight with Morgan in hy,	*right away*
	To sle him other he me	*slay; or*

---

[1]*As soon as he looked at it*

	With hand.	
	Erst schal no man me se	*Before [I do so]*
770	Ogain in Ingland."	

	Tho was Mark ful wo;	*very sorry*
	He sight sore at that tide.	*sighed*
	"Tristrem, thi rede thou ta	*be advised*
	In Inglond for to abide.	
775	Morgan is wick to slo;	*difficult to slay*
	Of knightes he hath gret pride.	*Among; great prowess*
	Tristrem, thei thou be thro,	*though you be bold*
	Lat mo men with the ride	
	On rowe.	*In an armed party*
780	Take Rohand bi thi side;	
	He wil thine frendes knawe."	

	To armes the king lete crie	*had called*
	The folk of al his land	
	To help Tristrem. Forthi	*For that occasion*
785	He made knight with his hand.	*knights*
	He dede him han on heye	*He provided him immediately*
	The fairest that he fand	
	In place to riden him by,	
	To don him to understand	*To counsel him*
790	So swithe.	
	Sorwe so Tristrem band	*constrained*
	Might no man make him blithe.	

	No wold he duellen a night —	*He would not remain*
	Therof nas nought to say.	
795	Ten hundred that were wight	*valiant*
	Wenten with him oway.	
	Rohand, the riche knight,	*powerful*
	Redy was he ay.	*always*
	To his castel ful right	
800	He sailed the sevenday	*seventh day*
	On rade.	*journey*
	His maister he gan pay;	*recompense*
	His sones knightes he made.	

178

	His frendes, glad were thai —	
805	No blame hem no man forthi —	
	Of his coming, to say,	*that is*
	Al into Ermonie,	
	Til it was on a day	
	Morgan was fast by,	
810	Tristrem bigan to say,	
	"With Morgan speke wil Y	
	And spede.	*succeed*
	So long idel we ly;	
	Miself mai do mi nede."	*I can attend to my own business*

	Tristrem dede as he hight.	*promised*
815	He busked and made him yare	*prepared; himself ready*
	His fiftend som of knight;	*a group of fifteen knights*
	With him yede na mare.	
	To court thai com ful right	*just*
820	As Morgan his brede schare.	*cut his bread*
	Thai teld tho bi sight	*counted*
	Ten kinges sones thai ware	
	Unsought;	*(see note)*
	Hevedes of wild bare	*Heads; boar*
825	Ichon to presant brought.	*Each one; as a gift*

	Rohand bigan to sayn,	*speak*
	To his knightes than seyd he,	
	"As woman is tuiis forlain,	*twice seduced*
	Y may say bi me.	*I may compare myself to*
830	Yif Tristrem be now sleyn,	*slain*
	Yvel yemers er we.	*Poor guardians*
	To armes, knight and swayn,	
	And swiftly ride ye	
	And swithe.	
835	Til Y Tristrem se,	
	No worth Y never blithe."	*I will never be happy*

	Tristrem speke bigan:	
	"Sir king, God loke the	*watch over you*
	As Y the love and an	*cherish*

840	And thou hast served to me."	*given aid*
	The douke answerd than,	
	"Y pray, mi lord so fre,	*noble*
	Whether thou blis or ban,	*wish well or curse*
	Thine owhen mot it be,	*own*
845	Thou bold.	
	Thi nedes tel thou me,	
	Thine erand, what thou wold."	

	"Amendes! Mi fader is slain,	*Retribution*
	Mine hirritage Hermonie."	
850	The douke answerd ogain,	*in reply*
	"Certes, thi fader than slough Y."	*Surely; slew*
	"Seththen thou so hast sayd,	*Since*
	Amendes ther ought to ly."	*Reparations; be due*
	"Therfore, prout swayn,	*proud young man*
855	So schal Y the, for thi	*As I may thrive*
	Right than	
	Artow comen titly	*directly*
	Fram Marke, thi kinsman?	

	"Yongling, thou schalt abide.	
860	Foles thou wendest to fand.	
	Thi fader thi moder gan hide;	*cohabit with secretly*
	In horedom he hir band.	*fornication; had intercourse with*
	Hou comestow with pride?	*By what right*
	Out, traitour, of mi land!"	
865	Tristrem spac that tide:	
	"Thou lext, ich understand	*lie*
	And wot."	*know*
	Morgan with his hand	
	With a lof Tristrem smot.	*palm; struck*

870	On his brest adoun	
	Of his nose ran the blod.	*From*
	Tristrem swerd was boun,	*Tristrem's; ready*
	And ner the douke he stode.	
	. . . .	
875	. . . .	

180

With that was comen to toun
Rohand with help ful gode
And gayn.   *useful*
Al that ogain hem stode   *against*
880 Wightly were thai slayn.   *Quickly*

To prisoun thai gun take
Erl, baroun and knight;
For Douke Morgan sake
Mani on dyd dounright.   *Many a one died outright*
885 Schaftes thai gun schake   *brandish*
And riven scheldes bright;   *cleave*
Crounes thai gun crake   *Heads; split open*
Mani, ich wene, aplight.   *in faith*
Saun fayl,   *Without fail*
890 Bituene the none and the night *noon*
Last the batayle.   *Lasted*

Thus hath Tristrem the swete   *gracious*
Yslawe the Douke Morgan.   *slain*
No wold he never lete   *cease*
895 Til mo castels wer tan;   *more; taken*
Tounes thai yold him skete   *yielded to him quickly*
And cités stithe of stan.   *strong*
The folk fel to his fet;
Againes him stode ther nan
900 In land.
He slough his fader ban.   *slew his father's murderer*
Al bowed to his hand.   *submitted to his authority*

Tuo yere he sett that land;   *set that land in order*
His lawes made he cri.   *he had proclaimed*
905 Al com to his hand
Almain and Ermonie,   *(see note)*
At his wil to stand
Boun and al redy.
Rohand he gaf the wand   *sceptre*
910 And bad him sitt him bi,
That fre.   *nobleman*

"Rohand lord make Y
To held this lond of me.   *hold [from a feudal lord]*

Thou and thine sones five
915 Schul held this lond of me;
Ther while thou art olive   *alive*
Thine owhen schal it be.   *own*
What halt it long to strive?   *avails; debate*
Mi leve Y take at te   *from you*
920 Til Inglond wil Y rive,   *arrive*
Mark, mi nem, to se   *my uncle (see note)*
That stounde."   *time*
Now boskes Tristre the fre   *prepares*
To Inglond for to founde.   *go*

925 Blithe was his bosking,   *preparation*
And fair was his schip fare.   *ship's rigging*
Rohand he left king
Over al his wining thare.   *conquest*
Schipmen him gun bring
930 To Inglond ful yare.   *readily*
He herd a newe tiding
That he herd never are   *before*
On hand.
Mani man wepen sare   *wept grievously*
935 For ransoun to Yrland.   *tribute*

Marke schuld yeld unhold   *had to give unwillingly*
Thei he were king with croun   *Though*
Thre hundred pounde of gold
Ich yer out of toun,   *Each*
940 Of silver fair yfold
Thre hundred pounde al boun,   *all prepared*
Of moné of a mold   *money cast in one mold*
Thre hundred pounde of latoun   *latten (see note)*
Schuld he.
945 The ferth yere, a ferly roun,   *fourth; a terrible requirement*
Thre hundred barnes fre.   *noble children*

182

	The truage was com to to	*tribute; take*
	Moraunt, the noble knight.	
	Yhold he was so	*Considered*
950	A neten in ich a fight.	*A giant*
	The barnes asked he tho	*children demanded he then*
	Als it war londes right.	*according to law*
	Tristrem gan stoutely go	
	To lond that ich night	*same*
955	Of rade.	*(see note)*
	Of the schippe thai hadde a sight	
	The day thai dede obade.	*wait for*

	Mark was glad and blithe	
	Tho he might Tristrem se.	*When*
960	He kist him fele sithe;	*many times*
	Welcom to him was he.	
	Marke gan tidinges lithe,	*hear*
	Hou he wan londes fre.	*conquered*
	Tristrem seyde that sithe,	
965	"Wat may this gadering be?"	*congregation*
	Thai grete.	*lamented*
	"Tristrem, Y telle it the,	
	A thing is me unswete.	*[that] is to me disagreeable*

	"The King of Yrlond,	
970	Tristrem, ich am his man.	*vassal*
	To long ichave ben hir bond.	*I have owed them fealty*
	With wrong the King it wan.	
	To long it hath ystond.	*lasted*
	On him the wrong bigan.	
975	Therto ich held min hond."	
	Tristrem seyd than,	
	Al stille,	
	"Moraunt that michel can	
	Schal nought han his wille."	*have*

980	Marke to conseyl yede	*went*
	And asked rede of this.	*advice about*
	He seyd, "With wrong dede	

The raunsoun ytaken is."
Tristrem seyd, "Y rede   *advise*
985   That he the barnes mis."   *fail to obtain the children*
Tho seyd the King in lede,   *among the people*
"No was it never his
With right."   *Rightfully*
Tristrem seyd, "Ywis,
990   Y wil defende it as knight."

Bi al Markes hald   *Throughout; domain*
The truwage was tan.   *tribute; collected*
Tristrem gan it withhald
As prince proude in pan.   *rich clothing*
995   Thai graunted that Tristrem wald,   *what Tristrem wanted*
Other no durst ther nan;   *[To do] otherwise; dared*
Nis ther non so bald   *Is not*
Ymade of flesche no ban,   *flesh nor bone*
No knight.
1000 Now hath Tristrem ytan   *undertaken*
Ogain Moraunt to fight.   *Against*

Tristrem himself yede
Moraunt word to bring
And schortliche seyd in lede,   *aloud*
1005 "We no owe the nothing."
Moraunt ogain sede,   *said in reply*
"Thou lexst a foule lesing.   *You lie a wicked lie*
Mi body to batayl Y bede   *in battle I offer*
To prove bifor the King
1010 To loke."   *As an offering*
He waged him a ring;   *He [Moraunt] gave as a pledge*
Tristrem the batayl toke.   *accepted the challenge*

Thai seylden into the wide   *sailed; open sea*
With her schippes tuo.
1015 Moraunt bond his biside,   *tied up*
And Tristrem lete his go.
Moraunt seyd that tide,
"Tristrem, whi dostow so?"   *do you*

184

	"Our on schal here abide,	*One of us*
1020	No be thou never so thro,	*valiant*
	Ywis.	
	Whether our to live go,	*Whichever of us stays alive*
	He hath anough of this."	

	The yland was ful brade	*wide*
1025	That thai gun in fight.	
	Therof was Moraunt glade;	
	Of Tristrem he lete light.	*He took Tristrem lightly*
	Swiche meting nas never non made	
	With worthli wepen wight.	*excellent; strongly constructed*
1030	Aither to other rade	*Each*
	And hewe on helmes bright	*struck*
	With hand.	
	God help Tristrem the knight!	
	He faught for Ingland.	

1035	Moraunt with his might	
	Rode with gret raundoun	*violence*
	Ogain Tristrem the knight	
	And thought to bere him doun.	*overthrow him*
	With a launce unlight	*stout*
1040	He smot him in the lyoun	*(see note)*
	And Tristrem that was wight	*valiant*
	Bar him thurch the dragoun	*Pierced*
	In the scheld.	
	That Moraunt bold and boun	*armed*
1045	Smot him in the scheld.	

	Up he stirt bidene	*quickly*
	And lepe opon his stede.	*leapt; horse*
	He faught, withouten wene,	*doubt*
	So wolf that wald wede.	*As; became mad*
1050	Tristrem in that tene	*rage*
	No spard him for no drede;	*fear*
	He gaf him a wounde ysene	*visible*
	That his bodi gan blede	
	Right tho.	

1055	In Morauntes most nede	*greatest need*
	His stede bak brak on to.	*His horse's back broke in two*
	Up he stirt in drede	
	And seyd, "Tristrem, alight,	*dismount*
	For thou hast slayn mi stede.	*horse*
1060	Afot thou schalt fight."	*On foot*
	Quath Tristrem, "So God me rede,	*May God keep me*
	Therto icham al light."	*willing*
	Togider tho thai yede	
	And hewen on helmes bright	
1065	Saun fayl.	*Ceaselessly*
	Tristrem as a knight	
	Faught in that batayle.	
	Moraunt of Yrland smot	
	Tristrem in the scheld	
1070	That half fel fram his hond	
	Ther adoun in the feld.	
	Tristrem, ich understond,	
	Anon the strok him yeld	*Instantly; requited*
	With his gode brond.	*sword*
1075	Moraunt neighe he queld,	*he nearly killed*
	That knight.	
	Marke the batayl biheld	
	And wonderd of that fight.	*was amazed at*
	Moraunt was unfayn	*troubled*
1080	And faught with al his might;	
	That Tristrem were yslayn	*might be slain*
	He stird him as a knight.	*conducted himself*
	Tristrem smot with main;	*with vigor*
	His swerd brak in the fight	*broke*
1085	And in Morauntes brain	
	Bileved a pece bright	*Remained; piece*
	With care.	*Unfortunately*
	And in the haunche right	*hip*
	Tristrem was wounded sare.	*grievously*

1090	A word that pended to pride	*tended towards*
	Tristrem tho spac he:	
	"Folk of Yrland side,	*region*
	Your mirour ye may se.	
	Mo that hider wil ride,	*More [of you]*
1095	Thus graythed schul ye be."	*treated*
	With sorwe thai drough that tide	
	Moraunt to the se	*sea*
	And care.	
	With joie Tristrem the fre	
1100	To Mark, his em, gan fare.	*uncle; did go*

	His swerd he offred than	
	And to the auter it bare.	*altar*
	For Markes kinsman	*As*
	Tristrem was loved thare.	
1105	A forward thai bigan	*agreement*
	Therto thai alle sware:	
	For that lond fre he wan,	*Since*
	That king he schuld be thare,	
	To say,	*That is*
1110	Yif he olive ware	*If; alive*
	After Sir Markes day.	

	Thei Tristrem light thenke,	*Though Tristrem might think little of it*
	He is wounded ful sare.	
	Leches with salve and drink	*Doctors; potion*
1115	Him cometh wide whare.	*Came to him from far and wide*
	Thai lorn al her swink:	*wasted; their labor*
	His pain was ay the mare.	
	No man no might for stink	
	Com ther Tristrem ware	*where Tristrem might be*
1120	Als than.	
	Ich man forsoke him thare	
	Bot Governayl, his man.	*Except; manservant*

	Thre yer in carebed lay	*Three years; sickbed*
	Tristrem, the trewe he hight,	*was called*
1125	That never no dought him day	*profited*

	For sorwe he hadde onight.	
	For diol no man no may	*pity*
	Sen on him with sight.	*Look*
	Ich man, for sothe to say,	*Each; truth*
1130	Forsoke tho that knight	
	As thare.	
	Thai hadde don what he might;	*(see note)*
	Thai no rought of his fare	*didn't care about his condition*

	Til it was on a day	
1135	Til Mark he gan him mene.	*complain*
	Schortliche, sothe to say,	
	This tale was hem bituene.	*conversation; between*
	"In sorwe ich have ben ay	*continuously*
	Seththen ich alive have ben."	*Since*
1140	Marke seyde, "Wayleway	
	That ich it schuld ysene,	*see*
	Swiche thing."	*Such a*
	Tristrem, withouten wene,	*without doubt*
	A schip asked the King.	*requested from*

	"Em," he seyd, "Y spille.	*Uncle; I am dying*
1145	Of lond kepe Y namare.	*I have no further use for land*
	A schip thou bring me tille,	*to*
	Mine harp to play me thare,	
	Stouer ynough to wille	*Provisions; at [my] disposal*
1150	To kepe me, son you yare."	*quickly; prepare*
	Thei Marke liked ille,	*Though Mark was displeased*
	Tristrem to schip thai bare	
	And brought.	
	Who wold with him fare?	
1155	Governayle no lete him nought.	*forsook*

	Tristremes schip was yare	*ready*
	And asked his benisoun.	*(see note); blessing*
	The haven he gan outfare —	*He sailed out of the harbor*
	It hight Carlioun.	*was called*
1160	Niyen woukes and mare	*Nine weeks and more*
	He hobled up and doun.	*He bobbed up and down [in his boat]*

	A winde to wil him bare	*as he wished*
	To a stede ther him was boun	*place where he was going*
	Neighehand.	*Nearby*
1165	Delvelin hight the toun,	*The town was named Dublin*
	An haven in Irland.	*port*

	A winde thider him gan drive;	
	Schipmen him seighe neighehand.	*nearby*
	In botes thai gun him stive	*boats; put*
1170	And drough him to the land.	*brought*
	A wounded man alive	
	In the schip thai fand.	
	He seyd bisiden a rive	*shore*
	Men wounded him and band	
1175	Unsounde.	*Unhealthy*
	No man might bi him stand	
	For stinking of his wounde.	

	Governail gan hem frain	*ask*
	What hight the se strand.	*What the sea coast was called*
1180	"Develin," thai seyd ogayn,	*Dublin; in reply*
	The schipmen that him fand.	*found*
	Tho was Tristrem unfain	*unhappy*
	And wele gan understand,	
	Hir brother hadde he slain	*Her [The Queen's]*
1185	That Quen was of the land	
	In fight.	
	"Tristrem" he gan doun lain	*He abandoned [the name] Tristrem*
	And seyd "Tramtris" he hight.	*was called*

	In his schip was that day	
1190	Al maner of gle	*entertainment*
	And al maner of lay	*music*
	In lond that might be.	
	To the Quen tho seyd thay,	
	Morauntes soster the fre,	
1195	Ywounded swiche a man lay	
	That sorwe it was to se	
	And care.	*sadness*

A miri man were he   *lusty*
Yif he olive ware.   *alive*

1200 Sche was in Develin,   *Dublin*
The fair levedi, the Quene,   *lady*
Lovesom under line   *Lovely; (see note)*
And sleighest had ybene   *most skillful*
And mest couthe of medicine.   *knowledgable about*
1205 That was on Tristrem sene.   *in the case of Tristrem made manifest*
Sche brought him of his pine,   *out of his suffering*
To wite and nought at wene,   *Indeed and without a doubt*
To say.   *That is*
Sche sent him a plaster kene   *strong poultice*
1210 To cast the stink oway.

A morwe when it was day,   *In the morning*
The levedy of heighe priis   *lady of great nobility*
Com ther Tristrem lay   *where*
And asked what he is.
1215 "Marchaund ich have ben ay;   *Merchant; always*
Mi nam is Tramtris.
Robbers, for sothe to say,   *truth*
Slough mine felawes, ywis,   *Slew my companions*
In the se.   *sea*
1220 Thai raft me fowe and griis,   *robbed; (see note)*
And thus wounded thai me."

An heye man he was like,   *great*
Thei he wer wounded sare.   *Though; grievously*
His gles weren so sellike   *musical instruments; marvellous*
1225 That wonder thought hem thare.   *it seemed to them*
His harp, his croude was rike,   *fiddle (see note); precious*
His tables, his ches he bare.   *chessboard; chess-men*
Thai swore by Seyn Patrike
Swiche seighe thai never are   *saw; before*
1230 Er than:
"Yif he in hele ware,   *health*
He wer a miri man."   *lusty*

	The levedi of heighe kenne	*noble kin*
	His woundes schewe sche lete,	*she had revealed*
1235	To wite his wo unwinne;	*know; grievous*
	So grimli he gan grete,	*weep*
	His bon brast under skinne,	*broke*
	His sorwe was unsete.	*painful*
	Thai brought him to an inne;	
1240	A bath thai made him sket	
	So lithe	*comforting*
	That Tristrem on his fet	
	Gon he might swithe.	
	Salves hath he soft	*comforting*
1245	And drinkes that er lithe.	*are agreeable*
	Thai no rought hou dere it bought	*They did not care how much it cost*
	Bot held him al so swithe.	*healed him as quickly as possible*
	He made his play aloft;	*He started to play music*
	His gamnes he gan kithe.	*skill in entertaining; exhibit*
1250	Forthi was Tristrem oft	*Therefore*
	To boure cleped fele sithe	*To a chamber called many times*
	To sete.	*For a feast*
	Ich man was lef to lithe,	*eager to listen*
	His mirthes were so swete.	*songs*
1255	The king had a douhter dere;	*beloved daughter*
	That maiden Ysonde hight	*was called*
	That gle was lef to here	*music; eager to hear*
	And romaunce to rede aright.	*stories; read indeed*
	Sir Tramtris hir gan lere	*teach*
1260	Tho with al his might	
	What alle pointes were,	*techniques*
	To se the sothe in sight,	
	To say.	
	In Yrlond nas no knight	
1265	With Ysonde durst play,	*dared*
	Ysonde of heighe priis,	*great nobility*
	The maiden bright of hewe	*fair of face*
	That wered fow and griis	*Who wore; (see note to line 1220)*

191

	And scarlet that was newe.	*fine clothes*
1270	In warld was non so wiis	*skilled*
	Of craft that men knewe	*art*
	Withouten Sir Tramtris	*Except*
	That al games of grewe	*From whom sprang all accomplishments*
	On grounde.	
1275	Hom longeth Tramtris the trewe,	*Homesick was*
	For heled was his wounde.	*healed*

	Sir Tramtris in Irlond	
	Duelled al a yere;	*Remained a full year*
	So gode likeing he fand	*contentment*
1280	That hole he was and fere.	*hale; healthy*
	The Quen to fot and hand	
	He served dern and dere.	*secretly; affectionately*
	Ysonde he dede understand	*caused to*
	What alle playes were	*stories*
1285	In lay.	*in song*
	His leve he asked at here	*from her*
	In schip to founde oway.	*sail*

	The Quen that michel can	*who is very knowledgable*
	To Tramtris sche gan say,	
1290	"Whoso fet uncouthe man,	*(see note)*
	He foundeth ever oway."	
	His hire thai yolden him than,	*payment; gave*
	Gold and silver, Y say.	
	What he wold, he wan	*Whatever he wanted, he got*
1295	Of Ysonde for his play	
	Saun fail.	*Without fail*
	He bitaught hem God and gode day;[1]	
	With him went Governail	

	Riche sail thai drewe	*Expensive; hoisted*
1300	White and red so blod.	*as*
	A winde to wil hem blewe;	*to their liking*

---

[1] *He commended them to God and [said] good day*

To Carlioun thai yode.
Now hat he Tristrem trewe   *is called*
And fareth over the flod.   *he journeys*
1305   The schip the cuntré knewe;   *the people of the region*
It thought hem ful gode   *It seemed to them*
As thare.
Of wrake thai understode   *About revenge; (see note)*
For on thai leten him fare.   *travel*

1310   Thai tolden to the King
That the schip had sain.   *seen*
Never of no tiding   *any news*
Nas Mark the King so fain.   *glad*
To toun thai gun him bring;
1315   The King ros him ogayn.   *rose to meet him*
Blithe was her meteing,   *their*
And fair he gain him frain   *(see note)*
That stounde: *time*
"Tristrem, nought to lain,   *truthfully*
1320   Heled is thi wounde?"   *Healed*

His em answer he yeld   *uncle; gave*
That litel he wald wene.   *doubt*
Of bot sche was him beld   *In [his] cure she was his healer*
That Moraunt soster had bene.   *Moraunt's sister*
1325   Hou fair sche hath him held   *healed*
He told hem al bidene.
And seththen Tristrem hath teld   *then*
Of Ysonde that was kene,   *wise*
Al newe,
1330   Hou sche was bright and schene,   *fair and lovely*
Of love was non so trewe.

Mark to Tristrem gan say,
"Mi lond bitake Y the   *I entrust to you*
To han after mi day: *have*
1335   Thine owhen schal it be.   *own*
Bring thou me that may   *maiden*
That ich hir may yse."   *see*

193

	This was his maner ay	
	Of Ysonde than speketh he	*when*
1340	Her prise,	*worth*
	Hou sche was gent and fre.	*highborn and noble*
	Of love was non so wise.	

	In Inglond ful wide	
	The barouns hem bithought	*planned*
1345	To fel Tristremes pride	*bring down*
	Hou thai fairest mought.	*might*
	The King thai rad to ride,[1]	
	A Quen to him thai sought	
	That Tristrem might abide	
1350	That he no were it nought,	*would not be*
	No king.	
	Thai seyd that Tristrem mought	*might*
	Ysonde of Irlond bring.	

	A brid bright thai ches	*beautiful woman; chose*
1355	As blod opon snoweing:	*blood; fallen snow*
	"A maiden of swiche reles	*(see note)*
	Tristrem may to the bring."	
	Quath Tristrem, "It is les	*a lie*
	And troweth it for lesing;	*believe; lying*
1360	To aski that never no wes,	*ask; was*
	It is a fole askeing	*foolish*
	Bi kinde;	*Naturally*
	It is a selli thing	*wondrous*
	For no man may it finde.	

1365	Y rede ye nought no strive.	*advise*
	A swalu ich herd sing.	*swallow; (see note)*
	Ye sigge ich wern mi nem to wive[2]	
	For Y schuld be your king.	*In order that*
	Now bringeth me atte rive	*at the shore*

---

[1] *They advised the King to rid [himself of a problem]*

[2] *You say I prevent my uncle from taking a wife*

1370	Schip and other thing.	
	Ye se me never olive	*alive*
	Bot yif ich Ysonde bring,	*Unless*
	That bright.	*fair one*
	Finde me min askeing,	*what I requested*
1375	Mine fiftend som of knight."	*fifteen knights in all*

	Knightes tho chosen thai	
	That were war and wise,	*skilled*
	Al that mest may	*might [do] the most*
	And heighest weren of priis.	*renown*
1380	A schip with grene and gray,	*green cloth and gray cloth*
	With vair and eke with griis,	*(see note); also*
	With alle thing, Y say,	
	That pende to marchandis	*pertain to buying and selling goods*
	In lede.	
1385	Thai ferden of this wise	*journeyed in this manner*
	Intil Yrlond thede.	*To the country of Ireland*

	In his schip was boun	*present*
	Al that mister ware.	*might be necessary*
	Out of Carlioun	
1390	Riche was his schip fare.	*ship's rigging (see note)*
	Thai rered goinfaynoun;	*raised; banner*
	A winde to wille hem bare.	*to their liking*
	Develin hat the toun	*The city was called Dublin*
	To lond thai comen thare,	*Where they came to land*
1395	The best.	
	The King present thai bare	*a gift*
	And asked leve to rest.	*permission*

	The King present thai brought,	*a gift*
	Another to the Quene;	
1400	Ysonde forgat thai nought,	
	To wite and nought at wene.	*Indeed and without a doubt*
	To schip when thai hem thought	*thought [to go]*
	That at the court hadde bene —	
	Swiche mayde nas never wrought	*created*
1405	That thai ever hadde sene	

With sight —
The cuntré alle bidene   *inhabitants [of the region]*
Thai seighe fle ful right.   *saw flee*

Out of Develin toun   *Dublin*
1410   The folk wel fast ran
In a water to droun,   *drown*
So ferd were thai than.   *frightened*
For doute of o dragoun   *fear*
Thai seyd to schip thai wan   *were going*
1415   To haven that were boun.   *a safe place; bound*
No rought thai of what man
In lede
That may him sle or can
Ysonde schal have to mede. [1]

1420   Tristrem, blithe was he.
He cleped his knightes stithe: *valiant*
"What man he is, las se,   *let's see*
That take this bataile swithe."   *might take; readily*
Alle thai beden lat be;   *asked to be left alone*
1425   Durst non himselven kithe.   *No one dared come forward*
"For nede now wo is me,"
Seyd Tristrem that sithe
Right than.
Listen now, who wil lithe   *hear*
1430   Al of an hardi man.

A stede of schip thai drewe,   *horse from the ship*
The best that he hadde brought.
His armes weren al newe,
That richeliche were wrought.   *richly*
1435   His hert was gode and trewe:
No failed it him nought.
The cuntré wele he knewe   *countryside*

---

[1] *They didn't care who the man might be / In all the world / Who might slay him [the dragon] or who knew how to; / He would have Ysonde as a reward.*

196

Er he the dragoun sought	*Before*
And seighe.	*saw*
1440 Helle-fere, him thought,	*Hell-fire it seemed to him*
Fram that dragoun fleighe.	*leapt forth*

Asaut to that dragoun	*Attack*
Tristrem toke that tide	*undertook*
As a lothely lioun	*fearsome*
1445 That bataile wald abide.	*would stand its ground in battle*
With a spere feloun	*deadly*
He smot him in the side.	
It no vailed o botoun;	*It availed not a bit*
Oway it gan to glide,	*It glanced aside*
1450 His dent.	*blow*
The devel dragouns hide	*fiendish*
Was hard so ani flint.	*as*

Tristrem, al in tene,	*rage*
Eft that spere tok he.	*Again*
1455 Ogain that dragoun kene	*Against; fierce*
It brast on peces thre.	*burst in three pieces*
The dragoun smot bidene;	*struck out quickly*
The stede he gan sle.	*He slew the horse*
Tristrem, withouten wene,	*doubt*
1460 Stirt under a tre	*Rushed*
Al stille	*securely*
And seyd, "God in Trinité,	
No lat thou me nought spille."	*die*

Ogain that fende dragoun	*fiendish*
1465 Afot he tok the fight.	*On foot*
He faught with his fauchoun	*sword*
As a douhti knight.	*bold*
His nether chavel he smot doun	*lower jaw; cut off*
With a stroke of might.	*powerful stroke*
1470 Tho was the dragon boun	*ready [with a response]*
And cast fere ful right	*fire*
And brend	*burned*
His armes that were bright;	

197

Schamliche he hath hem schent.   *Shamefully; disfigured*

1475   Swiche fer he cast ogain   *fire*
      That brend scheld and ston.   *burned*
      Now lith his stede yslain,   *lies*
      His armes brent ichon.   *each one*
      Tristrem raught his brain   *pierced*
1480   And brak his nek bon.   *neck bone*
      No was he never so fain   *glad*
      As than that batail was don.   *when*
      To bote,   *In addition*
      His tong hath he ton   *Its tongue has he taken*
1485   And schorn of bi the rote.   *cut off at the base*

      In his hose next the hide   *stocking; skin*
      The tong oway he bar.
      No yede he bot ten stride   *He didn't go even ten paces [when]*
      His speche les he thar.   *power of speech; lost*
1490   Nedes he most abide   *Necessarily; remain*
      That he no may ferther far.   *go*
      The steward com that tide;
      The heved oway he schar   *head; cut*
      And brought
1495   And tok it Ysonde thar   *To Isolt*
      And seyd dere he hadde hir bought.   *at a high price; won her*

      The steward wald ful fain
      Han Ysonde, yif he mought.   *Have; if; might*
      The King answerd ogain,   *replied*
1500   Fair the bataile him thought.   *seemed to him*
      Ysonde, nought to lain,
      Of him no wil sche nought.   *She didn't want him at all*
      There the dragoun was slain
      Hye and hir moder sought   *She*
1505   Al so
      Who that wonder wrought,
      That durst that dragoun slo.

      "Dede the steward this dede?"   *Did; deed*

"Certes," quath Ysonde, "nay.   *Surely; no*
1510   This ich brende stede   *very burned steed*
No aught he never a day,   *owned*
No this riche wede   *Nor; armor*
Nas never his, sothe to say."
Forther als thai yede,
1515   A man thai founde whare lay   *he lay*
And drough.   *had dragged [himself]*
"Certes," than seyd thai,
"This man the dragoun slough."   *slew*

His mouthe opened thai
1520   And pelt treacle in that man.   *put medicine*
When Tristrem speke may,
This tale he bigan
And redyli gan to say   *promptly*
Hou he the dragoun wan.   *defeated*
1525   "The tong Y bar oway;   *tongue; carried*
Thus venimed he me than."   *it poisoned me*
Thai loke.
The Quen that michel can   *who knows a great deal*
Out of his hose it toke.   *stocking*

1530   Thai seighen he hadde the right;   *saw he was in the right*
The steward hadde the wough.   *was in the wrong*
And yif he durst fight   *if he dared*
With him the dragoun slough,   *[who] slew the dragon*
Tristrem spak as a knight,
1535   He wold prove it anough.   *fully*
So noblelich he hem hight,   *nobly he vowed to them*
Therof Ysonde lough   *laughed*
That tide.
To his waraunt he drough   *He offered as a pledge*
1540   His schippe and al his pride.   *honor*

The Quen asked what he is
That durst the dragon abide.   *fight*
"Marchaunt icham, ywis;   *Merchant*
Mi schip lith here biside.   *nearby*

1545	He seyt he hath don this,	*He [who] says*
	Proven ichil his pride	*I will test his honor*
	Er he Ysonde kisse."	
	Ogaines him wald he ride	
	With might.	
1550	Ysonde seyd that tide,	
	"Allas that thou ner knight!"	*are not a knight*
	Her chaumpioun that day	
	Richeliche gun thai fede	
	Til hem think that he may	*it seems to them*
1555	Don a douhti dede.	*valiant deed*
	His armes, long were thai,	
	His scholders large on brede.	*in width*
	The Quen, for sothe to say,	
	To a bath gan him lede	*lead*
1560	Ful gayn,	*directly*
	And seththen hirself sche yede	*then*
	After a drink of main.	*potent drink*
	Ysonde, bright of hewe,	*fair of face*
	Thought it Tramtris ware.	
1565	His swerd, sche gan it schewe,	*examine*
	And broken hye fond it thare.	*she*
	Out of a cofer newe	
	The pece sche drough ful yare	*piece*
	And sett it to that trewe.	*fit it into that [sword] exactly*
1570	It nas lasse no mare,	*It was neither smaller or larger*
	Bot right.	*a perfect fit*
	Tho thought Ysonde with care	*sorrow*
	To sle Tristrem the knight.	*slay*
	Ysonde to Tristrem yode	*went*
1575	With his swerd al drain.	*drawn*
	"Moraunt, mi nem the gode,	*my uncle*
	Traitour, thou hast slain;	
	Forthi thine hert blode	
	Sen ich wold ful fain."	*See; gladly*
1580	The Quen whende sche were wode.	*thought she was mad*

200

	Sche com with a drink of main	*potent drink*
	And lough.	*laughed*
	"Nay, moder, nought to layn,	
	This thef thi brother slough.	*villain*
1585	"Tristrem, this thef is he;	
	That may be nought forlain.	*denied*
	The pece thou might her se	
	That fro mi nem was drain.	*my uncle; taken*
	Loke that it so be;	
1590	Sett it even ogain."	
	As quik thai wald him sle	
	Ther, Tristrem, ful fain,	
	Soth thing.	*True*
	In bath thai hadden him slain	*would have slain him*
1595	No were it for the King.	*Were it not for*
	And ever Tristrem lough	*smiled*
	On swete Ysonde the bright:	
	"Thou might have slain me ynough	
	Tho that Y Tramtris hight.	*When; was called*
1600	Ye witeth me with wough	*blame me wrongfully*
	Of Moraunt, the noble knight.	
	Y graunt wele ichim slough	*I slew him*
	In batayl and in fight,	
	Nought lain.	
1605	Yif he hadde had the might	
	So wold he me ful fain.	*would he [have slain] me*
	Tho Y Tramtris hight,	
	Y lerde the play and song,	*taught you*
	And ever with al mi might	
1610	Of the Y spac among	*conversed*
	To Marke, the riche knight,	
	That after the he gan long."	*he longed for you*
	So swore he day and night,	
	And borwes fond he strong	*he found sureties*
1615	Bidene,	
	Amendes of al wrong,	*compensation*

That Ysonde schuld be quen.

Tristrem swore that thing;
Thai seyd it schuld stand
1620 That he schuld Ysonde bring —
Thai token it under hand —   *They agreed to it*
To Mark, the riche king,
Olive yif thai him fand,   *Alive if*
And make hir with his ring
1625 Quen of Ingeland,
To say.
The forward fast thai band   *They firmly made the agreement*
Er thai parted oway.   *Before*

The steward forsoke his dede
1630 Tho he herd he Tristrem hight.   *was called*
The King swore, so God him spede,   *give him success*
That bothen schuld have right.   *justice*
The steward seyd wrong ther yede;   *(see note)*
Forthi nold he nought fight.   *Therefore he would not*
1635 Tristrem to his mede   *as his reward*
Thai yolden Ysonde the bright;   *gave*
To bring
To prisoun that other knight
The maiden biseketh the King.   *entreats*

1640 No asked he lond no lithe   *nor estate*
Bot that maiden bright.
He busked him al so swithe,   *prepared*
Bothe squier and knight.
Her moder about was blithe   *in turn*
1645 And tok a drink of might   *potent potion*
That love wald kithe   *induce*
And tok it Brengwain the bright   *entrusted*
To think,
"At er spouseing anight   *her wedding at night*
1650 Gif Mark and hir to drink."   *Give*

Ysonde, bright of hewe,   *fair of face*

	Is fer out in the se.	*far; sea*
	A winde ogain hem blewe	*against*
	That sail no might ther be.	
1655	So rewe the knightes trewe,	*rowed*
	Tristrem, so rewe he,	*rowed*
	Ever as thai com newe	*(see note to lines 1655–1659)*
	He on ogain hem thre,	
	Gret swink.	*labor*
1660	Swete Ysonde the fre	*noble*
	Asked Bringwain a drink.	
	The coupe was richeli wrought:	*cup*
	Of gold it was, the pin.	*(see note)*
	In al the warld nas nought	
1665	Swiche drink as ther was in.	
	Brengwain was wrong bithought.	*ill-advised*
	To that drink sche gan win	*went*
	And swete Ysonde it bitaught.	*gave*
	Sche bad Tristrem bigin,	
1670	To say.	*Indeed*
	Her love might no man tuin	*Their; separate*
	Til her ending day.	*their day of death*
	An hounde ther was biside	
	That was ycleped Hodain;	*called*
1675	The coupe he licked that tide	
	Tho doun it sett Bringwain.	*When*
	Thai loved al in lide	*(see note)*
	And therof were thai fain.	*happy*
	Togider thai gun abide	
1680	In joie and ek in pain	*also*
	For thought.	*(see note)*
	In ivel time, to sain,	*that is*
	The drink was ywrought.	*prepared*
	Tristrem in schip lay	
1685	With Ysonde ich night;	*each*
	Play miri he may	*Make love*
	With that worthli wight	*worthy person*

	In boure night and day.	*chamber*
	Al blithe was the knight,	*happy*
1690	He might with hir play.	*make love*
	That wist Brengwain the bright	*knew*
	As tho.	
	Thai loved with al her might	*their*
	And Hodain dede also.	

1695	Tuai wikes in the strand	*Two weeks; sea*
	No seyl thai no drewe.	*hoisted*
	Into Inglond	
	A winde to wille hem blewe.	*as they [had] wished*
	The King on hunting thai fand.	
1700	A knave that he knewe,	
	He made him knight with hand	
	For his tidinges newe	
	Gan bring.	
	Ysonde, bright of hewe,	
1705	Ther spoused Mark the King.	*wedded*

	He spoused hir with his ring;	
	Of fest no speke Y nought.	*the wedding feast*
	Brengwain, withouten lesing,	*in truth*
	Dede as hye had thought.	*she*
1710	Sche tok that love drink	
	That in Yrlond was bought.	
	For Ysonde to the King	*Instead of*
	Brengwain to bed was brought	
	That tide.	
1715	Mark his wille wrought	
	On bed Brengwain biside.	*In*

	When Mark had tint his swink,	*wasted his love-labor*
	Ysonde to bed yede;	*went*
	Of Yrlond hye asked drink; [1]	
1720	The coupe sche gan hir bede,	*offer*

---

[1] *She asked for the drink from Ireland*

204

Biside hir sche lete it sink.
Therof hadde sche no nede
Of non maner thing
Ogain Tristrem, in lede,   *With respect to Tristrem*
1725   As tho.
No might no clerk it rede,   *narrate*
The love bituen hem to.   *between those two*

Thai wende have joie anough;   *thought [they would] have*
Certes, it nas nought so.   *was not*
1730   Her wening was al wough,   *Their expectation; wrong*
Untroweand til hem to.   *False to the two of them*
Aither in langour drough   *Each fell into love-sickness*
And token rede to go;   *decided*
And seththen Ysonde lough   *(see note)*
1735   When Tristrem was in wo
With wille.
Now thenketh Ysonde to slo   *slay*
Brengwain and hir to spille.   *kill*

Sche thought, "Y may be wroth.   *angry*
1740   Sche lay first bi the King
For Y bihight hir cloth,   *promised*
Gold and riche wedding.
Tristrem and Y boathe   *both*
Beth schent for our playing.   *undone; intercourse*
1745   Better is that we rathe   *quickly*
Hir o live bring   *from life*
Al stille.
Than doute we for no thing   *fear*
That we ne may han our wille."

1750   The Quen bad her biside   *summoned to her*
To werkemen on a day.   *Two*
Sche told hem at that tide
What was her wille to say:
"Ye moten slen and hide   *must slay*
1755   Bringwain, that miri may."   *woman*
Sche seyd, "Ye schal abide   *You will live*

205

	Riche to ben ay	*To be rich forever*
	In lede.	
	No lete ye for no pay	
1760	That ye no do that dede." [1]	

	Into a grisly clough	*dreadful valley*
	Thai and that maiden yode.	*went*
	That on his swerd out drough;	*one; drew*
	That other bihinde hir stode.	
1765	Sche crid merci anough	*begged for mercy*
	And seyd, "For Cristes Rode!	*Cross*
	What have Y don wough?	*wrong*
	Whi wille ye spille mi blode?"	
	"Nought lain,	
1770	Ysonde, the levedi gode,	
	Hath hot thou schalt be slain."	*commanded*

	Brengwain dernly	*secretly*
	Bad hem say the Quen:	*Asked them to speak to the Queen*
	"Greteth wele mi levedy	
1775	That ai trewe hath ben.	*always*
	Smockes hadde sche and Y	*Chemises*
	And hir was solwy to sen,	*hers was dirty to look at*
	Bi Mark tho hye schuld ly.	*when she had to lie*
	Y lent hir min al clen,	
1780	As thare.	
	Ogain hir, wele Y wen,	*Against; expect*
	No dede Y never mare."	

	Thai nold hir nought slo	*slay*
	Bot went ogain to the Quen.	*back*
1785	Ysonde asked hem to,	*the two of them*
	"What seyd hye you bituen?"	
	"Hye bad ous say you so:	
	'Your smock was solwy to sen,	*chemise; dirty to look at*
	Bi Mark tho ye schuld ly;	

---

[1] *Do not forsake for any payment / Doing that deed*

206

1790 Y lent hir min al clene
   That day.'"
   Tho asked Ysonde the ken,   *wise*
   "Whare is that trewe may?"   *faithful woman*

   Tho seyd Ysonde with mode,   *passionately*
1795 "Mi maiden ye han slain."
   Sche swore bi Godes Rode   *Cross*
   Thai schuld ben hong and drain. *hanged; drawn*
   Sche bede hem giftes gode   *offered*
   To fechen hir ogain.   *bring her back*
1800 Thai fetten hir ther sche stode.   *brought*
   Tho was Ysonde ful fain,
   To say.   *Indeed*
   So trewe sche fond Brengwain
   That sche loved hir wele ay.   *always*

1805 Made was the saughtening   *reconciliation*
   And alle forgeve bidene.   *forgiven quickly*
   Tristrem, withouten lesing,
   Played with the Quen.
   Fram Irlond to the King
1810 An harpour com bituen.   *arrived*
   An harp he gan forth bring,
   Swiche no hadde thai never sen   *Such as*
   With sight.
   Himself, withouten wen,   *doubt*
1815 Bar it day and night.

   Ysonde he loved in are,   *in an honorable way*
   He that the harp brought.
   About his hals he it bare;   *neck*
   Richelich it was wrought.
1820 He hidde it evermare,
   Out no com it nought.
   "Thine harp whi wiltow spare, *Why won't you use your harp*
   Yif thou therof can ought   *If; know anything*
   Of gle?"   *music*
1825 "Out no cometh it nought

Withouten giftes fre."   *generous*

Mark seyd, "Lat me se   *Let me see*
Harpi hou thou can   *Play the harp*
And what thou askest me   *whatever*
1830   Give Y schal the than."
"Blethely," seyd he;   *Happily*
A miri lay he bigan.
"Sir King, of giftes fre,   *liberal in giving*
Herwith Ysonde Y wan   *earned*
1835   Bidene.
Y prove the for fals man
Or Y schal have thi Quen."   *Unless*

Mark to conseyl yede   *went*
And asked rede of tho to.[1]
1840   "Lesen Y mot mi manhed   *Lose; manly dignity*
Or yeld Ysonde me fro."   *surrender*
Mark was ful of drede;
Ysonde lete he go.
Tristrem in that nede
1845   At wode was, dere to slo,   *In the woods; to slay wild beasts*
That day.
Tristrem com right tho
As Ysonde was oway.[2]

Tho was Tristrem in ten   *in a rage*
1850   And chidde with the King: *scolded the King*
"Gifstow glewemen thi Quen?   *Do you give minstrels*
Hastow no nother thing?"
His rote, withouten wen,
He raught bi the ring;   *grasped*
1855   Tho folwed Tristrem the ken   *bold*
To schip ther thai hir bring
So blithe.

---

[1]*And asked advice about those two [alternatives]*
[2]*Tristrem came just / As Isolt had [gone] away*

208

Tristrem bigan to sing,
And Ysonde bigan to lithe.   *listen*

1860   Swiche song he gan sing
That hir was swithe wo.   *sorrowful*
Her com swiche lovelonging,
Hir hert brast neighe ato.   *nearly burst in two*
Th'erl to hir gan spring   *The earl*
1865   With knightes mani mo
And seyd, "Mi swete thing,
Whi farestow so,   *Why do you carry on so*
Y pray?"
Ysonde to lond most go   *had to*
1870   Er sche went oway.   *Before*

"Within a stounde of the day   *brief time*
Y schal ben hole and sounde.
Ich here a menstrel; to say,   *hear*
Of Tristrem he hath a soun."   *sound*
1875   Th'erl seyd, "Dathet him ay   *The earl; (see note)*
Of Tristrem yif this stounde.   *(see note)*
That minstrel for his lay
Schal have an hundred pounde
Of me   *From*
1880   Yif he wil with ous founde,   *If; go with us*
Lef, for thou lovest his gle."   *Beloved; music*

His gle al for to here
The levedi was sett on land
To play bi the rivere;
1885   Th'erl ladde hir bi hand.
Tristrem, trewe fere,   *companion*
Mirie notes he fand   *Delightful; played*
Opon his rote of yvere   *ivory*
As thai were on the strand   *shore*
1890   That stounde.   *time*
Thurch that semly sand   *Through; comforting message*
Ysonde was hole and sounde.

Hole sche was and sounde
Thurch vertu of his gle.   *efficacy of his music*
1895   Forthi th'erl that stounde,   *time*
Glad a man was he.
Of penis to hundred pounde   *(see note to line 420); two*
He gaf Tristrem the fre.
To schip than gun thai founde;   *go*
1900   In Yrlond wald thai be
Ful fain,
Th'erl and knightes thre
With Ysonde and Bringwain.

Tristrem tok his stede   *horse*
1905   And lepe theron to ride.   *leapt*
The Quen bad him her lede   *asked; bring*
To schip him biside.
Tristrem dede as hye bede;   *did as she asked*
In wode he gan hir hide.   *the woods*
1910   To th'erl he seyd, "In that nede
Thou hast ytent thi pride,   *lost*
Thou dote.   *fool*
With thine harp thou wonne hir that tide;
Thou tint hir with mi rote."   *lost*

1915   Tristrem with Ysonde rade   *rode*
Into the wode oway.
A loghe thai founden made   *dwelling*
Was ful of gamen and play.   *mirth*
Her blis was ful brade,   *abundant*
1920   And joieful was that may.   *woman*
Seven night thai thare abad   *remained*
And seththen to court com thai.   *then*
"Sir King,"
Tristrem gan to say,
1925   "Gif minstrels other thing."   *Give; something else*

Meriadok was a man
That Tristrem trowed ay.   *trusted*
Miche gode he him an.   *Much; wished*

	In o chaumber thai lay.	*one room*
1930	Tristrem to Ysonde wan	*went*
	A night with hir to play.	*make love*
	As man that miche kan,	*knew a great deal*
	A bord he toke oway	*board*
	Of her bour.	*From their room*
1935	Er he went, to say,	*Before*
	Of snowe was fallen a schour.	*shower*

	A schour ther was yfalle	
	That al the way was white.	*So that*
	Tristrem was wo withalle,	*distressed*
1940	With diol and sorwe and site.	*apprehension; sorrow; anguish*
	Bituen the bour and the halle	
	The way was naru and lite.	*narrow; constricted*
	Swiche cas him was bifalle	*predicament*
	As we finde in scrite.	*in writing*
1945	Ful sket	
	A sive he fond tite	*sieve*
	And bond under his fete.	*tied*

	Meriadok with his might	*with [all] his might*
	Aros up al bidene.	
1950	The way he went right	
	Til he com to the Quen.	
	The bord he fond of-tuight,	*removed*
	To wite and nought at wene.	
	Of Tristrem kertel the knight	*cloak*
1955	He fond a pece grene	*piece*
	Of tore.	*Torn off*
	Meriadok the kene	*bold*
	Wondred therfore.	

	A morwe he tolde the King	*In the morning*
1960	Al that he seighe with sight.	*saw*
	"Lord, withouten lesing,	*lying*
	With Ysonde lay Tristrem to night.	
	Thou schalt do swiche a thing,	
	Aske who her yeme might.	*who might take care of her*

1965   The croice to Jerusalem bring[1]

Say thou hast yhight,   *vowed*

Yif thou may.

'Tristrem the noble knight,'

The Quen hirself wil say."

1970   The King told the Quen,

Abed tho thai ware,

"Dame, withouten wene,

To Jerusalem Y mot fare;   *must go*

Loke now ous bituene   *Let's consider*

1975   Who may the kepe fram care."   *protect from harm*

"For al other bidene   *Instead of*

Tristrem," sche seyd thare,

"For than   *Because*

Y love him wele the mare

1980   He is thi kinsseman."

Al that Mark hir told

A morwe hye told Bringwain: *In the morning she*

"Of lond wil this bold.   *From [this] land will [go]*

Now we may be ful fain.

1985   Tristrem the court schal hold   *govern*

Til he com ogain."   *[he = Mark]*

Brengwain answere yolde,   *returned*

"Your dedes han ben sain   *observed*

With sight.

1990   Mark thiself schal frain   *ask*

Al otherloker tonight.   *Entirely in a different way*

"Wite thou wele his wille;   *Know well what he intends*

To wende with him thou say,   *go; (see note)*

And yif he loveth the stille,

1995   'Thou do Tristrem oway'   *send*

Biseche him he se thertille,   *see in addition*

Thi fo is Tristrem ay.

---

[1]*To go on a pilgrimage to Jerusalem*

	Thou dredest he wil the spille	*kill you*
	Yif he the maistrie may	*If he might control you*
2000	Above;	
	Thou lovedest him never a day	
	Bot for his emes love."	*uncle's*

	Ysonde the nexst night	
	Crid, "Mark, thi nore!	*your mercy*
2005	Mi fo thou hast me hight;	*entrusted me to*
	On me thou sinnes sore.	
	Gode yif thou hadde me hight[1]	
	Of lond with the to fare,	*From*
	And sle Tristrem the knight,	*slay*
2010	Yif love of the no ware,	*If it weren't for [my] love of you*
	This day;	
	For mani man seyt aywhare	*everywhere*
	That Tristrem bi me lay."	

	Mark is blithe and glad,	
2015	For al that trowed he.	*believed*
	He that him other tald,	*otherwise*
	He ne couthe him bot maugré.	*He bore him only ill-will*
	Meriadok him answere yald,	*gave*
	"In toun thou do him be.	*cause him to be*
2020	Her love laike thou bihald	*Their; play you will behold*
	For the love of me,	
	Nought wene.	*Without a doubt*
	Bi resoun thou schalt se	
	That love is hem bituene."	

2025	Mark departed hem to	*separated those two*
	And dede Tristrem oway;	*removed Tristrem*
	Nas never Ysonde so wo	*sad*
	No Tristrem, sothe to say.	*Nor; truth*
	Ysonde herself wald slo;	*slay*
2030	For sorwe Tristrem lay.	*lay [sick]*

---

[1]*[It would have been] good if you had commanded me*

213

Ysonde morned so
And Tristrem night and day
For dede.   *As a result*
Ich man it se may,   *Each*
2035   What liif for love thai lede.   *life*

Tristrem was in toun;
In boure Ysonde was don.   *put*
Bi water he sent adoun
Light linden spon.   *chip of linden wood*
2040   He wrot hem al with roun;   *inscribed characters*
Ysonde hem knewe wel sone.   *right away*
Bi that Tristrem was boun   *ready*
Ysonde wist his bone   *knew; request*
To abide.   *await [him]*
2045   Er amorwe none   *Before noon the next day*
Her aither was other biside.   *Each of them*

Quath Meriadok, "Y rede   *advise*
Thine hunters thou bid ride
Fourtennight at this nede   *Fortnight*
2050   To se thine forestes wide.   *inspect*
Tristrem thou hem bede.   *(see note)*
Thiself thou here abide,   *wait*
And right at her dede   *right in the act*
Thou schalt hem take that tide.
2055   In the tre,
Here thou schalt abide;
Her semblaunt thou schalt se."   *Their deceitful behavior*

In orchard mett thai inne,
Tristrem and Ysonde fre.
2060   Ay when thai might awinne,   *accomplish [it]*
Ther playd Ysonde and he.   *made love*
The duerve yseighe her ginne   *dwarf saw their trickery*
Ther he sat in the tre.
Mark of riche kinne
2065   He hight to don him se   *called on to make him see*
With sight

214

And seyd, "Sir, siker ye be, *convinced*
Thiself schal se that right."

His falsnesse for to fille *treachery; fulfill*
2070 Forth tho went he.
To Tristrem he com with ille *with malicious intention*
Fram Ysonde the fre.
"Mi levedy me sent the tille *to*
For icham privé, *I am discreet*
2075 And praieth the with wille *[she] beseeches you earnestly*
That thou wost hir se *wouldst*
With sight.
Mark is in other cuntré; *region*
Privé it schal be dight." *Secretly; arranged*

2080 Tristrem him bithought. *devised a strategy*
"Maister, thank have ye
For thou me this bode brought. *Because; message*
Mi robe give Y the
That thou no lete it nought *neglect*
2085 Say that levedy fre *To tell*
Hir wordes dere Y bought. *dearly I payed for*
To Marke hye bileighe me, *she slanders*
That may. *woman*
Tomorwe Y schal hir se
2090 At chirche, for sothe to say." *church*

The duerve toke the gate, *went away*
And Mark he told bidene,
"Bi this robe Y wate *know*
That michel he loveth the Quene. *greatly*
2095 Ysame we nought no sat. *We didn't agree*
He douteth me bituene. *feared*
It semeth by his lat *expression*
As he hir never had sene
With sight.
2100 Y wot withouten wene *know without a doubt*
He cometh to hir tonight."

Sir Mark sat in the tre
Ther metten thai to.   *Where those two met*
The schadowe Tristrem gan se
2105   And loude spac he tho,   *spoke*
That Ysonde schuld Mark se
And calle Tristrem hir fo: *enemy*
"Thou no aughtest nought here to be;   *ought not*
Thou no hast nought here to go
2110   No thing.
With right, men schuld the slo,
Durst Y, for the King.[1]

"Ysonde, thou art mi fo;
Thou sinnest, levedi, on me.
2115   Thou gabbest on me so   *lie about*
Mi nem nil me nought se.   *My uncle will not*
He threteneth me to slo.   *kill*
More menske were it to the   *honor*
Better for to do,
2120   Bi God in Trinité,
This tide.
Or Y this lond schal fle   *Otherwise*
Into Wales wide."

"Tristrem, for sothe to say,
2125   Y wold the litel gode,   *wished*
Ac Y the wraied never day,   *But I never accused you*
Y swere bi Godes Rode.   *Cross*
Men said thou bi me lay,
Thine em so understode.   *uncle*
2130   Wende forth in thi way;   *Go*
It semes astow were wode,   *as if you were mad*
To wede.   *rage*
Y loved never man with mode   *passionately*
Bot him that hadde mi maidenhede."

---

[1]*If [only] I dared, [but I don't] because of the King*

2135	"Swete Ysonde, thi nare!	*your mercy*
	Thou preye the King for me,	
	Yif it thi wille ware	
	Of sake he make me fre.	*blame*
	Of lond ichil elles fare;	*I will otherwise go*
2140	Schal he me never se."	
	Markes hert was sare	*distressed*
	Ther he sat in the tre	
	And thought,	
	"Ungiltles er ye	*Guiltless (see note)*
2145	In swiche a sclaunder brought."	*slander*

	"Thou seyst Y gan the wrie;	*I slandered you*
	Men seis thou bi me lay,	*say*
	Ac thei ich wende to dye,[1]	
	Thine erand Y schal say.	*message*
2150	Marke thi nem his heighe;	*your uncle is powerful*
	Anough he the give may.	
	No reche Y what Y lighe,	*I don't care how much I lie*
	So that thou be oway	
	With wille."	
2155	Marke tho thought ay,	
	"Yete he schal duelle stille."	*remain*

	Tristrem oway went so,	
	Ysonde to boure, ywis.	
	Nas never Mark so wo;	*sorrowful*
2160	Himself he herd al this.	
	Al sori Mark gan go	*sad*
	Til he might Tristrem kisse;	
	And dedely hated he tho	
	Him that seyd amis.	*spoke evil [about Tristrem]*
2165	Al newe	*All over again*
	Ther was joie and blis,	
	And welcom Tristrem trewe.	

---

[1]*But though I thought [myself] to die [as a result]*

Now hath Ysonde her wille:
Tristrem constable is heighe.   *(see note)*
2170 Thre yere he playd stille
With Ysonde bright so beighe.   *as a jewel*
Her love might no man felle,   *Their; destroy*
So were thai bothe sleighe.   *clever*
Meriadok with ille
2175 Waited hem ful neighe   *Spied on them very closely*
Of her dede.   *conduct*
Yif he might hem spille,   *If; undo them*
Fain he wald spede.   *Gladly would he accomplish it*

Meriadok wrayeth ay.   *makes accusations continually*
2180 To the King thus seyd he:
"Her folies usen thai ay;   *Their lechery they practice perpetually*
Wel yore Y seyd it the.   *Long ago*
Loke now on a day
And blod lat you thre.
2185 Do as Y the say,
And tokening thou schalt se   *evidence*
Ful sone.
Her bed schal blodi bene
Ar he his wille have done."   *Before*

2190 Blod leten was the King,
Tristrem and the Quene.
At her blod leteing
The flore was swopen clene.   *swept*
Meriadok dede floure bring
2195 And strewed it bituene
That go no might no thing
Bot yif it were sene
With sight.
Thritti fet bidene   *all together*
2200 Tristrem lepe that night.   *leapt*

Now Tristrem willes is   *Tristrem is of a mind (see note)*
With Ysonde for to play.
He no may hir com to kisse,

218

So ful of floure it lay.
2205 Tristrem lepe, ywis,   *leapt*
Thritti fete, soth to say.
As Tristrem dede this,
His blod bende brast oway   *bandage burst*
And bled;
2210 And seththen ogain the day   *then with the arrival of the day*
He lepe fram hir bedde.   *leapt*

Thritti fete bituene
He lepe, withouten les.   *in truth*
Sore him greved his vene,   *Grievously he injured his vein*
2215 As it no wonder nes.   *was not*
Mark her bed hadde sen,
And al blodi it wes.   *was*
He told tho Brengwain
Tristrem hadde broken his pes   *broken the peace he made*
2220 Bituene.
Anon of lond he ches   *from; went*
Out of Markes eiye-sene.   *sight*

Tristrem was fled oway,
To wite and nought to wene.   *Indeed and without a doubt*
2225 At Londen on a day,   *London*
Mark wald spourge the Quen.   *exonerate*
Men seyd sche brak the lay.   *law*
A bischop yede bituene.   *arrived*
With hot yren, to say,
2230 Sche thought to make hir clene   *prove her innocence*
Of sake.   *guilt*
Ysonde said bidene   *forthwith*
That dome sche wald take.   *sentence she would receive*

Men sett the merkes there   *(see note)*
2235 At Westeminster ful right,
Hot yren to bere   *carry*
For Sir Tristrem the knight.
In pouer wede to were   *Dressed in shabby clothing*
Tristrem com that night

219

2240	(Of alle the knightes here	
	No knewe him non bi sight	*None recognized him*
	Bidene)	*Indeed*
	To swete Ysonde bright	
	As forward was hem bituene.	*As they had agreed*
2245	Over Temes sche schuld ride,	*the Thames*
	That is an arm of the se.	*sea*
	"To the schip side	
	This man schal bere me."	
	Tristrem hir bar that tide	
2250	And on the Quen fel he	
	Next her naked side	
	That mani man might yse	*see*
	San schewe.	*Without [taking much] notice*
	Hir queynt aboven hir kne	*sexual organs*
2255	Naked the knightes knewe.	
	In water thai wald him sink	*drown*
	And wers, yif thai may.	*worse if*
	"Ye quite him ivel his swink,"	*repay; labor*
	The Quene seyd to hem ay.	
2260	"It semeth mete no drink	*food nor*
	Hadde he nought mani a day.	
	For poverté, methenk,	*it seems to me*
	He fel, for sothe to say,	
	And nede.	
2265	Geveth him gold, Y pray;	
	He may bidde God me spede."	*ask God to grant me success*
	Gold thai goven him thare.	*gave*
	The constori thai bigan.	*trial*
	Swete Ysonde sware	
2270	Sche was giltles woman:	
	"Bot on to schip me bare — [1]	
	The knightes seighe wele than	

---

[1]*Except for the one [who] carried me to the ship*

	Whatso his wille ware;	
	Ferli neighe he wan,	*Marvelously near he reached*
2275	Sothe thing —	*Truly*
	So neighe com never man	
	Bot mi lord, the King."	
	Swete Ysonde hath sworn	
	Hir clene, that miri may.	*That she is pure; fair woman*
2280	To hir thai had ycorn	*chosen*
	Hot yren, Y say.	
	The knightes were biforn;	*present*
	For hir tho praiden thai.	*prayed*
	The yren sche hadde yborn,	*carried*
2285	Ac Mark forgave that day	*And*
	And dede.	*(see note)*
	Meriadok held thai	
	For fole in his falshede.	*a sinner*
	Ysonde is graunted clene	*acknowledged [to be] pure*
2290	Meriadok, maugré his.	*(see note)*
	Never er nas the Quen	*Never before was*
	So wele with Mark, ywis.	*On such good terms with*
	Tristrem, withouten wene,	
	Into Wales he is.	
2295	In bataile he hath ben	
	And fast he fraines this	*eagerly he seeks this*
	Right thare.	
	For he ne may Ysonde kisse,	*Because*
	Fight he sought aywhare.	*everywhere*
2300	In Wales tho was a king	
	That hight Triamour.	*Who was called*
	He hadde a douhter ying,	*young*
	Was hoten Blauncheflour.	*named*
	Urgan with gret wering	*military force*
2305	Biseged him in his tour	*tower*
	To winne that swete thing	
	And bring hir to his bour	*hall*
	With fight.	

221

	Tristrem with gret honour	
2310	Bicom the Kinges knight.	
	Urgan gan Wales held	
	With wrong, for sothe to say;	*Wrongfully*
	Oft and unselde	*frequently*
	Of Triamour tok he pray.	*From; he seized booty*
2315	Triamour to Tristrem teld,	
	Opon a somers day,	
	Wales he wald him yeld	*give*
	Yif he it winne may	*conquer*
	Right than.	
2320	Tristrem, withouten nay,	*without fail*
	With were Wales wan.	*danger [to himself]; conquered*
	Tristrem mett Urgan	
	In that feld to fight.	*battlefield*
	To him seyd he than	
2325	As a douhti knight,	*bold*
	"Thou slough mi brother Morgan	*slew*
	At the mete ful right.	*(see note)*
	As Y am douhti man,	
	His deth thou bist tonight,	*you will pay for*
2330	Mi fo."	*enemy*
	Tristrem seyd, "Aplight,	*Indeed*
	So kepe Y the to slo."	*want; slay*
	Tuelve fete was the wand	*Twelve feet long was the club*
	That Urgan wald with play.	*fight*
2335	His strok may no man stand.	*withstand*
	Ferly yif Tristrem may!	*[It is] a wonder if*
	Tristrem vantage fand;	*opportunity*
	His clobbe fel oway;	*His [the giant's] club missed [Tristrem]*
	And of the geauntes hand	*off*
2340	Tristrem smot that day	*struck*
	In lede.	
	Tristrem, for sothe to say,	
	The geaunt gert he blede.	*made*

Urgan, al in tene, — *rage*
2345 Faught with his left hand
Ogain Tristrem kene. — *bold*
A stern stroke he fand — *mighty; experienced*
Opon his helme so schene, — *bright*
That to the grounde he wand. — *went*
2350 Bot up he stirt bidene — *leapt quickly*
And heried Godes sand — *praised God's grace*
Almight.
Tristrem with his brand — *sword*
Fast gan to fight.

2355 The geaunt aroume he stode; — *at a distance*
His hond he tint, ywis. — *lost*
He fleighe as he were wode, — *fled as if he were mad*
Ther that the castel is.
Tristrem trad in the blod — *trod*
2360 And fond the hond that was his.
Away Sir Tristrem yode. — *went*
The geaunt com with this
And sought
To hele his honde that was his.
2365 Salves hadde he brought.

Urgan, the geaunt unride, — *terrible*
After Sir Tristrem wan. — *went*
The cuntré fer and wide — *inhabitants [of the countryside]*
Ygadred was bi than. — *Assembled*
2370 Tristrem thought that tide,
"Y take that me Gode an." — *grants*
On a brigge he gan abide, — *bridge*
Biheld ther mani a man.
Thai mett.
2375 Urgan to Tristrem ran,
And grimli there thai gret. — *fiercely; attacked*

Strokes of michel might — *great force*
Thai delten hem bituene, — *exchanged*
That thurch her brinies bright — *through their coats of mail*

223

2380	Her bother blod was sene.	*Of both of them*
	Tristrem faught as a knight;	
	And Urgan, al in tene,	*rage*
	Gaf him a stroke unlight:	
	His scheld he clef bituene	*split*
2385	A tuo,	*In two*
	Tristrem, withouten wene,	*doubt*
	Nas never are so wo.	*before; distressed*
	Eft Urgan smot with main,	*Again; struck; force*
	And of that stroke he miste.	*with; missed*
2390	Tristrem smot ogayn	*struck back*
	And thurch his body he threste.	*through; pierced*
	Urgan lepe unfain;	*leapt unhappily*
	Over the bregge he deste.	*bridge; (see note)*
	Tristrem hath Urgan slain,	
2395	That alle the cuntré wist	*inhabitants knew*
	With wille.	
	The King tho Tristrem kist	
	And Wales tho yeld him tille.	*then gave to him*
	The King, a welp he brought	*puppy*
2400	Bifor Tristrem the trewe.	
	What colour he was wrought	
	Now ichil you schewe —	*I will*
	Silke nas non so soft —	
	He was rede, grene and blewe.	*red; blue*
2405	Thai that him seighen oft	*saw*
	Of him hadde gamen and glewe,	*pleasure and amusement*
	Ywis.	
	His name was Peticrewe;	
	Of him was michel priis.	*much worth*
2410	The King Triamour	
	Gaf him Tristrem the hende,	*Gave him [the dog] to Tristrem the courtly*
	For he brought out of dolour	*sorrow*
	Him and al his kende.	*people*
	Tristrem with gret honour	
2415	Kidde that he was hende:	*Revealed; noble*

He gaf to Blauncheflour
Wales withouten end   *in perpetuity*
Bidene,
And Peticrowe he gan sende
2420   To Dame Ysonde, the Quene.

Ysonde, withouten les,   *in truth*
Tho hye the welp had sain,   *When she had seen the puppy*
That sche had made his pes   *peace*
Sche sent word ogayn.   *in reply*
2425   Mark herd hou it wes
That Urgan had he slain.
Messangers he ches   *selected*
Tristrem for to frain,   *request to come*
That fre.
2430   Mark was ferly fain,   *wondrously glad*
And Tristrem kist he.

Mark gan Tristrem calle
And toke him al bidene   *entrusted to him*
Cités, castels alle,
2435   Steward as he hadde bene.   *As if he had been a steward*
Who was blithe in halle
Bot Ysonde the Quene?
Houso it schuld bifalle,   *However*
Thai playden al bituene,   *made love*
2440   Tho tuo.   *Those two*
So long of love thai mene   *complain*
That Mark seighe it was so.   *saw*

Mark seighe hou it is,   *saw how*
What love was hem bituene.
2445   Certes this thought was his,
Ful wele awreken to ben.   *avenged*
He cleped Tristrem with this   *called*
And bitoke him the Quene   *entrusted to him*
And flemed hem bothe, ywis,   *exiled*
2450   Out of his eiye-sene   *sight*
Away.

	Blither, withouten wene,	*Happier*
	Never ere nar thay.	*Never before were they*
	A forest fled thai tille,	*to*
2455	Tristrem and Ysonde the schene.	*beautiful*
	No hadde thai no won to wille	*dwelling at their disposal*
	Bot the wode so grene.	
	Bi holtes and bi hille	*woods*
	Fore Tristrem and the Quene.	*Lived*
2460	Ysonde of joie hath her fille	
	And Tristrem, withouten wene,	
	As thare.	
	So blithe al bidene	
	Nar thai never are.	*Were not; before*
2465	Tristrem and that may	*woman*
	Wer flemed for her dede.	*exiled*
	Hodain, soth to say,	
	And Peticrowe with hem yede.	*went*
	In on erthe hous thai lay;	*a cave*
2470	Tho raches with hem thai lede.	*Those hunting dogs*
	Tristrem hem taught o day	
	Bestes to take at nede	
	An hast.	*Quickly*
	In that forest fede	*(see note)*
2475	Tristrem Hodain gan chast.	*train*
	Tristrem with Hodain	
	A wilde best he slough.	*slew*
	In on erthe house thai layn	*a cave*
	Ther hadde thai joie ynough.	*Where; enough*
2480	Etenes bi old dayn	*Giants in the old days*
	Had wrought it, withouten wough.	*truly*
	Ich night, soth to sain,	*Each; say*
	Thertil thai bothe drough	*Thereto; approached*
	With might.	*Eagerly*
2485	Under wode bough	*In the woods*
	Thai knewen day and night.	*experienced*

	In winter it was hate;	*warm*
	In somer it was cold.	*cool*
	Thai hadden a dern gat	*secret entrance*
2490	That thai no man told.	
	No hadde thai no wines wat,	*liquid*
	No ale that was old;	
	No no gode mete thai at.	*ate*
	Thai hadden al that thai wold	*wanted*
2495	With wille.	
	For love ich other bihalt,	*(see note)*
	Her non might of other fille. [1]	

	Tristrem on an hille stode	
	As he biforn hadde mett.	*chanced upon*
2500	He fond a wele ful gode;	*well*
	Al white it was, the grete.	*gravel*
	Therto Tristrem yode	
	And hende Ysonde the swete.	
	That was al her fode	*their sustenance*
2505	And wilde flesche thai ete	*ate*
	And gras.	
	Swiche joie hadde thai never yete	
	Tuelmoneth thre woukes las.	*(see note)*

	Tristrem on a day	
2510	Tok Hodain wel erly;	
	A best he tok to pray	*as prey*
	Bi a dern sty.	*secluded path*
	He dight it, withouten nay,	*dressed; truly*
	And hom it brought an heighe.	*in haste*
2515	Aslepe Ysonde lay;	
	Tristrem him layd hir bi,	
	The Quen.	
	His swerd he drough titly	*drew quickly*
	And laid it hem bituene.	
2520	An hert Mark at ran	*hart; pursued*

---

[1] *Neither of them might be sated with the other*

227

Opon that ilke day;   *very day*
His hunters after wan;   *went*
A path tho founden thai.
Tristrem seighen hye than   *they saw*
2525 And Ysonde, sothe to say.
Seighe thai never swiche man
No non so fair a may
With sight.
Bituen hem ther lay
2530 A drawen swerd wel bright.

The huntes wenten right   *hunters; directly*
And teld Mark bidene.
The levedi and the knight
Bothe Mark hath sene.
2535 He knewe hem wele bi sight.
The swerd lay hem bituene.
A sonnebem ful bright   *sunbeam*
Schon opon the Quen
At a bore   *crevice*
2540 On her face so schene.
And Mark rewed therfore.   *had pity*

His glove he put therinne,
The sonne to were oway.   *ward off*
Wrethe Mark gan winne;   *Mark overcame [his] wrath*
2545 Than seyd he, "Wel ay,
Yif thai weren in sinne,
Nought so thai no lay.   *They would not lie thus*
Lo hou thai line atuinne!   *lie apart*
Thai no hede nought of swiche play,[1]
2550 Ywis."
The knightes seyden, "Ay,
For trewe love it is."

Tho waked Tristrem the trewe

---

[1] *They do not care about such sexual play*

	And swete Ysonde the schene,	
2555	The glove oway thai drewe	
	And seyden hem bituene	
	For Markes thai it knewe.	
	Thai wist he had ther bene.	
	Tho was her joie al newe,	*Then was their joy totally changed*
2560	That he hem hadde ysene	
	With sight.	
	With that com knightes kene	
	To feche tho to ful right.	*those two*

	To court were comen tho to	*those two*
2565	That in the forest were;	*had been*
	Mark kist Ysonde tho	*then*
	And Tristrem trewe fere.	*companion*
	Forgeven hem was her wo;	*them; their*
	No were thai never so dere.	
2570	Tristrem the bailif gan to	*office of bailiff; take*
	Swiftly for to stere	*govern*
	A stounde.	*For a time*
	Of love who wil lere,	*learn*
	Listen now the grounde.	*substance of the tale*

2575	So bifel bidene	
	Opon a somers day	
	Tristrem and the Quen	
	Stalked to her play.	*Walked cautiously; sexual play*
	The duerve hem hath sene;	*dwarf*
2580	To Mark gan he say,	
	"Sir King, withouten wene,	
	Thi wiif is now oway	
	And thi knight.	
	Wende fast as thou may,	*Go*
2585	Oftake hem, yif thou might."	*Overtake*

	Mark King after ran;	
	That thai bothe ysé.	*see*
	Tristrem seyd than,	
	"Ysonde, schent er we	*undone*

229

2590	For thoughtes that we can,	*(see note)*
	For hole no may it be."	*rectified*
	Nas never so sori man,	
	Tristrem than was he,	
	That hende.	*noble man*
2595	"For dout of deth Y fle,	*fear*
	In sorwe and wo Y wende.	*go*
	"Y fle for dout of deth;	*fear*
	Y dar no leng abide	*longer*
	In wo mi liif to lede	
2600	Bi this forestes side."	
	A ring Ysonde him bede	*gave*
	To tokening at that tide.	*As a token*
	He fleighe forth in gret drede	*fled*
	In wode him for to hide	
2605	Bidene.	
	To seken him fast thai ride;	*look for*
	Thai founden bot the Quene.	*only*
	Tristrem is went oway	*gone*
	As it nought hadde ybene.	
2610	Forthi the knightes gan say	
	That wrong Markes had sen.	
	For her than prayd thai	*pleaded*
	That Mark forgaf the Quene.	*forgave*
	Tristrem with Ysonde lay	
2615	That night, withouten wene,	
	And wok	
	And plaiden ay bituene.	*made love*
	His leve of hir he tok.	
	Tristrem is went oway	
2620	Withouten coming ogain	
	And siketh, for sothe to sain,	*sighs*
	With sorwe and michel pain.	*much*
	Tristrem fareth ay	*conducts himself*
	As man that wald be slain,	*wanted to be*
2625	Bothe night and day,	

Fightes for to frain,   *seek*
That fre.
Spaine he hath thurchsayn;   *searched through*
Geauntes he slough thre.   *Giants; slew*

2630   Out of Spaine he rade,   *rode*
      Rohande sones to se.
      Gamen and joie thai made;   *They were pleased and joyful*
      Welcom to hem was he.   *them*
      As lord he ther abade,   *resided*
2635   As gode skil wald be.   *As was reasonable*
      Thai boden him landes brade   *promised; spacious*
      That he wan hem fre.   *That he freed for them by fighting*
      He thought;
      He seyd, "Thank have ye.
2640   Your londes kepe Y nought."

      Into Bretein he ches,   *went*
      Bicome the Doukes knight.
      He set his lond in pes
      That arst was ful of fight.   *in the past*
2645   Al that the Doukes wes   *All that belonged to the Duke*
      He wan ogain with right.   *conquered*
      He bede him, withouten les,[1]
      His douhter that was bright   *beautiful*
      In land.
2650   That maiden Ysonde hight   *was called*
      With the White Hand.

      Tristremes love was strong
      On swete Ysonde the Quene.   *For*
      Of Ysonde he made a song
2655   That song Ysonde bidene.   *celebrated; indeed*
      The maiden wende al wrong   *thought entirely erroneously*
      Of hir it hadde ybene.   *About*

---

[1] *He [the Duke] offered him [Tristrem], in truth*

	Hir wening was so long,[1]	
	To hir fader hye gan mene	*she complained*
2660	For nede.	
	Ysonde with hand schene	*bright*
	Tristrem to wive thai bede.	*offered*

	Tristrem a wil is inne,	*Tristrem has formed an opinion*
	Has founden in his thought:	*[Which he] has arrived at in his sorrow*
2665	"Mark, mi nem, hath sinne;	*my uncle*
	Wrong he hath ous wrought.	*us*
	Icham in sorwe and pine;	
	Therto hye hath me brought.	*she*
	Hir love, Y say, is mine;	
2670	The Boke seyt it is nought	*Bible*
	With right."	
	The maiden more he sought	
	For sche Ysonde hight.	*was called*

	That in his hert he fand	*(see note)*
2675	And trewely thought he ay.	*continuously*
	The forward fast he band	*agreement; made*
	With Ysonde; that may	*maiden*
	With the white hand	
	He spoused that day.	*married*
2680	O night, ich understand,	*At night*
	To boure wenten thai	*bedroom*
	On bedde.	
	Tristrem ring fel oway	*Tristrem's*
	As men to chaumber him ledde.	

	Tristrem biheld that ring;	
2685	Tho was his hert ful wo.	
	"Ogain me swiche a thing	
	Dede never Ysonde so.	
	Mark, her lord, the King,	
2690	With tresoun may hir to.	*take*

---

[1] *Her hope [of receiving Tristrem's love] lasted so long [without fulfillment]*

Mine hert may no man bring
For no thing hir fro,
That fre.
Ich have tuinned ous to;   *separated the two of us*
2695   The wrong is al in me."

Tristrem to bedde yede
With hert ful of care.   *grief*
He seyd, "The dern dede,   *private act*
Do it Y no dare."
2700   The maiden he forbede
Yif it hir wille ware.   *If she should wish it*
The maide answerd in lede,
"Therof have thou no care   *Don't worry about that*
Al stille.   *Ever*
2705   Y nil desiri na mare   *will not*
Bot at thine owen wille."

Her fader on a day
Gaf hem londes wide
Fer in that cuntray —
2710   Markes were set biside.   *Boundary markers*
Bituene the Douke thai had ben ay
And a geaunt unride.   *fearsome*
No most ther no man play   *might; enjoy himself*
That he no dede him abide [1]
2715   And fight.
Lesen he schuld his pride,   *Lose*
Were he king or knight.

"Tristrem, Y the forbede,
For the love of me,
2720   No hunte thou for no nede
Biyond the arm of the se.   *sea*
Beliagog is unrede;   *fearsome*
A stern geaunt is he.   *fierce*

---

[1] *Without his [the giant's] waiting for him [for combat]*

233

Of him thou owest to drede;   *ought to fear*
2725 Thou slough his brether thre   *slew; brothers*
In fight:
Urgan and Morgan unfre   *ignoble*
And Moraunt the noble knight.

"Yif thine houndes an hare wele hayre   *pursue*
2730 And comen ogain to the fre,   *come back to you; (see note)*
Al so be thou bonaire   *courteous*
When his houndes comen to the."
The forest was wel faire
With mani a selly tre.   *marvellous*
2735 Tristrem thought repaire,   *set out*
Houso it ever be,   *Whatever the outcome*
To bide.
"That cuntré will Y se
What aventour so bitide."   *the chance arises*

2740 Tristrem on huntinge rade;   *rode*
An hert chaci bigan.   *hart to hunt*
Ther the merkes were made   *boundary markers (see note)*
His houndes, over thai ran.
The water was blac and brade.   *dark*
2745 Tristrem com as a man
Ther the douke was fade;   *(see note)*
Fast he folwed than
Right thare.
He blewe priis as he can   *(see note); knows how*
2750 Thre mot other mare.   *notes*

Beliagog com that tide
And asked wat he is.   *who he is*
"An hunting ther Y ride,   *A-hunting where*
Tristrem ich hat, ywis."   *am called*
2755 "O! thou slough Moraunt with pride —
Tristrem artow this? —   *Are you that Tristrem*
And seththen Urgan unride;
Unkinde were ous to kis   *It would be unnatural for us*
As kenne.   *As [if we were] relatives*

234

2760	Mendi thou most that mis,	*You must atone for that offense*
	Now thou mi lond art inne."	
	"Y slough Urgan, Y the telle.	*slew*
	So hope Y the to sla.	*to kill you*
	This forest wil Y felle	
2765	And castel wil Y ma.	*construct*
	Her is miri to duelle;	*pleasant to live*
	Forthi this lond Y ta."	*claim*
	The geaunt herd that spelle;	*discourse*
	Forthi him was ful wa	*angered*
2770	Unwise.	
	So bituen hem tua	*the two of them*
	The cuntek gan arise.	*conflict*
	Dartes wel unride	*powerful*
	Beliagog set gan.	*hurl*
2775	Tristremes liif that tide	
	Ferly neighe he wan.	*He very nearly took*
	Bituene the hauberk and side	*coat of mail*
	The dart thurch out ran.	
	Tristrem bleynt biside;	*turned quickly aside*
2780	God he thonked than	
	Almight.	
	Tristrem, as a man,	
	Fast he gan to fight.	*Vigorously*
	Beliagog the bold,	
2785	As a fende he faught.	*fiend*
	Tristrem liif neighe he sold,	*(see note)*
	As Tomas hath ous taught.	*us*
	Tristrem smot, as God wold,	*wished*
	His fot of at a draught.	*off with one blow*
2790	Adoun he fel yfold,	*defeated*
	That man of michel maught,	*great strength*
	And cride,	
	"Tristrem, be we saught,	*reconciled*
	And have min londes wide.	

235

2795	"Overcomen hastow me	
	In bataile and in fight.	
	Helden ogaines the	*Oppose you*
	No wil Y never with right."	
	His tresour lete he se	
2800	Tristrem the noble knight.	
	Tristrem knewe him fre.	*(see note)*
	Beliagog in hight,	
	Nought lain,	
	An halle to maken him bright	
2805	To Ysonde and Bringwain.	

	The geaunt him gan lede	
	Til he fond an hald	*shelter*
	The water about yede;	
	It was his eldren hald.	*shelter of his ancestors*
2810	The geaunt bad Tristrem belde	*Tristrem told the giant to build [the hall]*
	With masouns that were bald.	*powerful*
	Beliagog in that nede	
	Fond him riche wald	*forest*
	To fine.	*finish [his work]*
2815	Ysonde have there he wald,	*wanted*
	Luffsum under line.	*Beautiful in her clothing*

	The geaunt him taught that tide	*showed*
	A ford ther it was yare	*ready for use*
	There he might wele ride	
2820	When his wille ware.	*When he wanted to*
	In the hold he gan him hide,	*refuge*
	Seyd he nought he was thare.	
	Nold he nought long abide;	
	Ogain tho gan he fare,	*Back*
2825	That fre.	
	At the castel forthermare	
	His werkmen wald he se.	*would*

	Ogain went Tristrem than;	*Back*
	Beliagog had masouns sought.	
2830	Tristrem, that michel can,	*who knew much*

A werk hem hath ybrought.   *To*
Nas ther never yete man
That wist what other wrought.
Arere when thai bigan   *Build*
2835   Swiche a werk nas nought
At nede.
Thei al men hadde it thought,   *Though*
It nas to large no gnede.   *was not too large or too small*

At his des in the halle   *dais*
2840   Swete Ysonde was wrought;
Hodain and Pencru, to calle;   *(see note)*
The drink hou Brengwain brought;
Mark yclad in palle;   *dressed in fine clothing*
And Meriadok ful of thought;
2845   (So liifliche weren thai alle   *lifelike*
Ymages semed it nought
To abide); [1]
And Tristrem, hou he faught
With Beliagog unride.   *powerful*

2850   So it bifel a cas   *by chance*
In Seyn Matheus toun   *(see note)*
That a fair fest was   *celebration*
Of lordes of renoun.
A baroun that hight Bonifas   *was called*
2855   Spoused a levedi of Lyoun.   *married; (see note to line 2851)*
Ther was miche solas   *entertainment*
Of alle maner soun   *music*
And gle   *song*
Of minestrals up and doun
2860   Bifor the folk so fre.

The riche Douke Florentin
To that fest gan fare   *celebration; go*
And his sone Ganhardin;

---

[1] *It seemed as if they were not images / Standing there*

With hem rode Ysonde thare.

2865 Her hors a polk stap in;   *puddle stepped*
The water her wat aywhare.   *wet everywhere*
It was a ferly gin,   *strange happening*
So heye under hir gare   *high; dress*
It fleighe.   *splashed up*

2870 The levedi lough ful smare,   *laughed; contemptuously*
And Ganhardin it seighe.   *saw*

Ganhardin unblithe   *unhappily*
His soster tho cald he,
"Abide now, dame, and lithe.   *listen*

2875 What is ther tidde to the?   *has happened to you*
Do now telle me swithe,
Astow lovest me,   *As you*
Whi lough thou that sithe.   *laughed; time*
For what thing may it be?

2880 Withouten oth,   *(see note)*
Thi frendschip schal Y fle
Til Y wite that soth."   *know*

"Brother, no wrathe the nought;   *do not be angry*
The sothe Y wil the say.

2885 Mine hors the water up brought
Of o polk in the way.   *From a puddle in the road*
So heighe it fleighe, me thought,   *splashed it seemed to me*
That in mi sadel it lay.
Ther never man no sought   *reached*

2890 So neighe, for sothe to say,   *near*
In lede.
Brother, wite thou ay
That Y lough for that dede."   *event*

Quath Ganhardin, "Y finde

2895 That schamely schent ar we;   *shamefully disgraced*
To wive on our kinde   *take a wife in our family*
Hetheliche holdeth he.   *He holds in derision*
Ther he gan treuthe binde   *Where he pledged his troth*
Fain Y wald it se,

238

2900	For alle the gold of Ynde,	*India*
	Ybroken no schal it be.	
	To bete,	*To remedy [this]*
	His frendeschip wil Y fle.	
	Our on schal tine swete."[1]	

2905	Wroth is Ganhardin	
	And that Tristrem yses.	*sees*
	What thought he is in	*state of mind*
	Fast he asketh, ywis.	
	"Thou hast bi Ysonde lin	*lain*
2910	While thi wille is.	
	Whi nas hye never thine?	*she*
	Tristrem, tel me this	
	In lede.	
	What hath hye don amis?	*she*
2915	What wites thou hir of dede?"[2]	

	"Yif it hir wille ware	
	Forhole it might have be;	*Kept secret*
	Sche hath ytold it you yare:	*readily*
	Quite sche is of me.	*Free*
2920	Of hir kepe Y namare;	*About her I care no more*
	A gift Y geve the.	
	To a levedi wil Y fare	
	Is fairer than swiche thre	
	To frain."	*To seek [a lady's] favor*
2925	Ganhardin longeth to se	
	That levedi, naught to lain.	

	Ganhardin the fest fles.	*leaves the celebration*
	He bicom Tristremes frende;	
	He seyd his liif he les	*would lose*
2930	Bot he with Tristrem wende.	*Unless; went*
	Quath Tristrem, "Yif it so bes	

---

[1] *One of us shall lose his life-blood*

[2] *For what action do you blame her*

In Inglond that we lende,   *arrive*
No say nought what thou ses   *observe*
Bot hold, astow art hende,   *desist; noble*
2935   And hele.   *conceal*
Lay it al under hende,   *(see note)*
To steven yif thai it stele."

Ganhardin his treuthe plight;   *gave his word*
To ben his brother he bede,   *promised*
2940   To ben a trewe knight
In al Tristremes nede.
Bothe busked that night   *went*
To Beliagog in lede.   *(see note)*
Ganhardin seighe that sight   *saw*
2945   And sore him gan adrede.   *be afraid*
"To brink   *shore*
To sle thou wilt me lede   *slay*
To Beliagog, me think."   *it seems to me*

"Ganhardin, wrong have thou alle.
2950   Wel, whi seistow so?
Maugré on me falle   *Disgrace*
Yif Y the wold slo!   *slay*
The geaunt is mi thralle,   *servant*
His liif thei Y wil to."   *Even if I wanted to take his life*
2955   Tristrem tho gan him calle;   *then*
On a stilt he com tho   *peg leg*
Ful swithe.
"Lord, thi wille to do,
Tharto ar we blithe."   *happy*

2960   "Beliagog, go thare
And loke it boun be;   *ready*
Ganhardin and Y wil fare
The levedi for to se."
Swiche castel fond he thare   *Such*
2965   Was maked of ston and tre.   *wood*
Ganhardin wist nou are   *formerly*
Ther duelled Tristrem and he,   *Where*

240

	To lithe,	*(see note)*
	Ysonde for to se	
2970	In halle, bright and blithe.	
	To Ysonde bright so day	*as*
	To halle gun thai go.	
	Ysonde tho seighe thai	*saw*
	And Bringwain, bothe to,	*two*
2975	Tristrem, for sothe to say,	
	And Beliagog al blo.	*dark-skinned*
	As Ganhardin stert oway,	*drew back*
	His heved he brac tho	*head*
	As he fleighe.	*fled*
2980	Ganhardin was ful wo	*sad*
	That he com Ysonde so neighe.	*near*
	Ganhardin schamed sore;	*was ashamed*
	His heved ran on blod.	*was covered with blood*
	Ysonde he seighe thore	*saw there*
2985	And Brengwain fair and gode.	
	Brengwain the coupe bore.	*cup*
	Him rewe, that frely fode,[1]	
	He swore bi Godes ore.	*mercy*
	In her hond fast it stode	
2990	Al stille.	
	"Tristrem, we ar wode	*mad*
	To speken ogain thi wille.	*against*
	"Nis it bot hertbreke,	*heartbreak*
	That swithe wele finde we,	
2995	And foly ous to speke	*[for] us*
	Ani worde ogaines the.	*against you*
	Mi wille yif Y might gete,	*have*
	That levedi wold Y se.	
	Mine hert hye hath ysteke,	*pierced*
3000	Brengwain bright and fre,	

---

[1] *He was sorry, that noble young man*

That frende.
Blithe no may ich be
Til Y se that hende."

Tristrem and Ganhardin,
3005 Treuthe plighten thay | *pledged*
In wining and in tin, | *getting; loss*
Trewe to ben ay,
In joie and in pin, | *sorrow*
In al thing, to say,
3010 Til he with Brengwain have lin, | *lain*
Yif that Tristrem may, | *might [bring it about]*
In lede.
To Inglond thai toke the way, | *made their way*
Tho knightes stithe on stede. | *bold on horseback*

3015 Sir Canados was than
Constable, the Quen ful neighe. | *near*
For Tristrem Ysonde wan, | *Because; won*
So weneth he be ful sleighe, | *he expects to be very clever*
To make hir his leman | *lover*
3020 With broche and riche beighe. | *jewelry; gem*
For nought that he do can | *Despite all his efforts*
Hir hert was ever heighe | *proud*
To hold; | *To remain faithful*
That man hye never seighe | *saw*
3025 That bifor Tristrem wold. | *Who would [be] before Tristrem*

Tristrem made a song
That song Ysonde the sleighe | *celebrated; wise*
And harped ever among. | *continuously*
Sir Canados was neighe. | *near*
3030 He seyd, "Dame, thou hast wrong,
For sothe, who it seighe. | *whoever might consider it*
As oule and stormes strong | *owl; fierce*
So criestow on heye
In herd. | *At court*
3035 Thou lovest Tristrem dreighe; | *mightily*
To wrong thou art ylerd. | *instructed*

"Tristrem, for thi sake,
For sothe, wived hath he.   *married*
This wil the torn to wrake.   *turn you to vengeance*
3040   Of Breteyne douke schal he be.
Other semblaunt thou make,   *pretense*
Thiselven yif thou hir se.
Thi love hir dede him take
For hye hight as do ye   *is named as you are*
3045   In land.
'Ysonde' men calleth that fre   *noblewoman*
'With the White Hand.'"

"Sir Canados, the waite!   *watch out for yourself*
Ever thou art mi fo.
3050   Febli thou canst hayte   *Weakly; show hatred*
There man schuld menske do.   *do honor*
Who wil lesinges layt   *lies look for*
Tharf him no ferther go.   *It is necessary for him*
Falsly canestow fayt   *dissemble*
3055   That ever worth the wo.   *may grief come to you*
Forthi
Malisoun have thou also   *Curse*
Of God and Our Levedy.

"A gift ich give the:
3060   Thi thrift mot thou tine!   *good luck may you lose*
That thou asked me,
No schal it never be thine.
Yhated also thou be
Of alle that drink wine.
3065   Hennes yern thou fle   *From here quickly*
Out of sight mine
In lede.
Y pray to Seyn Katerine
That ivel mot thou spede."   *you may have bad luck*

3070   The Quen was wratthed sore;   *angered*
Wroth to chaumber sche yede.
"Who may trowe man more,   *trust*

243

	Than he hath don this dede?"	*When*
	A palfray asked sche there	*riding horse*
3075	That wele was loved in lede.	
	Dight sche was ful yare;	*Prepared; quickly*
	Hir pavilouns with hir thai lede	
	Ful fine.	
	Bifore was stef on stede	*strong*
3080	Tristrem and Ganhardine.	

	Ful ner the gat thai abade	*waited*
	Under a figer tre.	*fig tree*
	Thai seighe where Ysonde rade	*saw; rode*
	And Bringwain, bothe seighe he	
3085	With tuo houndes mirie made;	*charmingly*
	Fairer might non be.	
	Her blis was ful brade;	*abundant*
	A tale told Ysonde fre;	
	Thai duelle.	*linger*
3090	Tristrem that herd he	
	And seyd thus in his spelle:	*speech*

	"Ganhardin, ride thou ay.	
	Mi ring of finger thou drawe;	
	Thou wende forth in thi way	*go*
3095	And gret hem al on rawe.	*greet them all in turn*
	Her houndes praise thou ay;	
	Thi finger forth thou schawe.	*stretch out*
	The Quen, for sothe to say,	
	The ring wil sone knawe,	
3100	That fre.	
	Aski sche wil in plawe	*amiably*
	And say thou comest fro me."	

	Tho rode Ganhardin kene	*boldly*
	And overtaketh hem now.	
3105	First he greteth the Quen	*greets*
	And after Bringwain, Y trowe.	*believe*
	The knight himself bidene	
	Stroked the hounde Pencru.	*Petted*

	The Quen the ring hath sene	
3110	And knewe it wele ynough,	
	That fre.	
	Hye seyd, "Say me, hou	
	Com this ring to the?"	

	"He that aught this ring	*owned*
3115	To token sent it to the."	*As a token*
	Tho seyd that swete thing,	
	"Tristrem, that is he!"	
	"Dame, withouten lesing,	*truly*
	He sent it you bi me."	
3120	Sche sayd, "Bi heven King,	*heaven's*
	In longing have we be,	*distress*
	Naught lain.	
	Al night duelle we,"	*remain [here]*
	Seyd Ysonde to Bringwain.	

3125	Thai wende the Quen wald dye,	*thought*
	So sike sche was bi sight.	*sick; in appearance*
	Thai sett pavilouns an heye	*set up; in haste*
	And duelled, clerk and knight.	*remained [there]; (see note)*
	Ysonde biheld that lye	*that [one]*
3130	Under leves light.	
	Tristrem hye ther seyghe,	*she; saw*
	So dede Brengwain that night	
	In feld.	
	Ganhardine treuthe plight	*pledged [his] word*
3135	Brengwain to wive weld.	*as [his] wife to have*

	Tuo night ther thai lye	*Two; lay*
	In that fair forest.	
	Canados hadde a spie;	
	Her pavilouns he to-kest.	*surveyed (see note)*
3140	Ther come to Canados crie	*Canados' summons*
	The cuntré est and west.	*people of the region*
	Governayl was forthi	
	Therout, as it was best	*Outside*
	To abide.	*remain*

245

3145	He seyd Tristrem prest,	*quickly*
	"Now it were time to ride."	
	Governayl, his man was he,	
	And Ganhardine his knight.	
	Armed knightes thai se	
3150	To felle hem doun in fight.	*strike them*
	Governaile gan to fle;	
	He ran oway ful right.	
	Tho folwed bond and fre	*followed; (see note)*
	And lete the loge unlight	*left the shelter unhappily*
3155	That tide.	
	Oway rode Tristrem that night	
	And Ganhardine biside.	
	Sir Canados the heighe,	
	He ladde the Quen oway.	
3160	Tristrem, of love so sleighe,	*wise*
	No abade him nought that day.	*fought*
	Brengwain bright so beighe,	*as a jewel*
	Wo was hir tho ay.	
	On Canados sche gan crie	*Against; complain*
3165	And made gret deray	*disturbance*
	And sede,	
	"This lond nis worth an ay	*egg*
	When thou darst do swiche a dede."	
	Ganhardine gan fare	
3170	Into Bretaine oway;	
	And Tristrem duelled thare	
	To wite what men wald say.	*discover*
	Coppe and claper he bare	*(see note)*
	Til the fiftenday	*Until the fifteenth day*
3175	As he a mesel ware;	*leper*
	Under walles he lay,	
	To lithe.	*(see note to l. 2968)*
	So was Ysonde, that may,	*In such a state*
	That alle sche wald to-writhe.	*writhe about*

246

3180	Tristrem in sorwe lay;	*sorrow*
	Forthi wald Ysonde awede.	*Therefore; grow insane*
	And Brengwain thretned ay	*threatened constantly*
	To take hem in her dede.	*(see note)*
	Brengwain went oway;	
3185	To Marke the King sche yede	*went*
	And redily gan to say	
	Hou thai faren in lede:	
	"Nought lain,	
	Swiche knight hastow to fede	*do you have as an enemy*
3190	Thi schame he wald ful fain.	*desired*
	"Sir King, take hede therto:	*heed*
	Sir Canados wil have thi Quen;	
	Bot thou depart hem to,	*Unless; separate the two of them*
	A schame ther worth ysene.	*will become apparent*
3195	Hye dredeth of him so	*She is so afraid of him*
	That wonder is to wene.	*imagine*
	His wille for to do	
	Hye werneth him bituene	*denies him*
	Ful sone.	
3200	Yete thai ben al clene;	*Still; pure*
	Have thai no dede ydone."	*sexual act*
	Marke, in al thing,	
	Brengwain thanked he.	
	After him he sent an heigheing;	*in a hurry*
3205	Fram court he dede him be.	*caused him to be*
	"Thou deservest for to hing;	*hang*
	Miselven wele ich it se."	
	So couthe Brengwain bring	*knew how*
	Canados for to fle,	*flee*
3210	That heighe.	*proud [man]*
	Glad was Ysonde the fre	
	That Bringwain couthe so lighe.	*lie*
	Than to hir seyd the Quen,	
	"Leve Brengwain the bright	*Dear*
3215	That art fair to sene,	

247

	Thou wost our wille bi sight.	*know*
	Whare hath Tristrem bene?	
	Nis he no douhti knight?"	*bold*
	"Thai leighen al bidene	*lie*
3220	That sain he dar nought fight	*say*
	With his fo."	
	Brengwain biheld that right,	*understood*
	Tristrem to bour lete go.	*chamber*
	Tristrem in bour is blithe;	*chamber*
3225	With Ysonde playd he thare.	
	Brengwain badde he lithe,	*asked that he listen*
	"Who ther armes bare,	*Whoever [it was who] bore arms there*
	Ganhardin and thou that sithe	*time*
	Wightly oway gun fare."	*Quickly*
3230	Quath Tristrem, "Crieth swithe	*Announce*
	A turnament ful yare	
	With might.	
	Noither of ous nil spare	*Neither of us*
	Erl, baroun no knight."	
3235	A turnament thai lete crie.	*had announced*
	The parti Canados tok he;	*combat*
	And Meriadok, sikerly,	*certainly*
	In his help gan he be.	*On his side*
	Tristrem ful hastilye	
3240	Ofsent Ganhardin the fre.	*Sent for*
	Ganhardin com titly	*quickly*
	That turnament to se	
	With sight.	
	Fro the turnament nold thai fle	
3245	Til her fon were feld dounright.	*foes; overthrown*
	Thai com into the feld	*field*
	And founde ther knightes kene;	*bold*
	Her old dedes thai yeld	*(see note)*
	With batayle al bidene.	
3250	Tristrem gan biheld	*look*
	To Meriadok bituene.	

	For the tales he teld	
	On him he wrake his tene	*avenged; anger*
	That tide.	
3255	He gaf him a wounde kene	*painful*
	Thurchout bothe side.	*Throughout*

	Bituene Canados and Ganhardin	
	The fight was ferly strong.	*marvelously fierce*
	Tristrem thought it pin	*was displeased*
3260	That it last so long.	*lasted*
	His stirops he made him tine;	*lose*
	To grounde he him wrong.	*wrenched*
	Sir Canados ther gan lyn;	*lie*
	The blod thurch brini throng	*through [his] mail burst out*
3265	With care.	*grief*
	On him he wrake his wrong	*avenged*
	That he no ros na mare.	*arose*

	Her fon fast thai feld,	*Their foes; overcame*
	And mani of hem thai slough.	*slew*
3270	The cuntré with hem meld;	*people of the region; fought*
	Thai wrought hem wo ynough.	
	Tristrem hath hem teld	*reckoned with*
	That him to schame drough.	*Who dragged him into shame*
	Thai token the heighe held	*hill*
3275	And passed wele anough	*advanced*
	And bade.	*halted*
	Under wode bough	
	After her fomen thai rade.	*enemies; rode*

	Ther Tristrem turned ogain	
3280	And Ganhardin stithe and stille.	*valiant and unwavering*
	Mani thai han yslain	
	And mani overcomen with wille.	*eagerly*
	The folk fleighe unfain	*fled unhappily*
	And socour criden schille.	*aid; loudly*
3285	In lede, nought to layn,	
	Thai hadde woundes ille	
	At the nende.	*end*

The wraiers that weren in halle,   *accusers*
Schamly were thai schende.   *Shamefully; disgraced*

3290 Than that turnament was don,   *When; finished*
      Mani on slain ther lay.   *Many a one*
      Ganhardin went sone
      Into Bretaine oway.
      Brengwain hath her bone;   *has what she wanted*
3295 Ful wele wreken er thay.   *avenged are*
      A knight that werd no schon   *(see note)*
      Hete Tristrem, sothe to say.   *Was [also] called*
      Ful wide
      Tristrem sought he ay,
3300 And he fond him that tide.

      He fel to Tristremes fet   *feet*
      And merci crid he:
      "Mi leman fair and swete   *lover*
      A knight hath reved me,   *deprived me of*
3305 Of love that can wele let.   *(see note)*
      So Crist hir sende the.
      Mi bale thou fond to bet   *sorrow; undertake; make better*
      For love of Ysonde fre.
      Nought lain,
3310 Seven brethern hath he   *brothers*
      That fighteth me ogain.

      "This ich day thai fare   *very*
      And passeth fast biside.   *very near*
      Y gete hir nevermare
3315 Yif Y tine hir this tide.   *If; lose*
      Fiftene knightes thai are
      And we bot to, to abide."   *only two*
      "Dathet who hem spare,"   *(see note to line 1875)*
      Seyd Tristrem that tide.
3320 "This night
      Thai han ytint her pride   *lost*
      Thurch grace of God Almight."

250

	Thai gun hem bothe armi	*to arm [themselves]*
	In iren and stiel that tide.	*steel*
3325	Thai metten hem in a sty	*encountered each other on a road*
	Bi o forestes side.	
	Ther wex a kene crie	*arose a loud tumult*
	Togider tho thai gun ride.	
	The yong Tristrem forthi	
3330	Sone was feld his pride	
	Right thore.	*there*
	He hadde woundes wide	*gaping*
	That he no ros no more.	*arose*

	Thus the yong knight	
3335	Forsothe yslawe was thare.	*slain*
	Tristrem, that trewe hight,	*was called*
	Awrake him al with care.	*Avenged*
	Ther he slough in fight	*slew*
	Fiftene knightes and mare.	*more*
3340	Wel louwe he dede hem light	*brought them to the ground*
	With diolful dintes sare,	*painful blows*
	Unsounde.	*Unhealthy*
	Ac an aruwe oway he bare	*But; arrow*
	In his eld wounde.	*old*

[The leaf containing the ending of the poem is missing from the manuscript. In his edition, Sir Walter Scott wrote as a conclusion the following stanzas.]

3345	The companyons fiftene,	
	To death did thai thringe;	*throw down*
	And sterveth bidene,	*dies*
	Tho Tristrem the yinge;	*young*
	Ac Tristrem hath tene,	*But; anger*
3350	His wounde gan him wring,	*pain sharply*
	To hostel he hath gene,	*gone*
	On bedde gan him flinge	
	In ure;	*At that time*
	Fele salven thai bringe,	*Many salves*
3355	His paine to recure.	*cure*

But never thai no might,
With coste, nor with payn,
Bring Tristrem the wight,   *strong*
To heildom ogayn: *health*
3360 His wounde brast aplight,   *burst open quickly*
And blake was the bane;   *black; bone*
Non help may that knight,
The sothe for to sayne,
Bidene,
3365 Save Ysonde the bright,
Of Cornwal was quene.   *[Who] was queen of Cornwall*

Tristrem clepeth aye,   *calls*
On Ganhardin trewe fere;   *trusty companion*
"Holp me, brother, thou may,   *Help*
3370 And bring me out of care;
To Ysonde the gaye,
Of Cornwail do thou fare;
In tokening I say,   *As a sign*
Mi ring with the thou bare,
3375 In dern;   *secret*
Bot help me sche dare,   *Unless*
Sterven wol ich gern.   *Die; soon*

"Mi schip do thou take,
With godes that bethe new;   *which are*
3380 Tuo seyles do thou make,   *Two sails*
Beth different in hew;   *[Which] are; color*
That tone schall be blake,   *one; black*
That tother white so snewe;   *other; as snow*
And tho thou comest bake,   *when*
3385 That tokening schal schew   *sign*
The end,   *outcome*
Gif Ysonde me forsake,   *If*
The blake schalt thou bende."   *fly*

Ysonde of Britanye,
3390 With the white honde,
In dern can sche be,   *Was in hiding*

252

And wele understonde,
That Ysonde the fre,
Was sent for from Inglonde;
3395   "Y-wroken wol Y be   *Avenged*
Of mi fals husbonde
Saunfayle,   *Without fail*
Bringeth he haggards to honde,   *(see note)*
And maketh me his stale?"

3400   Ganhardin to Inglonde fares,
Als merchaunt, Y you saye;   *As a merchant*
He bringeth riche wares
And garmentes were gaye;
Mark he giftes bares,
3405   Als man that miche maye, [1]
A cup he prepares,
The ring tharein can laye,
Bidene;
Brengwain the gaye,
3410   Y-raught it the quene.   *Gave*

Ysonde the ring knewe,
That riche was of gold,
As tokening trewe,   *sign*
That Tristrem her yold;   *gave*
3415   Ganhardin gan schewe,
And priviliche hir told,   *privately*
That Tristrem hurt was newe,   *anew*
In his wounde that was old,
Al right:
3420   Holp him gif sche nold,   *Help; if; would not*
Sterven most that knight.   *Die must*

Wo was Ysonde than,
The tale tho sche hard thare;   *heard*
Sche schope hir as a man,   *disguised herself*

---

[1] *As a man who may do much (i.e., who is rich or powerful)*

3425   With Ganhardin to fare;
       O bord are thai gan,   *Aboard*
       A wind at wil thame bare;   *according to their will; carried*
       Ysonde was sad woman,
       And wepeth bitter tare,   *tears*
3430   With eighe:
       The seyls that white ware,
       Ganhardin lete fleighe.

       Ysonde of Britanye,
       With the white honde,
3435   The schip sche can se,
       Seyling to londe;   *Sailing*
       The white seyl tho marked sche,
       "Yonder cometh Ysonde,
       For to reve fro me,   *rob*
3440   Miin fals husbonde;
       Ich sware,
       For il tho it schal be,
       That sche hir hider bare."   *hither*

       To Tristrem sche gan hye,   *hasten*
3445   O bed thare he layne,   *where he lay*
       "Tristrem, so mot ich thye,   *as I might thrive*
       Heled schalt thou bene,   *Healed*
       Thi schippe I can espye
       The sothe for to sain,
3450   Ganhardin is comen neighe,   *near*
       To curen thi paine,
       Aplight."   *At once*
       "What seyl doth thare flain,
       Dame, for God almight?"

3455   Sche weneth to ben awrake,   *avenged*
       Of Tristrem the trewe,
       Sche seyth, "Thai ben blake,   *black*
       As piche is thare hewe."
       Tristrem threw hym bake,
3460   Trewd Ysonde untrewe,   *Believed*

His kind hert it brake,
And sindrid in tuo;   *split; two*
Above,
Cristes merci him take!
3465   He dyed for true love.

Murneth olde and yinge,   *Mourn; young*
Murneth lowe and heighe;   *low-born and noble*
For Tristrem, swete thinge,
Was mani wate eighe;   *wet eyes*
3470   Maidens thare hondes wringe,
Wives iammeren and crii;   *lament*
The belles con thai ring,
And masses con thai seye,
For dole;   *sorrow*
3475   Prestes praied aye,
For Tristremes sole.   *soul*

Ysonde to land wan,   *arrived*
With seyl and with ore;   *sail; oar*
Sche mete an old man,
3480   Of berd that was hore:
Fast the teres ran,
And siked he sore,   *sighed*
"Gone is he than,
Of Inglond the flore,   *flower*
3485   In lede;
We se him no more:
Schir Tristrem is dede!"   *Sir; dead*

When Ysonde herd that,
Fast sche gan to gonne,
3490   At the castel gate
Stop hir might none:
Sche passed in thereat,
The chaumbre sche won;   *reached*
Tristrem in cloth of stat
3495   Lay stretched thare as ston   *stone*
So cold.

Ysonde loked him on,
And faste gan bihold.

Fairer ladye ere   *before*
3500   Did Britannye never spye,
Swiche murning chere,   *sorrowful display (of emotion)*
Making on heighe:
On Tristremes bere,   *bier*
Doun con sche lye;
3505   Rise ogayn did sche nere,   *never*
But thare con sche dye   *she died*
For woe:
Swiche lovers als thei
Never schal be moe.   *again*

1   In the manuscript, a large capital I begins the romance. Large capitals also appear at the beginning of lines 34, 276, 452, 529, 573, 771, 1211, 1255, 1442, 1541, 1629, 1805, 1926, 2014, 2047, 2267, 2751, 2850, 3235, and 3290.

        Because of damage to the manuscript, probably due, as Scott suggests, to the cutting out of an illumination, the end of the first line is missing. However, the entire line appears as a catchphrase on the preceding page.

        Ertheldoun is Erceldoune, a village in Berwickshire, Scotland.

2   The *Tomas* referred to here (and again in lines 10, 397, 412 and 2787) as the purported source of the story of Sir Tristrem is Thomas of Erceldoune (fl. ?1220–?1297), a poet and prophet who is said to have predicted the death of the King of Scotland, Alexander III. Another work attributed to him but written long after his death is *The Romance and Prophecies of Thomas of Erceldoune*, edited by James A. H. Murray for the Early English Text Society (o.s. no. 61) in 1875.

3   The MED cites this line as an example of the use of the phrase *in roune* meaning "secretly" or "mysteriously." These meanings seem not to fit the context. The word probably has the meaning of "poem" or "song" in this context, and the author is here merely using the convention of citing an authority for his work.

20   McNeill notes that *to abide* is used here as "a mere expletive, which cannot be adequately translated."

23   McNeill notes that "Rouland" should be read for the manuscript reading of "Morgan," though he does not make the emendation in his text. I have followed Kölbing in making the emendation.

24   On *Morgan*, see the note to line 74.

39   Earlier editors agree on reading *pouer* as "the poor"; but it might also mean "the military force" or "the army."

44   On *Rouland Rise* (and also *Rouland Riis* on line 49), W. W. Skeat ("The Romance of Sir Tristrem," *Scottish Historical Review* 6 [1909], 59) says the "Rise" or "Riis" "is obviously the Welsh name *Rhys*, which has been Englished both as *Reece* and *Rice*."

74   *Ermonie* (which appears again in lines 762, 807, and 906, and as "Hermonie" in lines 532 and 849) as Tristrem's heritage is discussed at length by Ernst Brugger ("Almain and Ermonie as Tristan's Home," *MP* 25 [1927–28], 269–290). He suggests that in the Norse version of Thomas's story,

> Ermenia, Tristram's home, was a town and port in Brittany. Tristram was therefore a Breton as well as his enemy, Duke Morgan. . . . The English translation [i.e., *Sir Tristrem*] does not go so much into details as the Saga, is more vague in its geographical indications, but generally confirms, or does not contradict, those about Tristram's home in the Saga. Ermenie is not yet a town. Navigation is necessary for passing from King Mark's court in England to Ermenie or vice versa. . . . Brittany . . . may have been thought of as adjacent to Ermenie and to the country of Duke Morgan, though this is not expressly stated . . . " (pp. 272–273).

Brugger also suggests, however, that if Ermonie is original to the Tristan story, which he considers to have a Pictish origin, "Ermenie" should be identified with "*Manann-Manau* in Scotland" and goes on to say that a "confusion of Ermenie=Manann with *Ermenie*=Brittany . . . may have been the reason why Thomas transplanted Tristan's home from Scotland to the Continent; but I am inclined to think that this shifting was rather caused by the ambiguity of the name *Bretaigne*" (p. 289).

In another article ("Loenois as Tristan's Home," *MP* 22 [1924–25], 159–191), Brugger discusses the location of Tristan's home given in the Beroul (as opposed to the Thomas) tradition and identifies this place, Loenois or Lyonas, as Lothian, which he considers "far more important than *Ermenie*" (p. 190) because closer to what he sees as the Pictish origin of the legend.

80–81 The verse form and the sense suggest that there has been an omission by the scribe of two lines at this point.

95   Here and elsewhere throughout the manuscript, *gan* is an auxiliary verb indicating the past tense. Thus "gan he wende" means "he went."

146   The *goinfainoun* or "gonfalon" is a small pennon, here raised on the mast, or, as in line 173, suspended beneath the steel head of a knight's lance.

176–77 The paragraph mark used by the scribe to indicate new stanzas is erroneously placed before line 176, rather than before line 177, where the new stanza actually begins.

189   I follow Kölbing in emending the manuscript reading "Of" to "On."

247–49 The meaning of these lines is that Rohand, the steward of Tristrem's father Rouland, goes to his own wife's childbed and claims that his wife had two children, one of whom is Tristrem. Perhaps *wiif* is best taken as a dative form: he went "to his own wife" in her childbed. Rohand pretends the child is his own to protect Tristrem from his father's enemy Morgan. As part of the deception, he adopts the strategy referred to in lines 252–53 of disguising his name by reversing the syllables. In other versions of the legend, this strategy is adopted by Tristrem himself when he goes to Ireland in order that his identity as the slayer of the brother of the Queen of Ireland will not be revealed.

272   McNeill glosses *held his hert in an* as "kept his heart in one (*i.e.*, in equanimity, repressing his sorrow)." Kölbing glosses *"hielt sein herz in gleicher stummung, d.h. unterdrükte seinem kummer"* (held his heart in constant temper, that is, suppressed his grief). The sense is clearly that Rohand did not wear his heart on his sleeve.

291   McNeill's note summarizes the opinions of the previous editors on this line:

> This line defies interpretation as it stands. Scott in his glossary gives "Thede, apparently a contraction for *they gede*." But, as Kölbing points out, such a conjecture is untenable. Kölbing suggests that *thede* may be equivalent to the Old English theód, and proposes to read —
>   And everich play in thede,
> which would have the same sense as *in lede* in verse 64, so that the line would mean every game known to the people — every game in the country.

The sense of the line is surely something like: he taught him "the manner of playing of every nation" of the old law and the new. Such a reading might be achieved without emendation if "thede" is taken as a genitive form. The Old English "theod," from which the Middle English word derives, is a feminine noun which would have a genitive in *-e*, so it is possible to read "thede" as a genitive form in this line.

297   W. W. Skeat ("The Romance of Sir Tristrem," *Scottish Historical Review* 6 [1909]: 61) says of *Manerious*: "the great puzzle is the wonderful name *Manerious*, which no one (says the note [i.e., McNeill's note]) can explain. However, I explained it once somewhere some years ago. It should rather be Manerius; and it is nothing but the Old Norman and Middle English word *Manére*, touched up with a Latin suffix to imitate its original. For what is its original? It is merely a French translation, meaning 'manner,' of the Latin name *Modus*. But what is meant by Modus? It is to be feared that its fame has departed; yet it was at that time one of the most famous of all works, as well known as the *Roman de la Rose*, or as the name of Newton is now to the students of science. *Le Livre du Roi Modus et de la Reine Reson* (*The Book of King Manner and of Queen Reason*) was the chief authority on this very subject of 'venery' or hunting, containing all the precious terms of the chase and all the directions for the cutting up of the deer which, as the *Romance* informs us, Sir Tristrem knew so well. If he really knew more of hunting terms than even King Manner, he had great reason to be proud."

Skeat's explanation seems preferable to that of A. E. H. Swaen (*Anglia* 41 [1917], 182), who suggests reading "the puzzling name as *Manuredus*, i.e. Manfredus. Manfred, king of Sicily, wrote additional chapters to the Emperor Frederick the Second's famous treatise on falconry."

313   The OED notes that "aire" (of which *air* in this line is a variant) is "the earlier equivalent of aerie."

322   The MED entry on the word "assise" (of which *asise* in this line is a variant spelling) refers to H. J. R. Murray's *A History of Chess* (Oxford: Clarendon Press, 1913) p. 455, for an explanation of the term in this context. Murray writes: "In the Middle Ages there was no tribunal whose word on the game of chess could be final. All attempts at the improvement of the game were from the necessity of the case individual at the outset, and each had to win its way to universal or national acceptance. Hence the first result of such attempts was a loss of uniformity, and the rise of local rules which differentiated the game of one locality from that of another. It took time for a happy improvement discovered perhaps in Spain to reach Germany, England, or Iceland, and all the modifications did not commend themselves to players in other countries. This led to the growth of what were called *Assizes*, the different codes of rules by

which chess was played in different places or at different times. Thus we hear of the *Lombard assize* — the rules of the game as played by the famous players of Lombardy. We also hear in England of the *long* and *short assizes*, of which the former would appear to have been the ordinary mediaeval game, and the latter a game commencing from a different and more advanced arrangement of the pieces. We have a reference to the former in the Scotch version of the Tristram romance, *Sir Tristrem* . . . ."

325   The manuscript reads "Tristem." I have emended to "Tristrem." McNeill observes that "the sense of this and the following lines is very obscure. They seem to mean that Tristrem, doing as the wise do, looks upon the hawks on the one part, and the money on the other, as two separate parts, and lets the captain of the ship win as much money as he himself wins hawks." The problem with this interpretation is that in lines 340–41 we learn that Tristrem won 100 pounds. The MED, citing this line, glosses "delen a twinne" as "?act in two ways, work toward a double goal." However, in other instances cited by the MED the phrase means merely "to separate"; and it is possible that all that is meant is that Tristrem sets himself apart from Rohand in the process of playing the game. Lines 326–28, however, do seem to suggest that Tristrem plays wisely by allowing his opponent to win sometimes.

384   Kölbing glosses *weder* as *"wetter"* ("storm" or "bad weather" and McNeill glosses it as "weather"; but it seems to make as much or more sense to read it as "whither" or "wherever."

397   McNeill reads *tho* as "they, in the indefinite sense of people in general." It seems, however, that assigning it its more normal meaning of "then" yields better sense.

403–07   McNeill says that the sense of these difficult lines seems to be: "Whoever can say anything better (tell the story in a better manner), may say what he has to say (*his owhen*) here like a courteous man. But let each man praise what is pleasant to him at the end — *i.e.*, when I have finished my version of the story." (See the introduction for another reading of "As hende").

410   *Blihand* or "bleaunt" is a costly silk fabric.

412   *Toun* might mean "a town," but it might also mean an enclosed space, a garden or a courtyard, where a reading might occur.

420   A *peni* can be a coin of small value or, if used more exactly, an "English silver coin, weighing approximately 22 grains, decreasing in weight and value from about 1300 A.D., equal to 1/12 of a shilling or 1/240 of a pound" (MED).

431   The OED, citing this line, considers *temed* to be a form of *teem* (v. 1, definition 8) "to betake oneself, to repair, go, proceed to." McNeill glosses as "appealed"; Kölbing as *"berief sich"* (relied on); and Scott as "tamed." The last meaning makes little sense; however, the verb "teme" is defined by the OED as "subjugate," and the sense could be that Tristrem subjugated himself to (that is, put himself under the protection of) the king.

446   A *les* or "leash" is here a set of three hounds.

454   The MED and OED both take *Martirs* as an erroneous form of the plural of "mart," a slaughtered animal (originally "a cow or ox slaughtered at Martinmas and prepared for provision for the winter," MED). But, despite the fact that line 455 makes this the most plausible reading, it is likely that the poet also was suggesting (or that the scribe was thinking of) images of martyrs quartered for their faith.

464   The manuscript reads "Tristem." I have emended to "Tristrem."

472   The phrase *In lede is nought to lain*, which literally means "Among the people it not to lie" is basically a metrical filler. The best translation is an emphatic "truly."

476   McNeill defines the "heminges" as "a piece of the hide cut out to make brogues for the huntsmen."

485   Scott, McNeill and Kölbing all read "spande"; but, as the MED suggests, this is an error for *spaude* ("shoulder"). The two minims were read as *n* rather than *u*. McNeill and Kölbing also read *brede* as "breadth"; but it seems possible that the meaning intended is something like a "cut of meat" (from "brede" = "roasted or grilled meat; also a roast" [MED]).

486   The *erber* is the first stomach, as opposed to the "rede" (line 489), which is the fourth stomach. On the process of dressing or "dighting" the erber, see J. Douglas Bruce, "The Breaking of the Deer in *Sir Gawayne and the Green Knight*," *Englische Studien* 32 (1903), 23–36; the note to line 1774 in *English*

Hawking and Hunting in The Boke of St. Albans: A Facsimile Edition of Sigs. a2–f8 of The Boke of St. Albans (1486), ed. Rachel Hands (London: Oxford University Press, 1975) 141. The process is also referred to in *Sir Gawain and the Green Knight*, line 1330.

487   The *stifles* are the joints "at the junction of the hind leg and the body (between the femur and the tibia) in a horse or other quadruped" (OED).

491   The *noubles* or "numbles" are inner parts of an animal used for food. The word is also found in the form "umble" and the parts so designated are used in making "umble pie." The phrase "to eat humble pie" is from the word "humble," according to the OED, but perhaps with jocular reference to "umble pie."

499   The word *quirré*, which comes from the Old French "cuirée," meaning "skin," refers to "certain parts of a deer placed on the hide and given to the hounds as a reward" (OED).

502   M. Y. Offord, in her note to *The Parlement of the Thre Ages*, line 80 (EETS, o.s. 246, [London: Oxford University Press, 1959] 41), notes that "a small piece of gristle at the end of the sternum . . . was thrown up into a tree to crows or ravens, as a kind of luck-offering."

518   Hunting calls were used as a form of communication during and after the hunt. Presumably the *tokening* or signal referred to here is the "retraite," the signal used to announce the return of the hunters. On hunting calls, see John Cummins, *The Hound and the Hawk: The Art of Medieval Hunting* (New York: St. Martin's, 1998), pp. 160–71.

531   The MED, citing this line, glosses the phrase *spac biforn* as "spoke first," but the meaning here must be something like "spoke right up."

537   McNeill glosses the tag *For thought* as "that can be imagined."

564–65   These lines, which earlier editors do not explain, present a problem of interpretation. A possible reading of the lines might be: "They took leave [of Tristrem] in the hall, whoever might reach the young man." The suggestion would be that those in the hall honored Tristrem by taking their leave of him if they could get to him, which was difficult because of the throng of people wishing to reach him after the display of his talent.

615 The manuscript reads "Tristram," but, as McNeill notes, this is obviously an error for "Rohand," to which I have emended the text.

687 The MED defines *scarlet* as "a robe, an article of clothing, etc.: of fine quality, perh. of scarlet color."

736 Kölbing suggests emending "skete" to "swete."

743 McNeill glosses *with sight* as "with a glance." The MED, citing this line, glosses "with a sigh."

754 Kölbing suggests that the word "he" (referring to Tristrem) is needed to complete the line: Rohand tells how Tristrem was begotten by his parents.

823 *Unsought* seems to suggest that one could find ten sons of kings at Morgan's table without even looking for them, that is, that kings' sons were plentiful there.

851–58 Kölbing and McNeill both ascribe all of these lines to Morgan, but it seems as if they are an exchange: Morgan admits killing Tristrem's father; Tristrem replies that since he has admitted it, reparations are due; Morgan asks if it is for his rights (the reparations) that Tristrem has come from Mark.

874–75 Here, as in lines 80–81, the verse form and the sense suggest that there has been an omission by the scribe of two lines.

906 *Almain* is discussed by Ernst Brugger in his article on "Almain and Ermonie as Tristan's Home" (cited above in the note to line 74) and at greater length in the second part of that article (*MP* 26 [1928–29], 1–12). Brugger asserts in the former article that "Almain was not Morgan's duchy, but was, like Ermonie, occupied by Tristan as his heritage" (p. 269). Though in the English poem Almain must be adjacent to Ermonie, Brugger suggests in the latter article that if Almain is to be traced back to the original form of the legend, which he regards as Pictish, it must be a corruption of "Albaine," a "northern neighbor" of Lothian (10).

921 In the phrase *mi nem*, there is a transference of *n* from "min" to the following noun. It is not unusual for a similar transference to occur with articles and with other possessive pronouns. See, for example, "A neten" (for "An eten," ["A

giant"]) in line 950; "thi nore" (for "thin ore" [your mercy]) in line 2004; "thi nem" (for "thin em" [your uncle]) in line 2150; and "thi nare" (for "thin are" [your mercy]) in line 2135.

943   *Latoun* ("latten") is an alloy of copper, tin, and other metals.

948   *Moraunt* is the character who, in the French versions of the Tristan legend, is generally called le Morholt or le Morhot and, in Malory, Marhaus or Marhalt. In these versions, he is the Queen of Ireland's brother, whom Tristrem kills in combat to end the demand for tribute to the King of Ireland. In *Sir Tristrem*, Moraunt is presented as the brother of Ysonde (see line 1324) rather than her uncle.

955   The MED, citing this line, defines *rade* as "a protected place near shore where ships could lie at anchor."

968   As McNeill suggested, the word "tha" (after "thing" in the manuscript) seems to be crossed out.

1040   It seems fitting that Tristrem has a lion as the heraldic emblem on his shield, since the lion was the "Kyng and prince of alle bestes . . . . and some leouns . . . haven scharpe and fers hertes," as John of Trevisa writes in *On the Properties of Things: John of Trevisa's Translation of Bartholomæus Anglicus De Proprietatibus Rerum* (Oxford: Clarendon Press, 1975) II, 1214.

1093   McNeill reads "Zour," but the letter he reads as a "Z" seems to be comparable to the initial capital yogh as it appears elsewhere in the manuscript Thus I have transcribed it as "Y."

1132   McNeill suggests that following Kölbing's emendation of "thai" for "he" would improve the sense. It is possible to maintain the manuscript reading and to translate as: "Each of them had done what he might"; but perhaps a more suitable approach would be to emend "he" to "hie," an alternate form of "they," or to leave the manuscript reading and consider "he" as the third person plural pronoun. This form appears frequently enough in Middle English. See, e.g., *Havelok the Dane*, line 152 ("He [They] wrungen hondes, and wepen sore").

1150 McNeill says that for the manuscript reading of "son," "*send* must be read." The emendation is not necessary, however, if we read "yare" as a verb (meaning "to prepare").

1157 *His* is ambiguous in this line. It might refer to Tristrem: that is, Tristrem asked for a blessing for himself. It might also refer to Mark: Tristrem asked for his (Mark's) blessing. In either case, the subject (he=Tristrem) is understood.

1173 McNeill and the MED are probably correct in considering the manuscript reading "ride" an error for "rive," which is required by the rhyme. Thus I have emended to "rive."

1202 The phrase *under line* is used in Middle English, as the OED observes, as a mere expletive. Its literal meaning in something like "clothed in linen" or "in [one's] clothes."

1204 The manuscript reads "medicie." I have emended to "medicine," which is required by the rhyme.

1220 According to the MED, *fowe* is "a kind of particolored fur" and *griis* is a kind of gray fur, probably "fur from the back of the Russian gray squirrel in winter."

1226 *Croude* or "crowd" is "a name applied to various forms of the early fiddle: any of a class of stringed instruments with two to six strings, with bow, and later a fingerboard, in the shape of a rectangle, ellipse, or double ellipsoid, and played, depending on size, at the shoulder or across the knees" (*A Dictionary of Middle English Musical Terms*, compiled by Henry Holland Carter [Bloomington: Indiana University Press, 1961]).

1228 It is appropriate for the Irishmen to swear by St. Patrick, their patron saint.

1234 The first two letters of "sche" are not clearly legible in the manuscript; thus McNeill's text reads ". . he," though he does suggest that the word must be "sche."

1248 The phrase *maken aloft* means "to start or begin" something. In this line the word *play* means "music."

1290   *Fet* could be the third person singular of "feden" ("to feed" or "to nourish") or of "fetten" ("to rescue"). McNeill says the "sense" is "whoever cherishes an unknown man (is doomed to disappointment, for) he always goes away."

1308–9   Kölbing translates these lines: "Sie ahnten rache, weil sie ihn allein hatten fahren lassen" (They had a premonition about vengeance because they had let him travel alone).

1317   *Gain* is an alternate spelling of "gan." It gives a past sense to the word "frain" ("ask"). See the note to line 95.

1356   The MED, citing this line, glosses *reles* as "taste" and "? also beauty." McNeill glosses it as "description." Something like "beauty" is probably the sense intended, but it is possible that another sense of "reles" is intended either as the primary meaning or as a pun. The word can also mean "relief" or "abatement of distress" (MED). For the King and for the barons, a wife could relieve them of the problem of not having a direct heir to the throne.

1366   The point of this line is not immediately obvious. Perhaps the sense is something like "A little bird told me" that you are accusing me of preventing my uncle from marrying.

1381   According to the OED, *vair* is "a fur obtained from a variety of squirrel with grey back and white belly, much used in the 13th and 14th centuries as a trimming or lining for garments." On *griis*, see note to line 1220.

1390   The MED, citing this line, glosses *fare* as "rigging." However, the term might also refer to the "merchandise" of the ship.

1445   John of Trevisa (in *On the Properties of Things: John of Trevisa's Translation of Bartholomæus Anglicus De Proprietatibus Rerum* [Oxford: Clarendon Press, 1975] II, 1214) notes that when lions are pursued by hounds and hunters, "they lotyeth [lie concealed] nought nouther behuydeth [hide] hemself but sitteth in feldes where he may be seye [seen] and arrayeth himself to defens and renneth out of woode and covert with swift rennynge and cours, as though he wolde acounte vile schame to loty [lie concealed] and to huyde [hide] hymself. . . . Whanne he is ywounded he taketh wonderliche heede and knoweth hem that him furst smyteth, and reseth on [charges] the smytere though he nevere be in so gret multitude."

1520   Skeat, in his note to *Piers Plowman* C.II.147 (*The Vision of William Concerning Piers the Plowman in Three Parallel Texts* . . . [London: Oxford University Press] 1961, II, 27) defines "treacle" (*tryacle* in his text) as "a sovereign remedy" and says that "the chief point to be observed is that it was considered to be an antidote against poisons, because it contained the flesh of vipers."

1584   The manuscript reads "mi brother." I have emended to *thi brother*. McNeill notes the error, and observes that "it was the queen's brother, not Ysonde's, who was slain by Tristrem"; but he does not emend his text.

1586   McNeill reads "be," where the manuscript has "he."

1608   The manuscript reading of "lerld" is, as the MED suggests, apparently an error for "lerde," to which I have emended the text.

1633   The sense of this line seems to be that the steward claims he will not fight because "a wrong is being perpetrated there."

1645   See Sir Walter Scott's note on love potions in his edition of *Sir Tristrem* (313–315). Scott writes that "the noted hippomanes [a growth found at the forehead of a newborn foal and considered in antiquity to be an aphrodisiac] was the principal ingredient in these love-potions; but the bones of a green frog (provided the flesh had been eaten by ants), the head of a kite, the marrow of a wolf's left foot, mixed with ambergris, a pigeon's liver, stewed in the blood of the person to be beloved, and many other recipes, more or less nauseous, are confidently averred to be of equal virtue."

1655–59 McNeill gives the "sense" of these lines as: "Thus the true knights rowed, and Tristrem also rowed, and continued to row, all the time that they came fresh (having been relieved while Tristrem was still at the oar), though he was only one man to three of them — a great labour."

1663   The *pin* here refers to a pin or peg "inserted in a drinking vessel marking equal portions of the contents" (MED).

1677   *In lide* = "in lede," means literally "among the people" or "on earth;" but here it is a virtually meaningless tag.

1681   *For thought* is difficult to gloss in this context. In her translation of *Sir Tristrem*, Jessie Weston translates "Long as man's thought" (160). This seems too loose a gloss. The phrase may be seen as a nearly meaningless tag. Or the sense may be something like "when we think about it" (similar to McNeill's gloss "that can be imagined" for the phrase as it appears in line 537). It is also conceivable that what is intended is "for-thought," a participle from "forthinken" (*regret*). The sense would then be that Tristrem and Ysonde were together in joy and also in pain, which was to be regretted. This reading is supported by the "to sain" in the following line. The phrase suggests that the comment that the drink was made in an evil time explains what came before.

1720 ff.   In these lines Ysonde sneaks into bed to make Mark think he has slept with her rather than Brengwain. She asks for the drink from Ireland to make it seem to him that they have shared the love potion, but she lets the cup fall because she does not want to share it with Mark and she no longer needs it to strengthen her love of Tristrem, since their love is already sealed by the earlier drinking of the potion.

1734 ff.   The fact that Ysonde would laugh when Tristrem is in grief seems strange. Kölbing translates these lines: "Ysonde lachte, wen Tristrem in leid war, absichtlich" (Ysonde laughed when Tristrem was in sorrow, intentionally) and explains that her laughter was intentional so that no one would suspect the relationship between them. It might also be a sign that Ysonde's mind is affected by the love-sickness caused by their forced separation, the laughter being a kind of mad laughter. She does, after all, in the next line, plan to kill Brengwain. Susan Crane sees these and the surrounding lines as a "dramatization of feelings alternating between joy and sorrow, hope and disappointment" which "nearly captures Thomas's idea that love's contrary movements are reciprocal and inseparable" (p. 191).

1853   A *rote* is "a medieval stringed-instrument of the harp family consisting of a solid, triangular wooden frame with seven strings and played like a guitar with the hand." The harp of the Irish minstrel is, if the term is used technically (and not loosely to indicate a stringed instrument, as is sometimes the case), "a triangular-shaped diatonic instrument consisting of a small tripartite frame (body, front pillar, and arched neck with metal tuning pins) on which from eight to eighteen strings of twisted hair, gut, or wire were strung" (*A Dictionary of Middle English Musical Terms*, compiled by Henry Holland Carter [Bloomington: Indiana University Press, 1961], p. 414 and p. 185).

1854   The *ring* refers to a "metal ring attached to an object for fastening, lifting, etc."
        (MED).

1875   On *dathet,* John Edwards (*Scottish Historical Review* 1 [1904], 56) says, "This old
        imprecation is not Anglo-Saxon; it came over with the Conqueror, but early
        found an abiding place here. It is explained as coming from the Merovingian
        French, 'Deu hat,' meaning 'God's hate.'" Perhaps the best gloss on the word
        would be "damn" or "curses [on him]!"

1876   McNeill says that this line is "so corrupt as to be unintelligible." Perhaps some
        sense can be made of it by taking *stound* as a verb (as in "stound," OED v. 1)
        which means "to be painful" or "to cause great pain." Lines 1875 and 1876 then
        mean: "A curse on him always, / If this [his playing] cause [you] great pain
        concerning [that is, because it reminds you of] Tristrem." The earliest use of
        such a meaning recorded in the OED is 1500, but the parallel meaning of the
        noun "stound" dates back to 1300. There remains, however, an abrupt shift in
        the earl's thought, from cursing the minstrel for reminding Ysonde of Tristrem
        to rewarding him for traveling with them because his music pleases her.

1930   The manuscript reads "Tristren," which I have emended to "Tristrem," the form
        in which the name most frequently appears throughout the manuscript.

1940   I follow the suggestion of the MED in emending by adding "and" between the
        words "sorwe" and "site," which are contiguous in the manuscript.

1993   *Say* seems to govern both what comes before it and what follows. The sense is:
        "Ask to go with him, and say to him if he still loves you, 'send Tristrem away.'"
        The shift from indirect to direct discourse occurs frequently in Middle English
        romances.

2002   I follow Kölbing's suggestion in emending the manuscript reading of "thi
        nemes" to "his emes" ("his uncle's," i.e., Mark's).

2004   On *thi nore,* see the note to line 921.

2019   Meridok's plan is to trap Tristrem by separating him from Ysonde thus causing
        him to arrange a meeting with her which Mark can observe.

2051 McNeill says that "the line is unintelligible." Kölbing suggests emending to "Tristrem go with hem bede" ("Bid Tristrem to go with them"). This seems to be the sense of the line. Perhaps the emendation is not necessary, since it is not unusual for the verb "to go" to be understood.

2080–90 This stanza is typical of the compressed style of the poet. Tristrem sees through the dwarf's deception and immediately adopts the strategy of accusing Ysonde of harming him by slandering him to Mark. Tristrem's words are addressed to the dwarf, whom he calls "Maister," which may be used as a term of respect when addressing someone of a higher station or merely as a polite (or occasionally ironic) way of addressing someone of a lower station.

2135 On *thi nare*, see the note to line 921.

2138 The word *make* is repeated in this line of the manuscript.

2144 Kölbing notes that *Ungiltles* must be read as either "ungilti" or "giltles;" the sense is surely that Mark now believes Tristrem is not guilty of the accusations that have been made against him.

2169 A *constable* is "the chief officer of a ruler's household or court" (MED).

2184 In the Middle Ages, blood-letting was routine preventive medicine, a way of ridding the body of evil humors, as well as a cure for specific diseases. On this subject, see Stanley Rubin, *Medieval English Medicine* (Newton Abbot: David and Charles, 1974) 140 ff.

2199 Tristrem's leap of thirty feet is quite an accomplishment. The current record for the long jump, held by Carl Lewis, is twenty-eight feet, ten and a quarter inches.

2201 *Willes* is a genitive singular of "will" and is used here as a predicate adjective.

2229 ff. On the ordeal with the hot iron, see Ernest C. York, "Isolt's Ordeal: English Legal Customs in the Medieval Tristan Legend," *SP* 68 (Jan. 1971), 1–9. York notes that the ordeal "had gone out of use in England almost a century before" *Sir Tristrem* was written. For a more general literary context, see Ralph J. Hexter, *Equivocal Oaths and Ordeals in Medieval Literature* (Cambridge: Harvard University Press, 1975). For historical information about ordeals, see Robert Bartlett, *Trial by Fire and Water: The Medieval Judicial Ordeal* (Oxford:

Clarendon Press, 1988), and Henry Charles Lea, *The Ordeal*, with additional original documents in translation by Arthur E. Howland, ed. Edward Peters (Philadelphia: University of Pennsylvania Press, 1973).

2234   The *merkes* are the "posts by which the path of the accused is designated in a trial by ordeal" (MED).

2235   York (see note to lines 2229 ff.) notes that "Westminster was not a bishopric [the usual site of a trial by ordeal] until the sixteenth century and then only for a short time. But here an earlier Anglo-Saxon custom may be pertinent. According to the laws of Ethelred, 'every ordeal shall take place in a royal manor.' Westminster Abbey, from the time of the Confessor on, held numerous manors, many of which were royal ones" (8).

2280   *Ycorn* is the past participle of "chesan," "to choose."

2286   F. Holthausen (in "Zur Erklärung und Textkritik der ME. Romanze 'Sir Tristrem,'" *Anglia*, 39 [1915], 381) suggests reading "Hir" instead of "And." However, given the poet's tendency to use nearly meaningless tags, the manuscript reading should remain. The line then becomes a redundant (or perhaps emphatic) phrase meaning "and he did," but perhaps best translated by something like "indeed."

2290   *Maugré* is a preposition governing the genitive case. Thus *maugré his* means "in spite of him."

2296   McNeill translates "And he quickly gains intelligence of this (*i.e.*, of the reconciliation between Mark and Ysonde) . . ." But it seems more likely that *fraines this* refers to seeking battle. The poet uses "frainen" again in this sense in line 2626.

2327   Scott, McNeill and Kölbing all take *mete* as "meal," probably because Tristrem is said to have come upon Morgan as he began to cut his bread (see line 820). It is also possible that "mete" is related to the verb "meten" in the sense of encounter.

2329   *Bist* is from the verb "bien," which means "to buy" or, as here, "to pay for" or "to atone for."

2371   *An* is the third singular present of "unnen" ("to grant").

2393   *Deste* is the past tense of "dashen" ("to fall precipitously" or "to collapse").

2474   The OED, citing this line, defines *fede* as "Great, large" and notes that the etymology is unknown and that "the senses assigned are somewhat uncertain, and perh. the examples do not all contain the same word." The MED, also citing this line, suggests that the word may be related to the Old Icelandic "feyja" ("to rot, decay") and defines the term as "Decayed, withered; ?hoary (forest)."

2496   It seems possible to translate this line in two ways. It might mean: "On account of the love each had for the other." But it might also mean: "On account of love, each gazed on the other." The latter meaning would require the line to be punctuated: "For love, ich other bihalt;" rather than as it appears in the text.

2508   The line means "A year minus three weeks."

2548   McNeill reads "liue" (live), but the minims that he reads as *u* may also be read as an *n*. Reading "line" (as a form of "lien," "to lie,") makes much better sense in the context.

2557   This line appears at the bottom of the first column on folio 295 v. There is a sign after the fourth line of the column to indicate that this line should be inserted at that point.

2590   McNeill glosses this line: "In spite of the plans we are able to devise."

2628   McNeill glosses *thurchsayn* as "explored." Kölbing glosses it as "durchsuchen" ("search through").

2663–73 Of these lines, susan Crane says, "The whole of Tristan's debate on whether or not to marry Isolt of Brittany . . . is distilled into one stanza" (190).

2666   McNeill omits the word "ous," which appears in the manuscript between "hath" and "wrought."

2674   *That* refers to the intention to marry Ysonde of the White Hands.

2725   *Brether* is a plural form. Thus "brethern" (as in line 3310, for example) is a double plural (as is also the word "children"). The *n*-plural also appears in the word "fon" ("foes") in line 3245.

2730   The word *fre* as used in this line seems to have a legal connotation as it does, for example, in *The English Register of Godstow Nunnery, near Oxford*; ed. Andrew Clark; EETS o.s. 129 (London: Kegan Paul, Trench, Trübner and Co. for the Early English Text Society, 1905), 181]: "the fore-seyde syre Reynold & hys heyrys & hys men of woluerton, & the fore-seyde person & hys successours, shold haue alonly fre-goynge to her beestes to be warturde at the welle of the brech . . . ."

2742   The MED, citing this line, glosses *merkes* as "tracks (of an animal)"; but it seems preferable to read it as a variant of "markes" (which appears in line 2710), meaning "boundary markers." The point is that Tristrem's hounds run beyond the boundary markers into the giant's territory. The chance thus arising (see line 2739), Tristrem enters into the forbidden territory.

2744   I have emended the manuscript reading "blalc" to "blac." McNeill reads "blalc" but says in his glossary that it is erroneously written for "blac." Kölbing emends to "blac."

2746   McNeill suggests that Kölbing's emendation of "was fade" to "forbade" "would certainly make the sense more intelligible than it at present is." However, if "douke" is read in a general sense (meaning "knightly warrior") and taken as referring not to Duke Rohande but to the giant Beliagog, the line makes perfect sense. "Fade" would mean "eager for battle" in this context.

2749   *Priis* is the signal on the hunting horn that indicates that the quarry has been taken.

2779   *Bleynt* is the past tense of "blenchen" ("to move suddenly or sharply; jerk, twist; flinch, wince, dodge," MED). This line explains how Tristrem evaded the spear. By turning quickly aside, the spear passed between his hauberk and his body.

2786   The line, which translates literally as "Tristrem's life he nearly sold," means "He nearly killed Tristrem."

2801 ff.   McNeill translates this line: "Tristrem acknowledged him as a free man — *i.e.*, accorded him his freedom." Skeat ("The Romance of Sir Tristrem," *Scottish Historical Review* 6 [1909], 61) says, "This is a very harsh construction of *knewe*. I take *fre* in its usual sense of 'liberal' or 'bounteous.' Further, I alter the semicolon after *fre* to a comma, and place another comma after *Beliagog*. The sense is 'Tristrem knew him, Beliagog, (to be) liberal in his promise, (namely), if I am to conceal nothing, that he would make a bright hall for him.' Here is nothing forced or obscure. For *hight*, a promise, see the *Cursor Mundi*, l. 785. The semicolon after *fre* deprives the rest of the passage of its verb." Another possible explanation is to read 2801 either as McNeill does or as meaning "Tristrem knew him to be generous." In the next line, "hight" could be read as the past of "hien" ("to hasten or hurry"). The sense would then be: "Beliagog rushed right in, truly, to make him a bright hall for Ysonde and Brengwein."

2814   Kölbing glosses this line: "Sein werk zu ende zu führen" ("to carry through his work to the end").

2841   McNeill says that *to calle* is "an expletive with no more definite meaning than 'so to say,' 'so to speak'"; it is possible, however, that the phrase means something like "[ready] to be summoned" and is emphasizing the life-like quality of the statues of the dogs.

2851   York Powell ("A Few Notes on Sir Tristrem," *Englische Studien* 6 [1883], 464) says: "Sein Matheus toun is S. Mahé in Brittany on the coast, I fancy. This spot was well known to Englishmen and Scots at the date of the original poem. He is in *Bretein* l. 2641, and S. Mahé by Ushant i[s] [article reads "in"] not so far from S. Pol de Leon, the *Lyoun* of l. 2855. So we get an indication of travel or of knowledge of the Brittany coast such as a knight or bachiler serving in the wars or as ambassador might show. S. Mahé was well known from the Brittany wars of Ed. III and Rich. II to Englishmen."

2880   The MED, citing this line, notes that *Withouten oth* is used "as a tag or emphatic" to mean "assuredly, unquestionably, truly, indeed."

2936–37   McNeill seems to capture the sense when he glosses these lines: "Keep the whole matter under hand (*i.e.*, secret), lest they discover it from your voice."

2943   The phrase *in lede* (literally "in the [his] country" or "among the people" is here a rhyming tag with little real meaning.

2966   The word *are* in this line modifies "duelled" in the following line.

2968   The MED, citing this line and also line 3177, says that the phrase *to lithe* (literally "to hear" or "to listen") is "a more or less empty metrical tag."

2976   The word *blo*, meaning dark and thus virtually synonymous with "black," survives in the phrase "black and blue" where "blue" is "a corruption arising when *blo* became obsolete after 1550" (OED).

3050   The MED, citing this line, defines *hayte* as "?to fight, do battle"; but the more normal meaning of "to show hatred" seems more appropriate to the context.

3068   Catherine of Alexandria was a saint supposed to have lived in the fourth century who was "a noble girl persecuted for her Christianity, who despised marriage with the Emperor because she was a 'bride of Christ' . . . . Her protests were against the persecution of Christians by Maxentius; her tortures consisted of being broken on a wheel (later called Catherine wheel), but the machine broke down injuring bystanders; Catherine was beheaded." She was a patron of nurses ("because milk instead of blood flowed from her severed head") and of young girls (*Oxford Dictionary of Saints*).

3128   *Clerk and knight* is one of the contrasting pairs commonly used in Middle English to represent completeness. The sense of the phrase is "one and all."

3139   McNeill takes *to-kest* (his reading is "tokest" as meaning "destroyed." I prefer to read "to-kest," which I take as related to the verb "casten," which can mean "to cast one's eyes at" or "to look at something." Though the examples of this sense cited by the MED generally have a word meaning "look" or "eye" in conjunction with "cast," the sense of looking is suggested by the notion of spying. Thus "to-kest" would mean something like "looked over" or "surveyed."

3153   *Bond and fre* is another example of a contrasting pair used in Middle English to suggest completeness (see the note to line 3128). Thus the sense of the phrase is "everyone."

3173   The *claper* is the "lid or clapper of a beggar's clapdish" (MED). Scott (362) notes that lepers "usually carried the cup and clapper mentioned in the text. The former served to receive alms, and the noise of the latter warned the passenger to keep aloof, even while bestowing his charity."

3183   This line only makes sense if *hem* is taken as referring to Canados and Ysonde. Apparently her threats to catch them in the act are a way of preventing Canados from having his way with Ysonde. Although the antecedent is far removed from *hem* in this reading, the interpretation is supported by the following lines in which Brengwain complains about Canados to Mark.

3248   The sense of *yeld* in this line is something like "paid them back for." Tristrem and Ganhardin are paying back the bold knights (like Meriadok) for their old deeds, i. e., the harm done to Tristrem and Ysonde.

3261   In the manuscript the last letter of *stirops* is an "o." The word thus reads "stiropo," but the *MED* considers this an error for "stirops," to which I have emended the word.

3296   About the phrase *A knight that werd no schone* (wore no shoes), Scott says: "The knights often made whimsical vows, to forbear a certain part of their dress, armour, or habits of life, until they had executed a particular adventure . . . ." However, the line probably refers to the fact that the second Tristrem is a young and untested knight. To "win one's shoes" meant to prove oneself in combat. (See, e.g., *Rauf the Collier*, line 765: "It war my will, worthy, thy schone that thow wan . . . ."

3305–6   Kölbing is probably correct in reading *let* as a form of "leten" meaning "speak of" or "judge." This line makes best sense when seen as a continuation of the description of the beloved: "My beloved fair and sweet . . . who knows well how to speak of love." Line 3306 might be translated as "May Christ send her to you" (i.e., "May you save her"); or, if "hir" is taken to refer to Ysonde (named in line 3308), the line might mean: "May Christ send her [Ysonde] to you / [If] you undertake to make better my sorrow / For love of the noble Ysonde." If the latter reading is preferred, the period at the end of line 3306 should be changed to a comma.

3398   Scott defines *haggards* as "*wild hawks*, metaphorically, *loose women*." A *stale* is "a lover or mistress whose devotion is turned into ridicule for the amusement of a rival" but may also have the meaning of a "decoy-bird" (OED).

Glossary

abide *[stand to] fight; remain*
al-out *altogether*
and *and; if*
anon(e) *immediately, right away*
are *before*
arour *sin, error*
assemblee *battle, tournament*
at *that; from; at*
ather *either*
atuinne *apart*
aught *ought; owned*
ay *always, continually*

be *by; be*
bede *ask; offer; give; promise*
bidene *at once, quickly*
bitaught *entrusted; gave*
blithe *happy*
bold *valiant, valiant man*
boun *ready, prepared; armed*
bour *chamber, room*
bright *fair beautiful*
busk *prepare*
but *without; but*

can, gan *aux. verb indicating past tense*
care *sorrow*
chalmer *chamber*
chere *demeanor, manner, spirit*
ches *went; chose, selected; chessboard*
clepith *calls*

couthe *knew (how)*
crewell *cruel*
croun *crown*

dede *did; deed; dead; death*
dirk, dyrk *dark*
diverss *various*
dout *fear*
duerve *dwarf*
durst *dared*

eft *after, afterwards*
ek *also*
em *uncle; (in* mi nem / thi nem, *the* n
    *from "min" or "thin" attaches to
    "em")*
er *are*
er(e) *before*
erb *plant*

fain *glad, gladly*
fare *fair; go*
fer(e) *far; fire*
fere *companion*
ferly *marvelous, marvelously; terrible*
fleigh *fly; fled; leapt forth; splashed up*
flour(e) *flower; the best*
fo *enemy*
fois *foes*
forthi *therefore*
fra *from*

frain *ask (for); seek*
fre *noble; generous; noble person*

gan (*see* **can**)
gardinge *garden*
geaunt *giant*
gess *suppose*
gif *if; give*
gren *field*

haith *has*
hat *is called*
heighe *noble, proud; high; haste*
hem *them*
hende *courtly, noble*
her *her; their*
hevy *sad, distressing; heavy*
hevyness *sadness, grief, worry, anxiety*
hewe *color; face*
hie *high; hasten*
hight *is / was called, named; promised*
hole *hale, healthy*
hye *she*

ich *I; each; such*
ichon *each one*
if(ith) *give; if*
ilk *same, very, aforementioned; each*
ilkon *each one*
incontynent *immediately, at once*
into *in, into*
iwyss *indeed*

kene *bold, strong; wise; fierce, cruel; loud*

ladice *ladies; lady's*
lain, layn *to lie;* **noght lain** *not to lie,*

in truth
larges(s) *generosity*
lede *people; lead;* **in lede** *among the people, on earth*
leich *physician*
les *lie*
levedi *lady*
longith *pertains*
lough *laughed*
low *law; low*
luges, lugis *tents, lodgings*
lusty(e) *pleasant, comfortable*
lykith, likith *it pleases, it is pleasing*

magré *in spite of*
maid *made*
manhed *courage, valor*
mekil *much*
mene *speak*
michel *much; great, greatly*
mo *more*
morow *morning*

nas *was not*
nem (*see* **em**)
nocht *not, nothing*
nome *name; took*

o *a, an; one*
ogain *against; in reply; back*
one *one; on, upon*
one *one; a, an; on*
oneto *to, unto; until*
onon(e) *at once, immediately*
ost *host, army*
owhen *own*

pass *go*

pasing *surpassing, great, excellent*
plan(e) *plane, field*
play *play; have sexual intercourse*
pretend *aspire*
pri(i)s(e) *nobility, renown, worth*
puple *people*
pur *poor*
pwnyss *punish*

quath *said*
quhare *where*
quhat, qwhat *what*
quhen *when*
qu(h)ich *which, who*
quhill *until; while*
quhom *whom*
quod *said*

rathe *quickly*
rede *advice; advise; read*
resave *receive, accept*
reskew *rescue*
rid, ryd *ride*
ring(e), ryng(e) *reign*
ryne *run*

sal *shall*
salust *greeted*
samyne *same*
sare, sore *grievously*
say *say;* **to say** *that is, indeed*
schene *bright; beautiful, lovely*
schent *undone, disgraced; disfigured*
seighe *saw*
sen *since; seen*
sere *various*
set *although*
shir(e) *sir*

sich *such*
sithe *time*
sket(e) *quickly, immediately*
slo *slay*
slough *slew*
soth(e) *truth*
sown *sound*
spac *spoke*
sper *lance*
spille *kill, die, perish; spill*
spoused *married*
spreit *spirit; mind*
stede *horse; place*
stere *govern, control, command*
stounde *time*
strenth *strength*
suppos *although*
swiche *such*
swithe *quickly, directly*
synaris *sinners*
syne (adv.) *then*
syne (n.) *sin*

thar(e) *there; their*
the *you; they*
thede *country, people, race, nation*
thei *though; they*
ther *their; there*
thir *these*
throuch *through*
throue *through*
throw *through*
tho *then; when*
thurch *through*
tide *time*
til *to*
tint *lost; wasted; destroyed*
to *two; to*

toun *town*
tour *tower*
travel(l) *work, labor, effort; travail*
trewis *truce*
trowe *believe, trust*
tuech, twech *concern, relate to, touch on*
tuin *separate*
tyne *lose*

uicht *person*
uith *with*
unride *powerful*
unto *until; to*
uorship *honor*
urechit *wretched*
uroght *wrought*
uther *other*

vertew *virtue*
vertwis *virtuous*
vichsaif *vouchsafe, grant*

wald *would*
war(e) *were; war*
wende *thought, expected; go, went*
wene *thought, doubt; think, suppose*
were *were; wage war; war; peril; doubt*
wers *worse*
wex *grow; become; be*
whilk *which*
while, whill *until; while*
whois *whose*
wight *person*
wist *knew*
wite *know;* **to wite and nought at wene** *indeed and without a doubt*
wo *sorry, sad*

wondit *wounded*
worship *honor*
wot *knows*
wough *wrong*
wyss *way, manner; wise, wise one*

yare *readily, quickly*
yede, yode *went*
yhe *you*
yhit *yet*
yhon(e) *that*
yhoue, yhow *you*
yhour *your*
yif *if*
yold(e) *yielded, gave, given*
ywis *indeed*